The Myth That Made Us

The Myth That Made Us

How False Beliefs about Racism and Meritocracy Broke Our Economy (and How to Fix It)

Jeff Fuhrer

The MIT Press
Cambridge, Massachusetts
London, England

The MIT Press would like to thank the anonymous peer reviewers who provided comments on drafts of this book. The generous work of academic experts is essential for establishing the authority and quality of our publications. We acknowledge with gratitude the contributions of these otherwise uncredited readers.

This book was set in Stone Serif and Stone Sans by Jen Jackowitz. Printed and bound in the United States of America.

Library of Congress Cataloging-in-Publication Data

Names: Fuhrer, Jeffrey C., author.
Title: The myth that made us : how false beliefs about racism and meritocracy
  broke our economy (and how to fix it) / Jeff Fuhrer.
Description: Cambridge, Massachusetts : The MIT Press, [2023] | Includes
  bibliographical references and index.
Identifiers: LCCN 2022054393 (print) | LCCN 2022054394 (ebook) |
  ISBN 9780262048392 (hardcover) | ISBN 9780262375825 (epub) | ISBN
  9780262375832 (pdf)
Subjects: LCSH: Income distribution—United States. | Equality—United States. |
  American Dream. | Merit (Ethics)
Classification: LCC HC110.I5 F847 2023 (print) | LCC HC110.I5 (ebook) | DDC
  339.2/20973—dc23/eng/20230518
LC record available at https://lccn.loc.gov/2022054393
LC ebook record available at https://lccn.loc.gov/2022054394

10 9 8 7 6 5 4 3 2

Contents

A Note from Eastern Bank Foundation

When Jeff began this project in the summer of 2021, early in his term as a Foundation Fellow with us at Eastern Bank Foundation, he described to me the topic about which he planned to write. I was immediately taken with the thesis—having seen the tenets and tentacles playing out in our communities for decades and sensing, without the benefit of his scholarship, that our national and regional economy has been specifically constructed in ways that promote success for the few and failure for the many. Guided by false narratives about race, ethnicity, and gender; about the capacity of hard work to ensure success; and about businesses' blind, single-minded devotion to maximizing shareholder value without focusing on the consequences for workers, communities, and the environment, we have, deliberately or not, undermined the American dream. Given the times in which we live, and the importance of including more truth in the public narrative, it was clear to us that this vital, timely, and compelling book needed to be written, and I immediately volunteered to support Jeff while he was working on it.

Not that Jeff was telling me about the book in order to obtain our backing, but to us at Eastern, there seemed a natural partnership. This work is well-aligned with our foundation's mission and the bank's efforts to help people prosper. This is the third book project we have helped into this world. Each one is different, but all seek to advance a narrative for our time and focus on building racial equity and social justice in our communities.

For over 200 years, as a community-centered bank, Eastern Bank has been committed to providing appropriate and affordable financial services to our customers across all walks of life and to building communities that can thrive economically. As part of the local ecosystem, we understand that our bank can only be as strong as the communities we serve. Eastern Bank Foundation, created twenty-eight years ago and supported entirely by Eastern Bank, continues to carry out that mission. Each year the foundation supports more than a thousand not-for-profit organizations through philanthropy, volunteerism, advocacy, and collaboration, always with the clear goal of building strong, equitable, and just communities. Since 1994, Eastern Bank has donated more than $240 Million to local and regional nonprofit partners across Massachusetts, New Hampshire, and Rhode Island.

As we partner with the communities we serve, we have seen the effects that systemic racism, unequal opportunity, and the inability to obtain sustainable housing, employment, and prospects for wealth-building, have had on our neighbors. Jeff's book highlights the sources of these inequities but also provides compelling solutions that are rooted in providing opportunity to build human and financial capital, the long-run foundations of economic success. These are exactly the kinds of efforts our foundation supports in its key focal areas of advancing equity in the small business ecosystem, enriching early childhood development, securing safe and affordable housing, promoting workforce development that leads to careers and family-sustaining wages, and supporting innovation and collaboration within the nonprofit ecosystem.

We are proud to be partners in this effort to bring to light the structural weaknesses in our economy, and we remain committed to working together with our community partners to devise and implement solutions that build equity for all.

Nancy Huntington Stager

President and CEO

Eastern Bank Foundation, July 2022

Preface: A Mainstream Economist Discovers His Blind Spots

I spent more than three decades with the Federal Reserve System as an executive and as a widely cited research economist. My training was mainstream. I learned economics from leading scholars at Princeton and Harvard. The work I ultimately pursued married academic research into the workings of the macroeconomy with advising on real-time decision making about monetary policy. As director of the research department at the Federal Reserve Bank of Boston, I attended dozens of the Fed's monetary policymaking meetings—the Federal Open Market Committee meetings—in DC under each of the past five chairs, observing up close how the sausage is made. All of this was rewarding and fascinating.

Then, about fifteen years ago, the Fed initiated a new direction in its community development arm. The Boston Fed, where I was also executive vice president, partnered with a host of institutions in midsized, postindustrial New England cities to figure out how to bring back economic vitality. This data-based, collaborative, practical, on-the-ground effort, for which I served as a senior advisor, was enlightening for me. Most importantly for my personal journey, I was fortunate to be involved in numerous in-person discussions with residents and leaders of these low-income, often majority-minority, communities. The more I learned about their lives, the more I became aware of gaps in mainstream economics.

The problem in these communities was not a lack of industry, perseverance, or innovation. It was structural. Simply put, the economy itself had set them up to fail by denying opportunities for success.

*   *   *

By 2013, I was now responsible for the Fed's community development area when it embarked on a new project to measure the size of racial wealth disparities in the Boston metro area. This work, which followed in the footsteps of efforts by William A. Darity Jr. and Darrick Hamilton and was co-led by them and by Boston Fed staffer Ana Patricia Muñoz, once again exposed structural problems with our economy. A companion project brought together leaders from the region to discuss the roots of racial wealth disparities. Through those discussions and our reading of the sad history of institutional racism, it became clear to all of us that the racial wealth gap was the product of decades of *policy design* and *implementation* that boosted white families' wealth but largely excluded black families. While the troubling outcomes were *economic*, the sources were *political and were intentionally discriminatory*. Nowhere had I heard about this in my prior years as an economist.

Finally, in the fall of 2017, our community development group joined several other Reserve Banks in a project on the characteristics of low-wage work. Standard economic theory asserts that markets will efficiently determine the characteristics of jobs, including the compensation they offer, but that seemed far removed from the reality of low-wage jobs. Over time, employers had scaled back wages, reduced benefits, contracted out low-wage jobs, and dismantled the unions that had earlier provided voice and bargaining power to workers. While vast amounts of economic research have focused on improving education and skills to solve this problem—and while better training is no doubt part of the solution—it became clear that much of the blame lay with the norms our nation had come to accept for how employers treat their employees in many sectors of the economy.

*   *   *

As I learned about the broken parts of our economy, I felt compelled to speak up. In the course of my career, I had spoken to hundreds of groups about conditions in the national economy. I continued to do so but now devoted the latter half of my presentations to a discussion of the reality of low-income, disproportionately minority workers, along with the history of systemic racism and its impact on wealth accumulation among people of color. In all of those talks, I emphasized the role that corrosive (and ignorant) *narratives* have played in explaining away and perpetuating gross inequities—especially this narrative: that all you need to do is work hard and let the markets work their magic, and everything will be great.

These presentations seemed to fill a need among my audiences. Perhaps some already had an appreciation for our societal injustices and inequities, but few had been provided a blueprint of the economic engine that drove those injustices and inequities. At each talk, numerous attendees told me that they had never been confronted with the evidence, or that they knew things were wrong but they weren't sure just how or why. And many listeners thanked me for putting the big picture together in an accessible, albeit disheartening, way.

The feedback deepened my sense of purpose and convinced me that I needed to get this message out to more people. With the encouragement of colleagues, friends, and family who had also heard me speak about these issues (perhaps a bit too much), I decided that the best way to do so was to write this book. It is a labor born of passion for the subject, coupled with outrage that our economic system has been designed to leave so many, many behind. The widely held narrative that attributes lack of success to lack of effort is an embarrassment. It's not a lack of diligence or judgment that creates these miseries. We made it this way.

The good news, as the book will discuss, is that we can remake our country so that it more closely resembles the land of opportunity to which we all aspire. And I am proud to be a small part of that mission.

Interviews with Residents

This book examines hundreds of data sources to document the ways in which our economy is broken, fueled by false narratives about race, poverty, and the sources of success.

But the data can say only so much. To breathe life into these data, I conducted interviews with residents of low-income communities in Massachusetts, asking them to tell their stories of hard work, struggle, and, in some cases, success. I contacted interviewees through not-for-profit organizations that work with low-income communities and with which I already had a connection. The hope was that these organizations, with which residents were already familiar, could establish an initial bridge of trust between me and my interview subjects. They were asked to self-identify race, ethnicity, and gender. I asked a common set of questions of each interviewee, although the flow of the conversation determined to some extent what we ended up discussing. For those who requested it, a translator was provided to minimize the potential for misunderstanding. Conversations were recorded with interviewees' permission, so that I could ensure that any quotes I used were both accurate and documented for posterity. All the quotes and paraphrases used in this book were provided in advance to the interviewees for their approval.

It was not easy to arrange interviews, despite my institutional connections. These residents are busy working people with family obligations and health issues. It is telling that several of the residents I had hoped to interview were unable to participate—one because she had just been evicted and her life was in turmoil, one because she had just lost a child, and one because her child was in the process of being institutionalized.

A Note to My Economics Colleagues

This is not primarily a book for economists, nor is it about economists' theories or economics pedagogy. It is a book about how actors with wealth and power have used narratives to maintain the status quo in a system that slants outcomes dramatically toward the already successful. I have purposely simplified the description of standard economic theory because the finer points are not necessary to understand my main arguments. It is true that models of business objectives that go beyond maximizing shareholder value have been put forward since 1970—some will be discussed in chapters 1 and 2. And economists are now much more focused on the decades-long effects of systemic racism on labor market and wealth outcomes, examining the barriers that still prevent workers from achieving a reasonable measure of economic success.

But papers about business models—whether from the Business Roundtable or from business scholars like Michael Porter and others—and the excellent work on racial inequity by many economists have not fundamentally changed the outcomes in our economy. Indeed, we have, if anything, seen further slippage in the balance of power between workers and employers since economists and others began developing alternative ways to think about businesses. More importantly, what economists write has not changed the prevailing narratives among business leaders, politicians, and the general public about self-determination, the poor, institutional racism, or the appropriate role for government in the economy. I hope that the best research from economists exploring these aspects of how the world really works will help move us forward. But systemic change will take much more than that.

I want to emphasize—as I do throughout the book—that I am generally in favor of capitalism, and I believe capitalism, broadly construed, is likely the best system for the United States. However, I feel strongly that the way that we have implemented capitalism has been influenced by dominant narratives in a way that has left many behind, unnecessarily. And our brand of capitalism could be much improved through greater attention to the equal provision of opportunity, so that many more of our citizens have the chance to build life-changing human and financial capital.

This book presents a wide array of evidence in support of these propositions. It does not attempt to offer new research identifying underlying causal relationships. But it does examine data that highlight the magnitude of the problem, and it cites dozens of researchers whose work attempts to get at the underlying causes. One can argue with any piece of evidence or any one study, but it would be difficult to dismiss the overall pattern formed by the combination of data and research: our system is broken, we made it that way, and we have the choice to adopt policies and programs that will bring us closer to the ideal that most of us aspire to.

Introduction: Like Dives before Lazarus

It is human nature to tell stories to make sense of the world. But how much do these stories matter? In some domains, not much at all. You may choose to believe the world is flat. It won't make any difference in your daily life or those of others: you're unlikely to test the proposition by sailing far out into the ocean. Being wrong in this case has few if any negative consequences.

In other domains, stories matter quite a lot. Belief or disbelief in the efficacy of vaccines can affect not only our own health but also the health of all those with whom we come in contact. Belief that we can consistently pick winning stocks could lead us to lose our life savings. In these arenas, our beliefs can dramatically influence our life outcomes and those of others.

How about our beliefs about how the economy works? Here, the importance of beliefs may be less obvious. But this book tells the story of how our economy has been profoundly shaped by a system of beliefs that turns out to be terribly inaccurate. They are beliefs that I and many others held for far too long, beliefs that many still hold. I received key tenets as articles of faith through my mainstream economics training at Princeton and Harvard. Countless others absorb those tenets unconsciously through constant repetition in popular media. Critically, those like me, involved in policymaking at the Federal Reserve and other key public institutions, clung to these beliefs, which for too many years led us to take actions that unwittingly caused unnecessary economic harm to millions.

This set of beliefs—what I will call "The Myth"—is old and, as aspiration, deeply appealing. Its roots are inextricably entwined with those of our republic. In its simplest form, a key element of The Myth is this: success goes to those who work hard. Failure goes to those who do not.

*　　*　　*

The simple story of individual effort is only one piece of a more complete narrative that seeks to explain the behavior of individuals, businesses, and government. To briefly summarize, belief in the efficacy of individual effort is incomplete if individuals don't have the *opportunity* to exert the effort. And no individual will work hard unless the rewards to doing so are viewed as just. Thus complementary pieces of the individual-effort narrative include the belief that we live in the land of opportunity, and that this land is a meritocracy in which individual effort is appropriately rewarded. From a policy perspective—and this is critical—because the narrative links success to hard work, the poor are viewed with mistrust and suspicion: What did they do wrong to end up so poor? Why have they not worked harder? How many opportunities have they squandered? Can they be trusted with government-provided aid?

There is more to this narrative than individual striving. The economy also includes businesses and government. And beliefs matter a lot for actors in these two sectors, as they have the power to shape the economic environment that we all inhabit. And they certainly have done so.

So what role should businesses play, according to our national mythology? A widely held principle for guiding business activity is that "businesses must simply maximize shareholder value" by keeping their stock price as high as possible. "That and nothing else." Or, similarly, "businesses must maximize profit—full stop."[1] I will return to this particular narrative, proposed and propagated by Milton Friedman, a bit later because it is an important example of a narrative that has been used not only to make sense of our world but also to guide strategic decisions by business and government, and not always for the better.[2] Government's role, according to this narrative, is to make sure that markets operate freely, and to get out of the way of individual attainment—less government is more.

Layered over this narrative are the stories many of us believe, tell, and are told about our tortured racial history. Some hold to the narrative that we are a post-racist nation, that systemic and institutional racism never existed, no longer exist, or no longer affect outcomes for people of color. It is still the case that much of our nation's history—from genocide and displacement of Indigenous peoples, to broken promises for restitution to Blacks in the wake of the Civil War—is not taught to schoolchildren.[3] Curricula are censored and books are banned. Combined with other elements of The Myth, especially the notion that individual effort produces success, these narratives have been used to dismiss or diminish initiatives to address relative shortfalls in incomes, wealth, and employment among families of color. The Myth supports the conclusions that people of color achieve less success because they have not worked as hard as their white counterparts, or because they have made poor savings and investment decisions, or because they have taken advantage of government support programs instead of working.[4] In short, they merit the outcomes they receive.

The stories we tell to describe individual, business, and government behavior are the essential elements of The Myth. It is the purpose of this book to deconstruct those stories, demonstrate the vast damage they have done, and point the way toward a more generous national narrative that will aid in providing widespread opportunity to succeed.

The Myth as Excuser and Creator of Poor Outcomes

The system The Myth has built leaves millions behind. How does The Myth explain that? Lack of individual effort and initiative. Correspondingly, the rising cohort of billionaires in our country is the result of supreme intellect and Herculean effort on their part. For the low-income, the fault is in ourselves, not our stars. For the high-income, success also owes to our (better, more industrious) selves, not to our stars. In both cases, the role of our stars is grossly understated.

We see evidence of The Myth in action when we make excuses for the millions left behind. They are lower-skilled, less-trained, less-motivated, low-productivity workers. The Myth would insist that this is true. The simplest economic theories would immediately point to these excuses for poor outcomes.

This view of the world, The Myth, is corrosive. It is disrespectful to the millions in our country—disproportionately people of color—who are barred from achieving success, and it is grossly inaccurate. Every time we see or hear a news item or documentary that touts the "you can do anything you want—all you have to do is dream big and work hard" meme, The Myth rears its ugly head once more. It's everywhere.

Apart from the emotional responses they might induce, why do these rationalizations of lopsided outcomes matter so much at the national level? First, because they allow ordinary citizens to justify the existence of gross inequities, rather than rail against them. The Myth deflects attention from significant truths that provide alternative and factually accurate explanations for the outcomes. The truth of the claim that "all men are created equal" may indeed be self-evident. But after birth, do all people have equal *opportunity* to succeed? The answer is plainly no. Will free-market capitalism compete away income and wealth disparities? It has not so far, and it is not built to do so. The Myth fosters complacency about truly terrible economic outcomes, which makes it harder to build political will to address them. "It's just the way capitalism works," we are told. "Some aren't cut out to succeed."

A second reason that justifications of inequality matter is because they have been used systematically to design, build, and refine our system so that it continues to heap money and power on those who already have it and to deny everyone else access to the same. In shaping a host of public policies, programs, and institutions—tax policy, the safety net, labor unions, and critically, the array of policies that were designed to build wealth for white families—The Myth was used to exclude access to millions, while ensuring success for the wealthiest and whitest. The reasons for the inequality of outcomes lie not in differences in individual effort but in the economic structures we have designed to mete out opportunity and success, and most especially in the enduring effects of slavery and other forms of institutional racism in our country. Business and government decisions justified by The Myth have stalled earnings for many, limited their access to health care and other work-related benefits, reduced upward mobility within companies, and muted workers' voice in determining the conditions of their employment.

Adherence to The Myth would be more understandable if it were a reasonably accurate and representative depiction of reality. However, I will present ample evidence that the stories many of us tell ourselves about how the economy works—the narratives we hold—are at war with the facts about the outcomes our economy delivers. The key narratives held by many in the United States are not at all fair and accurate descriptions of reality. They may in some cases represent *aspirations* for the country, but they are quite far from representing reality.

Part of the narrative arc of this book consists in tracing how I and others like me—educated, white, privileged, male—came to recognize the falsehoods inherent in The Myth, most often with the help of those who had lived and/or studied the downside of The Myth. I will also discuss how key policy institutions in the United States—notably the Federal Reserve, my employer of over thirty-five years—began to recognize the same. For both people and institutions, that process of recognition was gradual and is still underway.

This book will explore the origins of The Myth in the formation of our national identity, the ways in which aspiration is distorted into description of reality, the reasons for The Myth's persistence in our national psyche, and most importantly the ways in which The Myth has been employed to design an economy that delivers grossly unequal opportunity and outcomes, decade after decade.

As compelling as the data on these issues are, I will also interweave the life stories of residents of low-income communities whom I have interviewed. Their voices will ground the statistics in reality, speaking eloquently to the truth about our broken economic systems.

Elements of Truth

Part of the reason for The Myth's success over the decades is that it contains kernels of truth. Does hard work matter? Of course. But while it is often required to succeed, it is far from sufficient in our economy. Is capitalism a good system? Generally, yes. But our nation has designed a particular flavor of capitalism that distributes success highly unequally, based on initial conditions that include race, ethnicity, place of birth, and socioeconomic class. Do markets do good things? Of course. In tranquil times, they allocate scarce resources pretty efficiently. But they are mute on issues of inequality or structural racism.

Is the economy broken, or doing just what it is supposed to? Ah, there's the rub. The contention of this book is that it has been designed to produce inequality, so in that sense it is not broken. It's doing what it was designed to do. But from the perspective of producing socially desirable outcomes, it's badly broken.[5]

A Nation Beginning to Notice

On an optimistic note, many in our country are becoming more aware of the distance between, on the one hand, our national myths and aspirations, and, on the other, the realities of our economic systems. And this awareness is reflected in key public institutions: my former employer, the

Federal Reserve System, initiated a system-wide effort called Racism and the Economy, which is committed to "understanding the implications of structural racism in America's economy and advancing actions to improve economic outcomes for all."[6] The Biden administration has proposed measures that would help to address some underlying sources of inequality, including a focus on universal free preschool, capping family expenditures on childcare, expanding the child tax credit, closing health care gaps, building affordable housing, increasing federal grants for students attending community and four-year colleges, and investing in historically Black and Native American universities.[7]

But reality has already hit the fan: the child tax credit expired at the end of 2021, and much of the administration's Build Back Better plan is awaiting congressional action as of writing. This highlights an important caveat concerning what might be characterized as a gradually awakening public and its institutions: awareness, at least in some respects, is heightened, but action—and more importantly the political will to take bold action—remains a work in progress.

And the degree of awareness varies quite a bit across key dimensions of the economy. Many people are now more cognizant of racial and ethnic injustice, especially with respect to the criminal justice system, but fewer are aware of the host of *economic* injustices suffered by people of color. And while awareness is growing, most are still woefully unaware of the historical, structural sources of current economic disparities accompanying differences of race and ethnicity. Some are aware but choose not to believe, perhaps swayed more by their post-racist narrative than by the historical research into systemic inequity.

Among those aware of the gaping disparities, those who—knowingly or not—adhere to The Myth may look to very different solutions from those I propose in this book. Critically, The Myth places responsibility for improving outcomes squarely on the individual. It is up to individuals to educate themselves, to gain skills, to pursue remunerative occupations, and to succeed. If they fail in any of these respects, the fault lies in themselves, not the systems in which they live. William Darity Jr. and Kirsten Mullen suggest that this

> dangerous line of thinking alleges the black-white economic gap is due not to an acutely unequal playing field but to blacks' deficient skills, training, and

motivation. Its defenders allege that group-based inequality ultimately can be eliminated if black Americans exercise enough willpower and do "the right thing."[8]

There are, to be sure, elements of political division in the story of our national mythology. Notably, many elements of The Myth have been more closely associated with conservative politicians and their adherents. However, the issue is not a pure red-versus-blue one. Many of The Myth's elements have gained considerable traction among moderate and some liberal politicians. An excessive faith in markets and a deep distrust of the poor shone through clearly in the design of welfare reform in 1996 and in our country's response to the financial crisis of 2007–2009, both Democratic-led efforts. In the latter case, our leaders rapidly mobilized resources to save the financial sector, lending trillions of dollars to the largest institutions. As for ordinary homeowners and workers, the response was halting and far less successful. In financial markets we trust.

Brokenness

This book documents many of the ways in which our economic systems are "broken," by which I mean that they deliver prosperity to the few and misery to the many. It must be said at the outset that nowhere is this clearer than in the gaping disparities between outcomes for whites and people of color, including Indigenous people, and I will return to that theme throughout this volume. Gaps in income, employment, education, health care, childcare, incarceration rates, and net worth—the last of which essentially sums up the cumulative effect of institutional discrimination through all of those channels and more—are stunning and disheartening.

Somewhat less attention is focused on the disparities of class that exist alongside the racial and ethnic disparities among our citizens. Millions of white families also suffer from unequal access to employment and wealth opportunities. In many cases, we hold to the same false narratives about the reasons for class disparities—that they are caused by lack of diligence, poor choices, or inappropriate government interference. I mention these class disparities not to divert attention from the tragic racial and ethnic disparities but to point out that our economy has been distorted in *many* ways, ways which harm both people of color and whites.[9]

Some will balk at my description of the world's second-largest economy as broken.[10] Our productivity is high; our output per person is among the highest in the world.[11] Our education system, particularly at the bachelor's-degree and graduate levels, is the envy of most countries around the world. Our medical, pharmaceutical, and IT sectors are world leaders in innovation. Many of the world's largest financial institutions, as measured by assets, are chartered within our borders.[12] How can this be deemed broken?

While these sectors are without doubt thriving, the income they produce, the jobs they create, and the wealth they amass accrue to a small minority of the country's population. Put differently, these measures of aggregate prosperity gloss over enormous schisms within the US economy. Our economy is indeed large, in absolute size or on a per capita basis; productive; and, in the aggregate, highly successful. Yet within our borders, tens of millions of residents struggle to survive—not just to thrive, but to stay alive.[13] Many families cannot take basic necessities—food, shelter, and medical care—for granted. Standard markers of economic success—access to effective secondary and higher education, employment, stable incomes, retirement security—are out of reach for millions.

The yawning disparities matter for two fundamental reasons. First, they matter to the cold-hearted accounting of lost economic potential: individuals and families who have suffered at the hands of a malfunctioning economy do not contribute all they could, considering their skills, capacities, and imagination. This lost potential has been calculated by many, but the exact magnitude is less important than recognition of the enormity of the problem. Whether it is $1 trillion or $10 trillion of lost annual "output," or $15 trillion of lost wealth, the loss is enormous.[14] This lost potential affects most directly those individuals who have never had a chance at success in our economy. But it also affects everyone else, by shrinking the size of the economic pie and reducing the level of demand for goods and services that the "winners" in our rigged system provide.

The second reason that disparities matter is at least as sobering as the first: the loss of human potential. Lives that do not flower or flourish, lives whose creative and innovative impulses are stifled or drowned, people who find it difficult to muster an ounce of hope for a better future—these are lives partly lost, whether the loss is captured in GDP measures or not. As a country, we should be embarrassed that, despite our aggregate riches, we allow such a combination of economic and human destruction to be the norm for millions of our fellow citizens. To me, it is unconscionable and totally inconsistent with the view we hold of our country as the land of opportunity. This situation is also completely at odds with any moral system that values all lives equally.

How can a country that is so wealthy in the aggregate be so comfortable with such outcomes? Are these outcomes consistent with the simplest stories about how our economy works—the narratives—that we hold dear? Aren't we the land of opportunity, a meritocracy in which hard work is sufficient for success, in which free-market capitalism delivers the best outcomes for all, given individual effort?

I believe the answer to that last question is emphatically no. We need to change the narrative held by many about how our economy really works. The narrative that attributes these horrendous outcomes to lack of individual effort or poor decision-making is in my view corrosive, disrespectful, and simply inaccurate. It will likely be impossible to take the significant steps required to improve economic structures if a large swath of the population believes that the current systems are fine, and that a change is unnecessary or even counterproductive. To fix our brokenness, we must reconsider and change our national mythology.

On Absolute versus Relative Outcomes

Much of the current debate focuses on the *inequality* of income and wealth—that is, the *relative* difference in economic outcomes across more- and less-successful people. I believe that concern, while important, is secondary. Even more important than these *relative* outcomes are the *absolute* outcomes for many in our economy. To be sure, it seems grossly inequitable that CEOs earn so much more than the median workers in their firms.[15] But that kind of unfairness is a small concern for millions of families who struggle to attain sufficient wages to *survive* without significant government assistance in the form of food, housing, and health care. If our country were to evolve so that all families had the opportunity to succeed, with the resources to achieve stable economic existence—not continuously terrified of losing employment, housing, and health care, not forced to cope with childcare disruptions that threaten to send them into a downward spiral toward abject poverty—that would be an enormous leap forward for our country. Even if CEOs were still paid generous (read: obscene) amounts.

Urgency

I believe our country has an economic and moral obligation to right the wrongs that it has perpetrated since its founding. To do so requires first and foremost a change in our national narrative—the stories we tell ourselves and each other about how our economy works, how our economic structure was designed and why, why poverty exists, how the racial and ethnic economic divides arose, and where economic success comes from. If we can reach some agreement on these narratives, we stand a chance of moving forward with changes to our economic structures that address the defects in design that we implemented earlier in our history.

Martin Luther King Jr. put it this way in 1967:

> We must honestly admit that capitalism has often left a gulf between superfluous wealth and abject poverty, has created conditions permitting necessities to be taken from the many to give luxuries to the few, and has encouraged small-hearted men to become cold and conscienceless so that, like Dives before Lazarus, they are unmoved by suffering, poverty-stricken humanity.[16]

We could opt for incremental, gradual approaches, which I frankly believe will do little to improve lives. Nor would gradualism properly reflect the urgency of the circumstances. Alternatively, we can choose bolder actions that directly address our long history of racial, ethnic, and class-based inequities. Such actions will be costly, but far less costly than leaving things as they are. We need to come to a reckoning about how and why our *systems* are broken and work to assemble new systems that will function better for us all.

Who Are "We"?

Throughout the book, "we" refers to the society that has created and perpetuated The Myth. Although some members of society now see The Myth for what it is, we as a society continue to use The Myth to excuse and create undesirable outcomes. This is why I use the collective "we." In other cases, where I am referring to a subset of the population, I will try to be explicit about whose perceptions and actions I am describing.

A Roadmap for the Book

Part I delves into our national economic mythology, defining and expanding on the components of The Myth described in this chapter. From there chapter 2 explores survey evidence on adherence to elements of The Myth among the population at large and among whites and people of color, low- and high-income people, conservatives and liberals. Chapter 3 provides an origin story for The Myth that traces back to the founding of our republic and earlier.

Part II offers evidence bearing on brokenness: the unequal distribution of income, the startlingly unequal distribution of wealth, the racial and ethnic disparities in both, and the prevalence and characteristics of "low-quality" jobs (chapters 4–6). Chapter 5 closes with a discussion of economic mobility—whether low income and wealth are transient or enduring. Chapter 7 briefly summarizes other dimensions of brokenness, including in the areas of housing, health care, education, incarceration, and access to financial markets.

Part III pits the facts against The Myth, drawing on economic evidence that contrasts the role of luck with the role of individual effort, evidence bearing on the trickle-down theory, and economic history that sheds light on the supposed inerrancy of free-market capitalism coupled with our bias toward rescuing the rich and powerful when they are in distress (chapter 8). Chapter 9 compares key outcomes across other free-market capitalist economies to demonstrate that ours are not the unavoidable outcomes of a free-market capitalist system.

Part IV traces the history of the use of The Myth in shaping key parts of our economy—institutional racism, carefully designed markets, tax policy, the safety net (including welfare reform), workplace norms, the rise and fall of unions, and macroeconomic policy. Part V surveys the wreckage that our system has left in its wake. Chapter 11 explores losses looking backward: destruction of Indigenous people and estimated losses due to slavery. Chapter 12 considers losses that we will bear in the future due to childhood poverty, inadequate earnings and benefits, wealth inequality, and deaths caused by all of the above.

Part VI proposes a way forward that concentrates on providing opportunity to build human and financial capital. Chapter 13 discusses the importance of changing the narrative about poverty and race, the psychological barriers to doing so, and promising means of overcoming those barriers. Chapter 14 details specific elements of a program to move forward, focusing on early childhood education, more effective use of our community college system, restructuring the workplace, providing much more affordable housing, enlisting white allies as mentors and coaches to build a more inclusive leadership corps, and instituting baby bonds and reparations. The chapter also estimates the costs entailed by these structural improvements. Chapter 15 discusses the other half of the battle: challenges in *implementation* that we must overcome if policy ideas are to become effective realities.

I The Myth

Narrative (n): a way of presenting or understanding a situation or series of events *that reflects and promotes a particular point of view or set of values.*
—*Merriam-Webster's Collegiate Dictionary* (emphasis added)

Narrative (n): a story that connects and explains a carefully selected set of supposedly true events, experiences, or the like, *intended to support a particular viewpoint or thesis.*
—Dictionary.com (emphasis added)

The real world is complicated. That's true of the physical world we inhabit and of the more abstract world of thoughts, ideas, philosophies, politics, art, music, and economics. To make sense of and make our way through the world, we constantly rely on simplifications that strip away the inessential and focus on the essential. Whether we're riding a bike, playing baseball, or making judgments about what's good or bad economic policy, we must use simplified renderings of complex realities to navigate and to make decisions.

Narratives constitute one of these simplifying tools. In making complex choices about how to conduct our business, or whether to augment or reduce government safety net programs, or whether the current degree of inequality is acceptable, we often fall back on underlying narratives.[1]

*   *   *

For the most part, I absorbed our national mythology as most of us do: through constant repetition. We hear it in the tale of our nation's founding commitment to equality. We hear it in the articulation of our unique global status as the land to which immigrants thronged to seize opportunity. We hear it in the adulation of industrial titans who supposedly succeeded through sheer force of will and intellect. And we hear it in the countless books, songs, and movies that tug at the particular heartstring that wants to believe that we can all succeed, regardless of where we start.

But I was also inculcated in this mythology through my mainstream economics training. I was taught that pay is market-determined and therefore both efficient and just. I was taught that businesses should maximize profits, an organizing principle that simplifies the host of complex roles they play in the economy and that yields the best outcomes for all. And the role of race in determining economic outcomes? That was barely mentioned in my formal training. All of this I learned diligently like the good student I was, and I believed like the acolyte I used to be.

It is still inspiring to read the words of the Declaration of Independence. That document sets forth many of the ideals to which our country has always aspired. I believe in those aspirations—indeed, it is because I believe in them that I find the current gulf between aspiration and reality so disheartening.

Because we have largely absorbed our mythology unconsciously, implicitly, I strive here to make the many elements of The Myth explicit. I hope it will become clear that The Myth has a powerful hold on us—across differences of race, gender and political party—and that it has been intimately involved in the construction of key aspects of our economic system.

1 Our National Economic Mythology

The Parable of the Self-Made Man

On September 11, 2017, CNBC—arguably a center-left media outlet—ran a story titled "10 Billionaires Like Oprah Winfrey Who Grew Up Poor." Rags-to-riches stories like these are not only the stuff of nineteenth-century authors like Horatio Alger. They remain common across media—TV news, films, theater, motivational books—to this day.

This particular story, which briefly chronicles the financial transformations of Oprah Winfrey; Ralph Lauren; J. K. Rowling; top executives from Oracle and Starbucks; and others, does more than report the facts of these truly remarkable transitions from poverty to billions. The story is peppered with aphorisms like these:

> Whether you're in need of some inspiration to start your own business, or you want to learn how to become a billionaire, take a look at how these famous folks made it to the top.

> Growing up poor didn't stop these CEOs, celebrities, and business experts from reaching the pinnacle of success—and it shouldn't stop you, either.

The story includes testimonials from the well-heeled, such as:

> I worked like hell to become part of the 1 percent. (Investor Kenneth Langone, worth about $6 billion)

> Everyone who works hard, and maybe a little cleverly, has the opportunity to make almost anything possible. (Larry Ellison, college dropout and cofounder of Oracle, worth about $90 billion)

To their credit, many of these "self-made" billionaires now give a substantial portion of their riches to the less fortunate.

The inspirational adages are not there by accident. They make a very specific point: Success is available to everyone. Opportunity is distributed equally. And the difference between success and failure is effort. You too can become a billionaire, if you dream big and work hard. "That's the American Dream, that anything here is possible," according to Ellison.[1]

This story encapsulates and caricatures a narrative so dominant in the United States that we often are not aware that it's there: success is determined by individual effort, and everyone can achieve it. But the narrative is not only about the sufficiency of individual effort. The individual must have the *opportunity* to exert effort in exchange for just compensation. Thus a key component of the narrative is that we truly are the land of opportunity, in which the chance to succeed is available to everyone. And not only is opportunity universally available, but also the reward for taking the opportunity and working hard is just compensation—otherwise, why do all the work? Put differently, we live in a meritocracy—a system in which people get what they deserve, where all workers from janitors to CEOs are paid according to their true value to the economy.[2]

So far, the narrative focuses on individuals—their opportunities, efforts, and rewards. But there are other key actors who complete this view of the world: businesses and government. This narrative has a particular view of how businesses and government are best structured to allow individual flourishing. As for businesses, they do best for everyone when they obey the categorical imperative for firms, as articulated by Milton Friedman in a 1970 *New York Times* essay: maximize shareholder value by maximizing profits, and nothing else.[3] As for government, its job is to promote the free operation of markets and more generally to minimize its interventions in the economy—to get out of the way of individual achievement.

The roles of the individual and of government intersect when politicians consider aid for families and individuals. The government, it is said, should help the "deserving poor," and, of course, not the undeserving. The precise definition of who is deserving has evolved somewhat over time, but in nineteenth-century America as in fifteenth century Europe, the deserving poor were those who *could not* work, who were physically disabled. Those who *could* work were seen as undeserving, regardless of the economic circumstances that working afforded them, and therefore did not merit assistance from the government. The deserving/undeserving distinction and the distrust of the poor that it breeds have shaped policy discussions right up to the present day.[4]

Finally and critically, while the narrative may acknowledge to some extent the racial injustices of the past, it embraces the belief that racism is now behind us and today plays little role in determining economic outcomes.[5] These are the key elements of The Myth: All individuals have the opportunity to succeed, and their success is proportionate to their own effort. Business's one task is to maximize profits. Government's primary task is to ensure that markets remain free, and its secondary task is to provide minimal aid to only the deserving poor. Race plays no role in determining who prospers.

While The Myth largely focuses on the ingredients for success, it also implies explanations for failure. Poor economic outcomes—the yawning inequities in income, wealth, education, criminal justice, housing, and health care—are best explained by lack of effort and poor decisions by individuals, or by inappropriate government interference that prevents markets operating freely and efficiently.

This narrative and its constituent components play two important roles in our economy. First, the narrative is used to explain and justify—to excuse the array of outcomes that are documented in this book. If you trust that free-market capitalist economies featuring minimal government intervention produce the best economic outcomes, then the outcomes we observe must be the best we can achieve. Tinkering with those outcomes—especially via government policy—is dangerous!

Second, the narrative is used to shape the economy so as to perpetuate and augment the disparate outcomes that it has produced to date, by advocating for hands-off government policy and by structuring the workplace. As will be made clear in Part II, the system works really well for a small subset of the population. As a consequence, there is strong financial and political interest among the wealthy and powerful in keeping it that way.

I find far more realistic an alternative narrative that challenges the premises underlying The Myth. Briefly, this alternative narrative recognizes that we do not live in the land of opportunity, as opportunity is far from equally available to all. As an obvious corollary, most people simply cannot achieve whatever they may dream. Differences in outcomes are not best explained by differences in individual effort. There is no such thing as a free market that operates without significant government support and/or intervention. Decades of systemic racism have indeed caused the enormous gaps in wealth and other outcomes that we observe across demographic groups. CEOs do not merit the vast multiples of their employees' salaries that they are paid. A slavish devotion to shareholders is the hobgoblin of the small-minded firm and has likely caused tremendous damage to the welfare of low-to-moderate-income workers.

Perhaps most importantly, this alternative narrative holds that the rich and powerful have consciously *created* the economy we have, designing it to deliver outlandish returns to the few and a teetering economic existence to the many. It did not happen because that's the way capitalist economies have to work.[6] It happened because some of us chose to make it that way. Looking on the bright side, this implies a glimmer of hope. We have a *choice* about how our system works. We broke it, we can fix it.

Consider how one might frame policy and business choices from the perspectives of The Myth and its opposing view. Will an expansion of the safety net lead the poor to misuse more scarce resources and avoid work, or will it facilitate opportunities to succeed? Will an exclusive focus on profits raise a firm's stock price, or will it reduce wages and benefits for employees? Will increased regulation of financial markets reduce efficiency, or will it prevent excessive financial risk-taking from spilling over to Main Street, harming businesses and households? These examples may seem oversimplified, but in fact these tradeoffs appear quite explicitly in key episodes in our nation's economic history, and I discuss them in greater detail later in the book.

In a refreshing counterpoint to the billionaire stories cited above, CBS ran a 2022 story about Pete Kadens, a businessman who donated the cost of college tuition and fees to the graduating classes at five Chicago-area high schools. While Kadens had worked hard and amassed considerable wealth, he balked at being called a self-made man. In an interview with reporter Steve Hartman, he showed considerable awareness of the weakness of that narrative: "This country was built on the notion that no matter where you come from, you can become successful and wealthy—that just factually is not true." Thank you, Mr. Kadens, for that concise summary of this book![7]

Why Do We So Mistrust the Poor?

A theme that is woven throughout our nation's history is a deep mistrust of the poor. It flows from the belief that the poor are lazy. For those who believe they have authored their own success, unaware of the many good fortunes that have brought them that success, it can seem puzzling that there are so many who struggle with poverty. Why didn't they just work harder? There must be something wrong with them. We can't just give them aid and support; they can't be trusted to use the money wisely.

Beliefs about the sufficiency of hard work can be employed in a particularly pernicious way to interpret the effects of systemic racism on economic outcomes for families of color. Rather than admit the ways in which our country as a matter of policy has barred people of color from equal opportunity to achieve success, the individual-effort narrative instead asserts that racial and ethnic differences in economic outcomes reflect defects in individuals' efforts, as well as their choices about education, housing, and criminal activity.[8]

Mistrust of the poor is compounded when immigration status is involved. Not only are many immigrants poor, but they're also "not from here." As part of this book project, I conducted interviews with lower-income residents of Massachusetts, with the goal of adding the human experience reflected in their voices to the dispassionate facts presented in the data.[9] Three of the interviewees—Mariela M., Rosada S., and Brenda R.—emigrated from Central America to escape gangs that had repeatedly attacked them and had murdered family members, forcing them to relocate multiple times within their home countries. They arrived in the United States in different ways—one with the help of an international aid agency, another by crossing the Rio Grande on foot, the third via a more circuitous route. Some family members have been able to join them, others have been left behind.

Their stories are harrowing, and it was difficult for them to describe their lives to me without breaking down. Their experiences are still raw, the pain very near the surface. Some of their family members were granted refugee status fairly quickly, but others' status is still in limbo as courts continue to assess their circumstances years after they arrived here. Their stories are like those of many other low-income families: they are struggling, working as much as possible, trying to provide for their children, worried about how to get health care and pay the rent, relying on food banks, and unable to save much. Their access to benefits is limited. As Rosada put it, "Many who come into this country can't feed their kids and can't apply for food stamps, because they're undocumented." Their finances are precarious. Brenda worries that "the economy isn't getting better, but rent is getting higher. . . . Things could turn worse for the economy, making it harder to balance everything." The interviewees wonder why benefits are not available to them. "Every taxpayer should have the same benefits as anyone else," one told me. "[We're] paying the taxes."[10]

Our nation has, of course, a long and painful history with immigrants. Emma Lazarus's poem at the base of the Statue of Liberty famously welcomes the refugee:

> Give me your tired, your poor,
> Your huddled masses yearning to breathe free,
> The wretched refuse of your teeming shore.

The "Mother of Exiles," as Lazarus calls her, also commands, in a rebuke to European elites,

> Keep, ancient lands, your storied pomp![11]

In spite of Lady Liberty's focus on the downtrodden, as a nation, we are generally more comfortable welcoming the educated elite from around the world than the poor immigrant, although there is some debate about allowing either type of immigrant into the country.[12] In part, this is because, like the stories many of us tell about the poor and about racial disparities, our narratives about immigrants—the rationale behind our resistance to their incorporation into our country—is deeply flawed, despite centuries of successful integration for many waves of immigrants. "They will take our jobs." "They abuse the welfare state." "They won't assimilate." "They increase crime." All of these claims have been shown to be mistaken: immigrants *increase wages and income* for US citizens; immigrants are less likely to use key government programs, even as they contribute significantly to the funding of Medicare and Social Security through payroll taxes; today's immigrants are no less likely to integrate than those of the past; crime rates among immigrants, both documented and undocumented, are significantly lower than among native-born residents.[13]

Meanwhile, misperceptions about poor families and about communities of color are facilitated by the geographic segregation of demographic and economic subgroups in the United States. The flight of white families from urban to suburban residences, which caused a rise in the concentration of people of color in urban settings, is well documented. Today, whether in the cities or the 'burbs, neighborhoods remain segregated by race, ethnicity, and income. The average white person lives in a neighborhood that is about 70 percent white. The average Black person lives in a neighborhood that is about 45 percent Black and 17 percent Hispanic. The average Hispanic person lives in a neighborhood that is 47 percent Hispanic and 32 percent Black.[14] Segregation by income follows a similar pattern: there is little mixing of low- and high-income residents in most neighborhoods, and that tendency has increased in recent decades. However, the extent to which families of different *incomes* reside in the same neighborhood varies by race and ethnicity: low-income people of color are more likely than low-income whites to live in neighborhoods that meet the federal statutory definition for low-income communities. When we don't live near one another, we are freer to construct our own narratives about those who differ from us along racial, ethnic, or class lines.[15]

The Eternal Hope That Riches Will One Day "Trickle Down" from the Top

The phrase "trickle down" has been so widely used that it now has an economics-specific entry in the dictionary:

> **trickle-down theory** (noun): a theory that financial benefits given to big business will in turn pass down to smaller businesses and consumers.[16]

I will examine the evidence bearing on this theory—which applies to the wealthy as much as to big business—later in the book. The phrase appears to have originated with the comedian Will Rogers, who used it to berate President Herbert Hoover's economic stimulus efforts during the Great Depression.[17]

> Mr. Hoover was an engineer. He knew that water trickles down. Put it uphill and let it go and it will reach the driest little spot. But he didn't know that money trickled up. Give it to the people at the bottom and the people at the top will have it before night, anyhow. But it will at least have passed through the poor fellows' hands.

The phrase was subsequently mocked by Samuel Rosenmann, President Franklin D. Roosevelt's speechwriter, and by detractors such as the economist John Kenneth Galbraith to describe President Ronald Reagan's "supply-side" economic policies.[18] While few conservatives would label their own policies "trickle-down," many would subscribe to the notion that less regulation, and tax cuts for corporations and the wealthy, can be expected to raise output and create jobs.

This theory is commonly used to justify tax cuts for corporations and wealthy individuals—indeed, the Tax Cuts and Jobs Act of 2017 incorporates some elements of supply-side economics. The importance of this element of The Myth lies exactly in its power to motivate politicians to pursue specific policies that overtly benefit the already-wealthy and successful. Without an appeal to the benefits such a policy might yield for the lower and middle classes, it would be more difficult to garner political backing. But if the supply-side effects really do kick in, well then, it's a win-win proposition for the rich and the poor! Unfortunately that is very far from reality.

How Organizations Value Their Workers

Economists have often been less than helpful in their rigid adherence to simple theories about how the economy works. Basic economic theory would suggest (loosely) that if the addition of a worker to a firm's rolls adds $1,000 of value to the firm's output, then in a perfectly competitive world, the worker would receive something like $1,000 in total compensation for her effort. This element of The Myth has implications for both the low and the high end of the compensation scale.

On the low end, this principle can be used to justify poor compensation. The argument is that low compensation *must* reflect a relatively low contribution to the firm. That contribution may be low because the position occupied by the worker is inherently a low value-added position. Or it could be that the *specific* worker brings relatively little skill and experience to the job and thus will contribute relatively little to the firm's welfare. There should of course be some truth to both propositions. Jobs that require fewer skills and less training will on average pay less than those that require more skills and training, a prediction borne out in numerous studies of actual earnings.[19] And within a specific job type, workers who bring lower skills, training, or effort to the job will over time likely accrue less pay, as they add less value to the firm.

But to determine if a worker is paid fairly, we need to know not only their value *relative* to other workers, but their *absolute* value to the firm. Is fair pay for a maintenance worker $25,000 per year or $40,000 per year? In reality, it is very difficult to measure the true value a worker adds to a business—the output added by the worker per hour worked—because output is hard to judge. How do we measure the output of a lawyer? Or a health care aide? Or a secretary? Or a teacher? We can certainly measure the *hours* spent on a task, but that tells us nothing about the output produced per hour. Indeed, in the cases of many occupations, output is estimated mostly from hours worked, so that the measurement of output-per-hour is hopelessly circular. You can't independently measure both hours and output if all you know is hours! So there's no terribly firm foundation for determining appropriate pay for many workers.[20] This allows a lot of leeway and subjectivity in assessing whether workers are paid appropriately.[21]

On the high end of the compensation scale, the same basic argument is often applied, with some embellishments. Sky-high CEO compensation is also justified by reference to the value-added principle: it must be that the value CEOs contribute is many multiples of their firm's average worker. If they did not, no firm would pay them the salaries they receive, often in the tens of millions of dollars. It wouldn't be "rational." Recent estimates of CEO pay show an increasing spread between CEO and average worker compensation. A series of studies by the Economic Policy Institute, for example, shows top executive pay increasing from a multiple of 20–30 in 1965 to over 350 in 2020.[22]

Theoretical arguments that seek to justify huge gaps may focus on the value of CEO's "rolodexes" (professional networks); the increasing importance of digital-platform companies that have typically paid their CEOs lucrative salaries; the increasing array of complex skills now required to function as a CEO, including an understanding of financial markets, public relations, and navigating a globalized marketplace and supply chain; and the effect of increasing firm size.[23] Other empirical research that blends theory and practice notes that the actual link between CEO compensation and firm performance is weak and that CEO compensation may be better explained by the "social psychology of the boardroom." That is, because CEOs serve on the boards of one another's companies, they pay each other well, knowing that generosity toward their colleagues will return to benefit them.[24]

To me, the stories that justify outlandish CEO pay reflect the business profession's self-serving desire to rationalize outcomes that most would view as simply absurd. As a good friend of mine quipped, "Do you think that Mark Zuckerberg would have abandoned his Facebook project if he knew that his net worth would be a mere $100 million, instead of $100 billion?" CEO compensation seems well out of proportion with any true value added, either to the company in question or to society, and way out of line with the incentives needed to motivate hard work and innovation. The rationalization of very low salaries seems similarly suspect, although unlike unbounded CEO salaries, there is a limit to how low pay can go.

Hijacking Horatio: Alger's "Rags-to-Riches" Stories

Horatio Alger published a series of Gilded Age stories that are now commonly called "rags-to-riches" tales. A brief digression into these Alger stories will illustrate what Alger actually wrote, and how his writings have been adapted to fit The Myth. The recastings of his writing again reflect our deep desire to believe that individual effort in a land of opportunity makes anything possible for anyone.

Alger wrote his stories, often in serial form, in the last third of the 19th century. While his novels for boys are often characterized as rags-to-riches stories, in fact they most often focused on the *virtues* of the protagonist, who usually began in disadvantaged circumstances. In most of the stories, the protagonist got a boost from a wealthy benefactor who helped him escape his initial circumstances. Alger described these interventions as the result of divine providence—God had looked favorably on the youth of high virtue and rewarded him with material prosperity. Alger did not suggest that providence was likely to be available to the average person, so his wasn't in fact a self-help prescription for widespread economic success. Instead, it was a morality play that ended well for the virtuous protagonist, due to divine intervention via the benefactor. Today, some might change the source of individuals' success from "providence" to "luck." In short, hard work did not lead to wealth. Good luck did.

Alger's novels fell out of favor in the early twentieth century as wealth inequality rose and as labor unions and labor disputes became more prominent features of the economy.[25] But even today, the Horatio Alger Society annually presents its Strive and Succeed Award to "promising young people who emulate the ideals of Horatio Alger, Jr.," namely "the concept that success is earned and character is developed by following principles of honesty, integrity, hard work, industry, and good sportsmanship."[26] No one could fault the society for promoting these virtues.

But judging by Alger's self-proclaimed intent for these stories, we have promulgated a distorted interpretation of his morality plays. Interestingly, in Alger's preface to *Ragged Dick*, first published as a serial and then collected into a single volume, he frames his stories as follows:

The author hopes that, while the volumes in this series may prove interesting stories, they may also have the effect of enlisting the sympathies of his readers in behalf of the unfortunate children whose life is described, and of leading them to co-operate with the praiseworthy efforts now making by the Children's Aid Society and other organizations to ameliorate their condition.[27]

Rather than a self-help manual for the indigent, Alger's book was a plea for compassion—and aid—to the many who were born into poverty. The link others have mistakenly drawn between Alger's novels and the efficacy of bootstrapping oneself to prosperity reveals our deep desire to believe that that's how our economy works. We have distorted Alger's meaning to suit our love of The Myth.

The Role of Institutional Racism in Our Economy

With the Supreme Court's ruling in *Brown v. Board of Education* in 1954, the passage of the Civil Rights Act in 1964, the Fair Housing Act of 1968, and the executive orders that spurred the use of affirmative action in employment and university admissions, many believed we were entering a post-racial era of US history. Following the election of the country's first Black president in 2008, many were eager to confirm that race was no longer a factor in the most important decisions we make as a country.

Because it has been more than fifty years since the passage of these key pieces of legislation, any effects of previous discrimination should have faded or reversed, The Myth might say. The laws should remain on the books (perhaps), but the use of affirmative action to achieve employment or school admissions goals is no longer necessary. After the election of Barack Obama in 2008, the *Wall Street Journal*, for example, published an editorial averring, "One promise of his victory is that perhaps we can put to rest the myth of racism as a barrier to achievement in this splendid country."[28]

That the *Journal* identified racial barriers to achievement as a myth reflects an underlying pillar of The Myth itself. If racism is not to blame for disparities in economic outcomes, something or someone else must be. Blame lies with individuals rather than institutions.

Mattie, a Black woman living in Roxbury, Massachusetts, who grew up in Boston worked for the city for decades, describes herself as "borderline poor." Asked about whether she feels economically stable, she said, "I don't feel like I'm in a comfortable place financially, but I know how to make it work." Unprompted, she began our conversation by pooh-poohing The Myth: "You can't just work harder to achieve your own goals. We live in a time of systemic racism, with many inequalities . . . We're still struggling to this day, in the land of plenty."[29]

The Appropriate Role for Government

The Myth maintains that the combination of capitalism with unfettered markets does the best job of allocating the nation's resources among its people. The genius of markets is that they provide a mechanism for allocating economic resources without the need for government interference. Relative scarcities produce increased prices—for goods, services, labor, financial assets—enticing suppliers to produce more of what is scarce, in turn reducing scarcity and lowering the price. In the long run, those goods and services that yield the greatest benefit to society will be in highest demand, yield the most profit, and draw the most resources, producing the most beneficial outcome. Government policies that interfere with unfettered capitalism will distort the price signals needed to clear markets and lead to worse outcomes overall. Or so we have been told.

To be clear, in criticizing The Myth, I am not taking the position that capitalism per se is a problem. Capitalism and (relatively) free markets can work well in many circumstances. The problem lies in our particular brand of capitalism, a brand the wealthy and powerful have worked hard to create and sustain.[30]

A strong corollary to the free markets religion is the belief that smaller government is better, *because the private sector—"markets," in many cases—does most things better than government can.* The private sector is of course better suited to the basic provision of many goods and services in normal times. Very few today seriously advocate a move toward Soviet-style government control of resources.[31] But The Myth expands the scope of private-market expertise to many arenas. A 1981 remark by President Reagan to the National Alliance of Business sums up this position nicely:

> There is a legitimate role for government, but we mustn't forget: before the idea got around that government was the principal vehicle of social change, it was understood that the real source of our progress as a people was the private sector. The private sector still offers creative, less expensive, and more efficient alternatives to solving our social problems. Now, we're not advocating private initiatives

and voluntary activities as a halfhearted replacement for budget cuts. We advocate them because they're right in their own regard. They're a part of what we can proudly call "the American personality."[32]

Attributing the "real source of our progress" to the private sector is playing a bit fast and loose with history. Many of the world's most profound and life-changing improvements—reliable water supplies, electrification, public secondary schools, life-extending medical breakthroughs—have arisen through government-funded basic research and through public policy.[33] But most jarring to my ear is the proclamation that the private sector "offers creative, less expensive, and more efficient alternatives to solving *our social problems*." If that were true, the social problems of the 1960s ought long since to have been eradicated. But that is far from true.

The argument over the size and appropriate role of government continues today, and it is not restricted to debate across party lines. There is significant disagreement within the two major parties about that role, as evidenced by the disputes within the Democratic Party as it tried to move forward the Biden administration's historically large and far-reaching social-programs bill in the fall of 2021.

The Role of Shareholder Value in Guiding Businesses

Maximizing shareholder value, maximizing profits, keeping the company's stock price high—these are the overarching goals for the firm. As Milton Friedman wrote in 1970, revealing some of the ideological underpinnings that motivated his view,

> The businessmen believe that they are defending free enterprise when they declaim that business is not concerned "merely" with profit but also with promoting desirable "social" ends; that business has a "social conscience" and takes seriously its responsibilities for providing employment, eliminating discrimination, avoiding pollution and whatever else may be the catchwords of the contemporary crop of reformers. In fact they are—or would be if they or anyone else took them seriously—preaching pure and unadulterated socialism. Businessmen who talk this way are unwitting puppets of the intellectual forces that have been undermining the basis of a free society these past decades.[34]

Note the emphasis in this passage on "socialism," and on undermining a "free society." Maximizing shareholder value is not just a nice idea. Pursuing other goals undermines the basis of a free society. Them's fightin' words.[35]

Adherence to this element of The Myth has caused significant damage. Note that increasing shareholder value is roughly equivalent to maximizing the stream of profits generated by a company—this generally raises stock prices, so is good for the shareholder. In fact, most formal models of stock prices posit exactly this linkage.[36]

So how is a firm to raise profits? Well, profits are approximately equal to revenues minus costs. One can either raise revenues by increasing prices or expanding markets or market share, or one can lower costs. Costs may be lowered by finding new and more efficient ways to produce goods or offer services—by increasing productivity, economists would say. But costs may also be lowered by reducing expenditures on inputs to production—labor, machinery, utilities, and so on.

The US economy is already pretty productive. Finding ways to significantly increase productivity—innovating—is not easy, although companies are striving to do so all the time. However, keeping down the largest cost of producing most any good or service—labor, which amounts to about 60 percent of all costs—may be easier.[37] It is fair to argue that the relentless drive to raise profits, in large part by keeping labor costs down, has much to do with the distribution of wages and income that we observe in the United States today. The goal of increasing profits has been accomplished by dramatically reducing the power and membership of unions, nearly eliminating the provision of defined-benefit pensions, shifting health-care costs toward workers and away from firms, and keeping wages from rising, all of which generally harm workers.[38]

While workers' productivity—output produced per hour of labor effort—has continued to rise moderately over the past several decades, and while profits have increased significantly over the same period, the share of income going to labor has declined significantly over the past thirty years, in part as a consequence of the cost-reducing actions mentioned above.[39] Another way of putting this is that, although businesses have increased their efficiency and therefore profits, the benefits of increased efficiency have largely not gone to workers. Shareholders, however, have benefitted, as larger profits generally translate into higher stock prices. And shareowners are lopsidedly those in the highest-income and wealth deciles.

In an encouraging sign, some business leaders have lately called into question the principle of shareholder-value maximization. In 2019, the Business Roundtable issued the following proclamation:

Americans deserve an economy that allows each person to succeed through hard work and creativity and to lead a life of meaning and dignity. We believe the free-market system is the best means of generating good jobs, a strong and sustainable economy, innovation, a healthy environment and economic opportunity for all . . . We commit to . . . investing in our employees. This starts with compensating them fairly and providing important benefits . . . supporting them through training and education . . . We foster diversity and inclusion, dignity and respect. . . . Each of our stakeholders is essential. We commit to deliver value to all of them, for the future success of our companies, our communities and our country.[40]

In the same Business Roundtable report, JP Morgan/Chase CEO Jamie Dimon suggests, with a mix of understatement and hyperbole, "The American dream is alive, but fraying . . . Major employers are investing in their workers and communities because they know it is the only way to be successful over the long term." Recent academic work has similarly revisited Friedman's maxim. Of note here is a paper by economists Oliver Hart and Luigi Zingales, which advocates that "companies should maximize shareholder welfare not market value."[41] Shareholder welfare here refers to a broader business objective that takes into account the benefit to society when a company (for example) reduces the environmental impact of its activity or treats its workers more humanely.

These are indeed encouraging signs, although academic articles and business-lobby proclamations do not by themselves alter economic reality.[42] However, they indicate some awareness on the part of some business leaders that all is not right with the US economy. Jamie Dimon might alternatively have said, "The Myth is alive, but fraying." Let's hope so.

The Myth's Logical Fallacies

The Myth's individualist bent is subject to several logical pitfalls. First, attribution of success on the basis of individual effort makes sense only if we limit our sample to the few individuals who started out poor and have become successful. It is easy to make this mistake, because the wealthy and powerful are highly visible precisely because of their wealth and power. They are the ex post winners in our economic lottery.

Focusing only on the few individuals who began life in poor families and end up wealthy, one might infer that being poor poses no barrier to success. But that of course ignores the millions who start out poor and sadly have

little chance at improving their lot, as the data on economic mobility suggest. Unless you believe that none of those millions have worked hard—a
dubious proposition—then you have to conclude that poverty is indeed a
barrier. Those few very successful who started out poor are the exceptions
that prove the rule.

A second misapplication of logic lies in how we misinterpret cause and
effect, especially when multiple causes are at play. Success depends on
many factors. Given a number of other conditions—an economically stable upbringing, familial wealth support, access to a good education, being
white, and some luck—hard work sometimes, though not always, leads
to success. In this context, with a complex set of causal factors at work,
it is extremely hazardous to draw the common *backward* inference: that
the absence of success implies hard work didn't occur, or at least that not
enough of it occurred. Anyone who is not successful simply has not worked
hard enough. In that mistaken way, the hard-work narrative imputes to the
less-successful personal deficiencies that account for their lack of success.

An alternative, and probably more accurate, inference is that less prosperous people typically do not enjoy the same beneficial accidents of birth
and life that the successful do, or that they have labored in an economic
system that denies them the opportunity that it affords others. I have long
asserted the following postulate:

Laziness is uniformly distributed across income deciles.

A rich person is just as likely to be lazy as a poor person is. Effort may
account for some differences within groups of richer and poorer people, but
it is not what distinguishes the truly successful from the struggling.

It is less insulting, even if it is still inaccurate, to infer that everyone who
accrues the outward trappings of great success must have worked very hard,
and often, is assumed to be brilliant as well. Few people will get upset if I
falsely impute to them a strong work ethic and smarts, based on their success.

A third common error of inference is the "I know a person" argument.
In support of the notion that hard work can overcome initial conditions,
no matter how bad, some will point to a person they know who has indeed
succeeded despite objectively poor initial conditions. Therefore, one can
succeed if one works hard. You only need one counterexample to rebut the
claim that hard work is not enough, so the argument goes.

But of course, this is almost always misleading, for two reasons. First, upon further examination, it often turns out that this person had the benefit of a mentor or other benefactor, an unusual schooling or employment opportunity, or some other "leg up" that helped them, despite the odds, to succeed. That is the point of Horatio Alger's stories. Second, the points that this book strives to make pertain to the bulk of the population, not to the few outliers from the norm. We should delight in those who find a way to achieve success despite a difficult start. But it is a mistake to generalize from those rare examples to the plight of the far larger population. There are tens of millions who are finding it difficult to succeed in our economy. It's great that there are a few hundred who make it despite rough starts, but this *highlights the scale of the problem*. It does not reveal a hidden solution.

Tierra, a Boston resident and Afro-Latina single mother of four children, recognizes well that one cannot attribute success solely to the diligence or brilliance of the successful. Born to poor immigrants from Honduras and raised by her two grandmothers, she struggled in early adulthood to muster the resources needed to provide for her children. She accumulated significant debt following a divorce and faced a sharp rise in her rent to $4,400 per month, which would have eaten up most of her take-home pay. Forced to leave her apartment, she was offered the chance to move into a church-owned home for $500 per month. That much-reduced housing cost allowed her to pay down almost $14,000 of her debt. Tierra appreciates the impact that community support had on her current success:

> I think about my two years where I was able to live for $500 a month, and how much that really just shifted my financial [circumstances]. . . . And I think about that, because . . . I've had community, I've had people who support me. I know that there are so many people who do not have that.[43]

Tierra now lives comfortably, with more than $10,000 in the bank to cover emergency expenses and a government pension that will provide $40,000 per year in retirement. She needs no financial support from government programs, family members, or her community. She has always worked hard, but she knows that her success also required significant support from others. And she knows that many others never get that support, and will not succeed despite their hard work.

A Personal Connection

My paternal grandfather, Herbert Fuhrer, could well be cited to support the self-made man element of The Myth. Born in 1906 to a family of quite modest means, he was high school educated, graduating at age sixteen, a self-taught engineer who became president of a successful firm, Viking Pump Company of New York. For a variety of reasons, he received little support from his family after the 1930s. He designed a number of novel pump applications for military and private use, including fuel-handling pumps for oil companies. He recounted to me stories of some of the difficult engineering problems that he and his colleagues solved—pumping viscous liquids like toothpaste around factories, for example. He received a patent for an articulated invalid bed in 1956.[44] He clearly had engineering aptitude, and I'm quite sure he worked very hard.

But he had advantages as well. He had the good fortune to be born white and likely benefited from the work of some very capable partners in his business endeavors. He also had a receptive ear with the senior management at Viking Pump. One can imagine how a high school–educated Black, Hispanic, or Asian man negotiating the same world of work in the 1930s and 1940s might have fared. Herbert did not become a billionaire, but he was well-off, with two houses and a comfortable life.

Despite my close connection to this rags-to-riches story, I now find it difficult to see this story as representative of the fate of many people who start off in challenged economic circumstances. The rags-to-riches narrative simply is not borne out in the data. As alluring as that part of The Myth may be, it is critical that we not use it as a guide to interpreting our country's economic circumstances, nor as a benchmark against which to judge competing economic policies.

2 Public Belief in The Myth: A Survey of Polling Results

How widely held is The Myth among the general public? According to public opinion polls that bear on matters of self-determination, sources of poverty, economic mobility, and the appropriate roles of business and government, the short answer is: quite.

A fascinating 2009 Pew survey, "Economic Mobility and The American Dream," provides some insight into the public's thinking on these issues.[1] The data were collected in the midst of the Great Recession and Financial Crisis, an episode that highlighted some of the perils of a slavish adherence to The Myth. The build-up to the crisis featured a different category of narratives—the cyclical narratives that Nobel laureate Robert Shiller has shown often propel economic crises—along with elements of The Myth. Key cyclical narratives include: housing will always be a good investment; housing prices have never fallen nationally; and you can't prove that big increases in housing prices are indicative of a bubble. Relevant narratives related to The Myth include: financial entities are staffed with (wealthy and therefore) brilliant people who know what they're doing with mortgage-related securities, among other things; and too much financial regulation will stall economic progress.[2]

The crisis could well have shattered those narratives. It did not. The summary accompanying the Pew survey report speaks to the resilience of The Myth even amid severe economic circumstances that could plausibly have shaken its foundations:

> In the midst of an historic economic crisis, Americans insist that despite the recession it is still possible for people to improve their economic standing, and most believe that they control their economic destiny. Americans believe ambition, hard work and education primarily drive mobility, rather than outside forces like the current state of the economy.[3]

That is some sticking power! Many millions of lives were seriously disrupted by unemployment and foreclosure due to external forces—a collapsing financial market, falling housing prices, a deep recession. Yet their belief that individual effort, not these forces, drives mobility was unshaken.[4] Some of the specific findings of the poll highlight strong adherence to important elements of The Myth.

- 71 percent of respondents believe that "personal attributes, like hard work and drive, are more important to economic mobility than external conditions, like the economy and economic circumstances growing up," versus 21 percent who believe otherwise. Belief in the importance of these success factors is held almost equally by Blacks and Hispanics.

- In ranking factors affecting economic mobility, the top-rated response is "hard work" at 92 percent of respondents; second is "having ambition." Luck is third-to-last, selected by 21 percent of respondents.

- Sadly, dead last in factors influencing economic mobility are race and gender, despite the facts about racial disparities and the history of institutional racism.

- There is a distinct (and, to me, disturbing) symmetry in respondents' beliefs about what determines outcomes: the most common explanations

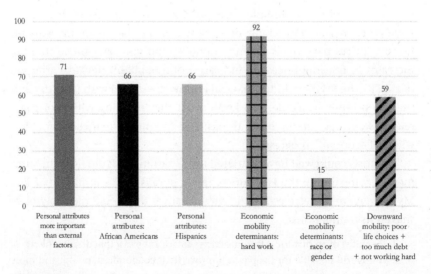

Figure 2.1
Poll results on factors determining economic mobility, 2009. Fraction responding "yes."

for *downward mobility* in the survey were personal attributes and decisions such as "poor life choices," "not working hard" and "too much debt" (the sum of these is presented in the rightmost bar).

- Respondents across all income categories agreed that it is more important to give people "a fair chance to succeed" (71 percent, overall) than it is directly to "reduce inequality" (21 percent). It is not clear whether this implies that Americans largely believe that their compatriots already have a fair chance, and fail because of lack of individual effort, or that they believe we need to restructure our economy to provide more of a fair chance. But there is little willingness to directly address existing inequality.

- In strong contradiction to the evidence on economic mobility, 55 percent of respondents disagreed with the statement: "In the United States, a child's chances of achieving financial success are tied to the income of his or her parent."

- In striking confirmation of the individual-effort aspect of The Myth, one respondent, a father in the 35–49 age range, offered, "People manage to pull themselves up from their bootstraps all the time." Another said, "The Apple guys started the computers in the garage; [people] still do that today, if you've got the smarts and the drive." Yup. That's all it takes.

Overall, this survey demonstrates the remarkable resilience of The Myth among the general public despite an ongoing crisis in which circumstances well beyond individuals' control had mightily disrupted their economic lives. Homeowners who had regularly made their mortgage payments lost their homes when prices fell below the amount they still owed and their incomes were disrupted due to job loss or other causes. Bootstraps clearly provided insufficient lift for many during this episode, yet belief in self-made success persisted. On top of this, the priorities of economic policymakers were made quite clear: financial institutions were quickly rescued, while ordinary households suffered for many years after 2009.

A more recent Pew survey, from 2019, showed that little changed in the decade after the financial crisis. Sixty percent of respondents agree with the statement, "Most people who want to get ahead can make it if they're willing to work hard." That is The Myth in a nutshell, and while political affiliation strongly correlated with views on the Alger narrative (as it has been construed), it has many adherents among both Democrats (45 percent) and Republicans (78 percent).[5]

Closely related to views on the sources of economic success are perspectives on causes of poverty. Views on this topic split strongly across political parties. In response to a 2019 question about whether and why poor families' lives are easy or hard, 74 percent of Republican and Republican-leaning respondents agreed with the statement, "Poor people today have it easy because they can get government benefits without doing anything in return." Yikes. On the other side of the great divide, 72 percent of Democrats and Democrat-leaning respondents agreed with the statement, "Poor people have hard lives because government benefits don't go far enough to help them live decently." That view has grown in favor among Democratic respondents over the past quarter-century: Fewer than 50 percent of Democrats held the same view in a 1994 poll. Republican agreement with this statement has held fairly steady, around 25 percent, since 1994.[6]

Respondents differed widely on their assessments of the key contributors to economic inequality, as summarized in the table below, reproduced from a 2020 Pew report.

Table 2.1
Major contributors to economic inequality

Explanation	"Contributes a great deal"
Outsourcing of jobs to other countries	45
The tax system	45
Problems with the educational system	44
The different life choices people make	42
Some people start out with more opportunities	40
Not enough regulation of major corporations	37
Some people work harder than others	34
Discrimination against racial minorities	32
Automation of jobs	30
Current US trade policies	29
The growing number of legal immigrants working in the US	23
Too much regulation of major corporations	15

Source: Pew Research Center, January 9, 2020. Data collected Sep. 16–29, 2019.

Outsourcing of jobs, the tax system, and the educational system top the list, in recognition of the contributions of these systemic factors to inequality. But just behind are factors conforming to the individual-initiative story—inequality stems from the "different life choices that people make," and "some people work harder than others." Just 40 percent believed that inequality results from "some people start[ing] out with more opportunities than others," in spite of ample evidence supporting this conclusion. Just under one-third attributed inequality to "discrimination against racial and ethnic minorities," an improvement relative to the 2009 survey, although the phrasing of the question is somewhat different.[7]

A more recent 2020 Pew survey—"Why People Are Rich or Poor"—contained a sign of hope. More than half of respondents said they believed that rich people are rich because "they have had more advantages in life than most other people," while one-third believed that they are rich because "they have worked harder than most other people." With respect to why people are poor, the responses are similar, with 71 percent answering that poor people "have faced more obstacles in life than most other people," as opposed to having "not worked as hard as most other people."[8] The results varied dramatically by political affiliation: 80 percent of Democrats attributed being rich to having more advantages in life; among those self-reported as Republican or "leaning" Republican, only 29 percent attributed wealth to having more advantages, and 42 percent believed the source of poverty was not working as hard as most other people.[9] Democrats are even more likely now to attribute wealth to advantages than they were in the recent past. In a 2018 survey, 62 percent of Democrats pointed to advantages, a share that had been quite stable since 2014, compared to the 80 percent reported in the 2020 survey. While the experience of COVID may have changed some Democrats' views about how advantaged the wealthy are, Republicans have not experienced a similar change of heart.[10]

How *important* are such issues to the general public, compared to other economic and social issues? A January 2022 Gallup poll found that only *1 percent* of respondents believed the "gap between rich and poor" was "the most important problem facing the country today." In general, economic problems registered much lower than non-economic problems, by a margin of 80 percent (noneconomic) to 22 percent (economic). But even within the subset of economic problems, the "high cost of living/inflation," the "economy in general," unemployment, and the federal budget deficit/debt ranked ahead of the gap between rich and poor. Issues such as poor government leadership, COVID-19, unifying the country, the judicial system, and race relations/racism (fortunately!) ranked well ahead of the gap between rich and poor, with anywhere from 23 to 5 percent of respondents placing them as their number-one concerns.[11]

In spite of some shifts in attitudes, our population retains great faith in the availability of opportunity and the power of self-determination. That faith remained intact even after two of the largest disruptions in a century—the Great Recession and the COVID pandemic and associated recession—powerfully highlighted inequality of opportunity and the role of external factors in determining individual success.

On Meritocracy: Are Workers Paid What They Are Worth?

A 2021 McKinsey study surveyed 25,000 Americans about the state of economic opportunity. Only one-third of respondents agreed that "most people are fairly recognized and rewarded for their work." Only one-quarter of women agreed with this statement, perhaps reflecting the widely documented gender pay gap. There were only small differences across responses by race and ethnicity. When asked whether "the pay that most people receive allows them a good quality of life," more than a third of men agreed and one-quarter of women agreed. Again, racial and ethnic differences were immaterial. There was a greater divide between low- and high-income workers: about 30 percent of those earnings less than $75,000 agreed with the statement, versus 40 to 47 percent of workers earnings $100,000 or more.[12]

Employers may well believe that they are paying workers according to their value, given competition and cost pressures. Their workers feel differently.[13] Even more importantly, most workers believe they are not paid enough to afford a good quality of life. This represents another tension in adherence to The Myth: the ones cutting the paychecks (employers) believe it; the ones receiving the compensation aren't so sure.

Beliefs about Whether We Live in a Post-Racist Economy

The same 2021 McKinsey survey found that individuals' identities are perceived as affecting their careers. Whites and males appear to be doing okay, not surprisingly. More than one-third of women with family obligations felt that their job prospects were negatively affected by these aspects of their identities. Among Black respondents, 41 percent felt that their race hurt their job prospects and 35 percent that it negatively affected compensation. About 30 percent of LGBT men and women felt their identity had negatively affected job prospects and compensation.

The country more broadly disagrees on whether we are a post-racist nation or not, with opinions dividing across racial and ethnic lines. A 2021 Pew survey found that most respondents, 57 percent, understood that "white people benefit from societal advantages that Black people do not." But respondents didn't see a need for institutional change: just over half wanted to see "little or no change," and only one-quarter thought institutions "need to be rebuilt." Only 42 percent of Whites thought there's "a lot to be done," as compared to more than three-quarters of Blacks.[14]

More focused studies of perceptions of racial equity find that we tend to overestimate both the degree of racial equality *and* the progress our nation has made in improving equality. Americans generally overestimate racial equality in health benefits, wages, income, and wealth, and they overestimate the progress we have made in these dimensions. Black and white Americans, both high- and low-income, overestimate current racial equality, although the extent of overestimation is larger for whites than for Blacks and for high-income whites than for low-income whites.[15] Other research found that, in 2016, Americans on average underestimated the racial wealth gap by about *80 percentage points*.[16]

A 2016 Pew survey, "Views of Race and Inequality," found striking misperceptions about progress on racial equity. Uniformly, far fewer whites than Blacks believed that Blacks were treated less fairly in dealings with the police, in the courts, by mortgage lenders, in the workplace, in retail establishments, or when voting. Seventy percent of Blacks pointed to racial discrimination as "a major reason that some Blacks have a harder time getting ahead," versus 36 percent of whites. Seventy percent of whites saw individual racism as a bigger problem than institutional racism, while only 19 percent held the opposite view. The corresponding proportions for Black respondents were 48 and 40 percent. Strikingly, 38 percent of Black respondents believed that Blacks were as well off or better off financially than whites, in stark contrast to the facts.[17]

Thus as to whether we are a post-racist nation, it depends on who you ask and what your question is. Many believe white privilege is real, but fewer believe institutions need to change. Many white survey respondents (and many Republicans; there is of course overlap) believe we are essentially post-racist—that little good will come from focusing more on the history of slavery and racism and that relatively little work remains to be done, given the progress already made. Importantly, both Blacks and whites grossly underestimate the size of economic inequities. The populace generally understates the size of the disparities and in so doing may reduce the urgency of addressing these inequities.

What Do People Believe the Role of Government Should Be?

The Myth holds that a minimalist, noninterventionist government serves us best. This view derives in part from a longstanding and widely held mistrust of government. According to a 2020 Pew survey, trust in government is at near-record lows, although the level of trust has not changed much since 1980. This view is generally shared by Democrats and Republicans, although Republicans had a modestly more optimistic assessment, at least at the end of the Trump presidency: 28 percent of Republicans said they "trust the federal government to do what is right just about always/most of the time," as compared to 12 percent of Democrats.[18]

While the perceived appropriate role for government varies by partisan affiliation, some broad patterns are consistent across parties. Poll respondents believed strongly that government should play a "major role" in addressing threats to public health (not surprising given that the survey was conducted in the midst of a pandemic), responding to natural disasters, ensuring safe food and medicine, managing immigration, keeping the country safe from terrorism, and strengthening the economy. This last item registered the smallest gap between Republicans and Democrats.

Considerably lower numbers of respondents felt the federal government should play a "major role" in "helping people get out of poverty," although here the partisan split was especially wide. Republicans scored the poverty category lowest of all options. Few thought the government does a good job getting people out of poverty—60 percent rated its performance "somewhat bad" or "very bad," versus 36 percent "good" or "very good." Only 18 percent of Democrats believed the government is doing a very or somewhat good job in helping people escape poverty.[19]

Across religious affiliations, Buddhists, Hindus, Jews and Muslims were much more likely than Christians to believe that "government aid to the poor does more good than harm," with 60 percent or more seeing more good done by aid. The population overall is evenly split on this question. Mainline Protestants responded similarly to the general population. Interestingly, members of historically Black Protestant denominations and Jehovah's Witnesses believed strongly that government aid to the poor does more good than harm, by two-to-one margins. Evangelical Protestants, on the other hand, were less convinced, with 38 percent seeing more good than harm and 56 percent seeing more harm than good.[20] Evangelical Protestants are of course closely affiliated with the Republican party, supporting the GOP by a two-to-one margin.[21]

In sum, nobody really trusts our government, and support for aid to the poor is middling at best. The scorecard for the government's handling of aid needs improvement. These views are generally consistent with an electorate that is skeptical about whether the government can or should do something to reduce poverty.

What Do People Believe the Role of Business Should Be?

The answer depends on whom you ask. CEOs, academic researchers, and business writers are actively debating the role that maximizing shareholder value, à la Milton Friedman, should play, as opposed to maximizing the broader "stakeholder value" or practicing corporate social responsibility. The Business Roundtable and associated discussions mentioned above reflect the growing awareness that shareholder value may not be the be-all-and-end-all of business objectives. By and large, this is a discussion among the very largest business owners, who have the overhead and profit margins—the luxury, really—to consider new goals.

Michael Porter and Mark Kramer of Harvard Business School see hope for businesses that expand their horizons beyond shareholder value. They recommend embracing the goal of creating "shared value," which fosters economic value "by creating societal value."[22] Some of their suggestions amount to means of improving productivity by involving new voices in the design and production of goods and services, taking into account the variety of effects that a company's products and production processes may have on the communities in which it operates. Porter and Kramer also recommend investing in employee well-being and engagement, which have been shown to improve productivity. "Not all profit is equal" in their view. "Profits involving a social purpose represent a higher form of capitalism—one that will enable society to advance more rapidly while allowing companies to grow even more. The result is a positive cycle of company and community prosperity, which leads to profits that endure."[23] Evolving our capitalist system to a "higher form" sounds like a good antidote to the slavish devotion to shareholder value.

But Stanford political economist Neil Malhotra points out the difficulty in implementing a new paradigm like this: How does one trade off the competing objectives inherent in a shared-value or multiple-stakeholder approach? The simplicity and clarity of shareholder value, which is relatively easy to measure, is one reason that this maxim continues to dominate business thinking.[24] Porter and Kramer's goal is laudable, but it is not yet clear that it has pulled business away from the alluringly shiny object of profit maximization. Some nagging questions arise from their thinking: How do we get most or all businesses to agree to coordinate on a new set of objectives? Will they do it themselves, especially if that involves meeting costly goals and if success is difficult to measure? Or does the change to a shared-value approach require some form of government coordination?

As for the public, to begin with, their trust in business is only a bit higher than their trust in government, as Gallup and Pew surveys confirm. In a 2019 Pew survey, respondents ranked business leaders as the second least trusted major figures in American society, just a bit better than elected officials. Gallup has asked similar questions about trust for four decades, and the responses are similar. In 2021, 18 percent of respondents placed "a great deal or quite a lot" of confidence in "big business," versus 12 percent for Congress. Confidence has been consistently low for decades. The best results for business came in 1975, when 34 percent of respondents expressed high confidence. High confidence in government has not exceeded 25 percent since 2001.[25]

Small business, in contrast, has received among the *highest* scores in Gallup polls, peaking recently with a "great deal/quite a lot" confidence rating of 70–75 percent. Small businesses have consistently received a vote of high confidence since 1997, when this question was first asked. So it may be wise not to lump all businesses together in thinking about how business fits into the public's narrative about the economy.[26]

The dichotomy in opinions may stem in part from obvious differences between publicly traded and privately owned companies. Publicly traded companies may be more likely to follow the principle of maximizing profits and shareholder value—in part because they all have shareholders, and the value of their shares is readily observed—and as a consequence may over time have lost public trust. Thus, while large-business executives, boards, and stockholders still hew to much of the Milton Friedman doctrine—to the chagrin of employees and the general public—a smaller business is perhaps viewed as "one of us." Proximity and relation to the community likely also matter. Large corporations may be seen as distant and abstract, while small businesses operate in your town, owned by your neighbors. It's easier to trust your local hair salon than it is to trust Alphabet or Meta, the parent companies of Google and Facebook, respectively.

So trust in business depends on size and likely on proximity. But trusting or not, most still feel that businesses should be left alone to do what they do best. Since 1994, Pew has tracked views on whether government regulation of business is necessary "to protect the public interest" or whether regulation instead "usually does more harm than good." Both shares hovered near 50 percent from 1994 to 2017, the last time this question was asked, with a small rise in the "protects public interest" share over that period and a correspondingly modest decline in the "does more harm than good" share.[27] In the most recent Gallup poll on the subject, from September 2021, 43 percent of respondents said there was "too much" government regulation of business, one-quarter said there was too little, and one-third thought there was just the right amount, implying that three-quarters would oppose any increase in business regulations.[28] However the question is asked, a substantial share of the public is generally opposed to business regulations. One exception is the recent rise in calls for regulation of large tech and social media companies, a concern that is shared by members of both political parties.[29]

In sum people do not trust big business, and they never have. The only institution with lower trust is government. People really trust small businesses, and they have for a long time. People on balance would prefer no further regulation of most businesses, and a substantial segment of the public would like to see less. It seems likely that survey-takers are thinking primarily of small businesses when they say they want to maintain or reduce regulation. This might suggest the door is open for a bipartisan agreement to keep regulation on small business light while tightening regulation of larger businesses where necessary. Of course, a fly in this ointment is that people don't trust government, so it's unclear whether they would entrust government with the responsibility to regulate big businesses.

Other Countries' Beliefs about the Sources of Success and Failure

It is difficult to compare attitudes about the sources of economic success and failure across countries, as there are few surveys that ask such questions over time and across countries. But we can gain insights from the World Values Survey (WVS), which has asked a variety of questions bearing on economic and social well-being since 1981. A number of questions have been asked of only a subset of countries in a handful of years, however.

Still, the survey covers relevant questions across a broad array of more- and less-developed economies, including the United States. The first such question, which was fielded between 1995 and 1998, asks, "Why, in your opinion, are there people in this country who live in need?" The survey offers a limited set of choices: "because of laziness or lack of willpower," "because of an unfair society," or "other answer."

Figure 2.2 displays the percentage of respondents who responded "laziness or lack of willpower" across dozens of countries.

The share in the United States responding that laziness lies at the core of why people are in need corresponds very closely to the 2019 Pew survey in which 60 percent agreed that most anyone can get ahead if they work hard.

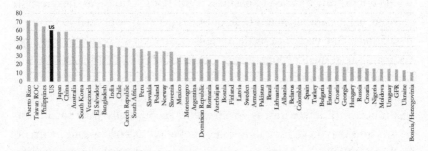

Figure 2.2
Why are people in need? Percent responding "laziness or lack of willpower."

There are a few countries that hew even closer to that narrative than does the United States, including Taiwan and the Philippines, which have close historical and political ties to the United States. (Puerto Rico, a US territory, is surveyed separately from the rest of the country and also follows The Myth even more strongly than the rest of the United States, in the survey.) Few countries share the US's confidence in this explanation for why people are in need.[30] In most countries, far less than half of respondents attributed "need" to "laziness." More than half the countries registered less than 30 percent support for this linkage.[31]

In the 2017–2021 wave of WVS polling, the survey asks a subset of countries whether economic success is due more to "hard work" or "luck," rating those options on a ten-point scale with "1" corresponding to strong belief in the hard-work explanation and 10 to a strong belief in luck (figure 2.3). Here the results are a bit more even across countries, but still the United States winds up on one end of the distribution, registering a median response of 3. The most common median response among countries is a 5, which, loosely speaking, puts equal weight on hard work and luck. The United States' near neighbors on this issue include Bangladesh, Kyrgyzstan, and Zimbabwe, countries in which the lack of a robust safety net may well mean that hard work is the *only* option available to attain success, however unattainable success may be. Other developed economies—Germany, Japan, South Korea, Taiwan, Australia—register responses from 4 to 6 on this scale.[32]

One might wish to interpret these results—and some of those above—as suggesting that, relative to the rest of the world, the US safety net is great and opportunity is widely available, so the distinguishing factor in the

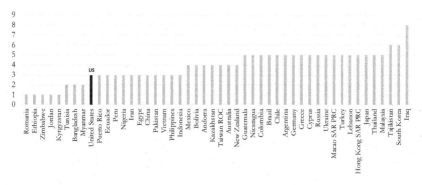

Figure 2.3
Success due to hard work (1) or luck (10). Median response, 1–10 scale.

economy really *is* whether one works hard or not. That's certainly an internally consistent way of thinking about these results. The problem is that income data do not at all support such a conclusion. Neither do the international comparisons of government spending on key human capital–building programs, which we will come to later.

On balance, the United States appears to have an attitude toward poverty and success that is rather unusual among developed, capitalist countries. How do other countries view the US approach to the distribution of economic success within its borders? A recent survey asked residents in established and aspiring democracies: "America's style of democracy would be more attractive in my country if ___," offering ten possible responses. Across ten geographically diverse countries—Brazil, China, Egypt, Germany, India, Japan, Mexico, Nigeria, Poland, and Russia—the most highly ranked response was "the gap between the incomes of rich and poor people was smaller."[33] American views toward poverty and its sources are extreme, and people elsewhere are aware of it. They see a need for improvement. Perhaps we will too.[34]

*   *   *

It should by now be clear that this narrative resonates deeply with us—all of us want to believe in the efficacy of individual effort, in the opportunities inherent in a meritocracy, in our country as the land of opportunity, and in the American Dream. We have rewritten Horatio Alger's works to conform to our version of reality, and our leaders and media spout versions of the self-made-man story at every opportunity. As Richard Reeves puts it:

> Only in America is equality of opportunity a virtual national religion . . . Americans are more tolerant of income inequality than the citizens of other countries, in part because of this faith that in each generation, the poor run a fair race against the rich, and the brightest succeed.[35]

Markets may treat individuals of equal education, training, and ability equally, but the opportunity to obtain education, training, *and access to markets* differs radically by race, ethnicity, income, and wealth.

Rarely do stories of self-made success make clear that these are far and away the *exceptions* to the most common experience: starting in poor circumstances usually leads to poor outcomes later in life. In other words, as I document below, economic mobility is low. Thus rags-to-riches stories reveal a triumph of belief over reality in the mind of the average American.

3 An Origin Story for The Myth: Roots in the Founding of the Republic

From America's founding—and before—elements of The Myth have been at play in our national identity. By the early nineteenth century, there was a general expectation that white men should, and could successfully, strive for self-mastery and improvement: that a hard-working, right-living youth could become a prosperous self-made man. Implicit disapproval of the poor has an even longer history, rooted in debates over colonial poor laws. As a nation, we have absorbed and employed these narratives for generations.

In tracing the roots of these narratives, two caveats are in order. First, what the average person thought about individual achievement and opportunity at the beginning of the nineteenth century is difficult to say. What exists are the accounts of those who succeeded, those wealthy enough to have had political power and thus be included in the historical record. Second, this topic is much too broad to cover adequately in this book. Many have written about the nation's evolving sense of itself in the wake of independence and during the years in which the republic solidified. I will borrow from their insights and heavily summarize the import of their work for this discussion of the origins of The Myth.

What did well-off Americans believe about opportunity and individual achievement when our nation was young? What narratives did they employ both to make sense of their newly forming country and to guide their decisions in the formative period before the Civil War? The principles of freedom and equality loomed large in the writings of the time, in part because they contrasted strongly with the constraints on freedom of choice that prevailed under Crown rule and in part because issues of liberty had been so intensely debated during the Revolutionary Era. As Harvard economist Benjamin Friedman notes, by the time observant foreign visitor

Alexis de Tocqueville commented on American society in the 1830s, he could conclude that Americans' devotion to the ideal of a free and equal society "created the belief that *anyone* could get ahead; and while not everyone would succeed in doing so, this belief fostered an attitude that *everyone* should at least try."[1]

And the country was indeed more "open" then than now—at least for non-enslaved and non-Indigenous people. Following the Revolution, as territory west of the Appalachians opened for settlement, there was simply more land available, even though much of it was already occupied by Indigenous people. Available lots could be purchased through the Land Office, an 1800 creation of Congress that was designed to administer land sales.[2] But following the War of 1812 Congress also granted veterans of the war 160-acre parcels located between the Illinois and Mississippi rivers.[3]

Independence from Britain also released some Americans from hierarchical limits on work choices.[4] An expanding world of commerce and manufacturing created new choices and opportunities for some. The opening of trade to India and other markets similarly provided new opportunity for a few to amass wealth in markets that had been inaccessible under colonial rule. For some white men there was an almost giddy sense of opportunity to improve, to rise, to achieve wealth and standing. Tocqueville inferred that mid-nineteenth-century America's wealthy men were mostly self-made, observing, "In America, most of the rich men were formerly poor."[5]

American belief in self-determination was bolstered by a religious imperative. By the 1820s, the religious revival known as the Second Great Awakening rocked the nation. The awakened soul was urged to perfect himself and society, an imperative that emphasized *individual* striving. Young revivalist ministers not only reinvigorated "flagging religious affections," they simultaneously spread "lessons about personal strength" and urged "self-reliance the basis of liberty," which "worked to undermine people's dependence upon authorities."[6] Religion bolstered economic striving throughout the nineteenth century. A Baptist minister who preached the same sermon over 6,000 times, reaching millions of listeners in late nineteenth century America, proclaimed:

> Never in the history of the world did a poor man without capital have such an opportunity to get rich quickly and honestly as he has now in our city. . . . I say that you ought to get rich, and it is your duty to get rich . . . to make money honestly is to preach the gospel."[7]

In many ways, our earlier national narrative echoed the rhetoric of the current one: those whom we know about through remaining written record—white men—felt they had achieved much through their own hard work.[8] This perception is somewhat understandable, as many had migrated to new lands to the West and cleared, cultivated, and maintained them through back-breaking labor. "There must have been something wondrous about growing up when the pinebreaks and forests, teeming with game, yielded to the plough, the ax, and the managed fires of frontier farmers," Joyce Appleby writes.[9]

Like the narrative of the current period, this narrative suffers from selective memory—limitations of the extant historical record—as well as a focus on exceptions rather than statistical norms and scant attention to the effects of success on people of color. The older narrative doesn't recognize the people left behind during the great progress of the nineteenth century—the many failures that accompanied the few recorded successes. For example, the likelihood of business survival in the nineteenth century was low: businesses in many places had a one in three chance of survival after three years.[10] The old narrative also ignores the Indigenous people who suffered for the sake of progress. Not only were Indigenous people displaced from the land they had occupied for centuries in order to make way for the westward migration of white men and their families, they were further dislocated or murdered by US troops who were sent to support the settlers establishing themselves in this "new" land.[11] And, in a rather glaring omission, nor does the story take account of the fate of the enslaved during this period.

Similarly, current debates about the appropriate role of government are presaged in the republic's early history. Tocqueville reported that 1830s Americans believed "their chief business [was] to secure for themselves a government which will allow them to acquire the things they covet and which will not debar them from the peaceful enjoyment of those possessions which they have acquired."[12] Government served best when it stayed out of the way of the attainment of the emerging American Dream—except when it came to slaughtering the pesky Indigenous people who inconveniently stood in the way of the attainment of that dream.

Attitudes toward the poor followed an ancient narrative, which divided the destitute into the pitiful who deserved compassion and aid and the indolent or "vicious" poor, addicted to sloth and vice, who deserved nothing but disdain. This taxonomy of the poor is laid out in debates that date back centuries:

> Distinguishing between the worthy and unworthy poor had been customary in Europe since the fourteenth century. The worthy poor were indigent through no fault of their own and deserved aid. The unworthy poor had contributed to their own decline and thus were not, properly speaking, poor at all but *criminal and deserved nothing more than correction.*[13]

Indeed, even before the formation of the Republic, prominent citizens expressed views about the poor that might well have appeared in last week's *Washington Times*. Benjamin Franklin came from humble beginnings in a large family (his father had 17 children with two wives), but this experience hardly left him sympathetic. In 1767, he wrote:

> I am for doing good to the poor, but I differ in opinion of the means. I think the best way of doing good to the poor, is not making them easy *in* poverty, but leading or driving them *out* of it. In my youth I travelled much, and I observed in different countries, that the more public provisions were made for the poor, the less they provided for themselves, and of course became poorer. And, on the contrary, the less was done for them, the more they did for themselves, and became richer.[14]

Numerous examinations of early poor relief in the colonies find the same expressions of English tradition, and the same distinction between the deserving and undeserving. Nian-Sheng Huang's examination of poor relief in eighteenth-century colonial Boston noted:

> The town could not ignore provincial laws mandating that it care for the indigent and dispose of the idle or able-bodied poor, *a traditional Elizabethan distinction.*[15]

Eric Nellis and Anne Cecere's introduction to their collection of the records of the Boston Overseers of the Poor similarly suggests:

> As to the question of who was therefore responsible for the relief of the poor, the answer then was the poor themselves if they were able-bodied and the community or state if they were not.[16]

In devising what he considered a just system of poverty relief for Massachusetts in 1821, Josiah Quincy authored a report that distinguished between the two classes of the poor: the "impotent" poor, "who are wholly incapable of work, through old age, infancy, sickness or corporeal debility," and the "able" poor, who are "capable of work, of some nature, or other; but differing in the degree of their capacity." Were all of the poor of the first kind, Quincy testified, there "would be little difficulty, either as to the principle, or as to the mode of extending relief." These are, of course, the "deserving" poor. Quincy believed that many of the poor were in fact able, at least until they got on the dole: he noted the tendency of the 1818 English Poor Laws to "encourage the worthless and audacious . . . to lessen their honest exertions; to deprave their morals . . . to multiply their number, offering a premium for indolence." Once they have received aid, the able poor "begin to consider it as a right; next they calculate upon it as an income."[17] Nowhere does Quincy imagine that some who are able to work might also deserve assistance, perhaps because circumstances beyond their control have left them unemployed, or underemployed, or employed in miserable conditions.

Thus, The Myth runs deep in our history: men can and should rise to success in this land of opportunity, and those who do not are to blame for their failure. To a degree, this position is understandable. There was a time when—the exceptions noted above notwithstanding—the country *was* more open, provided more opportunity, and, for those whose records remain, was perhaps more likely to reward individual effort with material success. The republic's founding principles of liberty and equality, along with the Great Awakening's emphasis on individual achievement, harmonized well with the themes of opportunity, meritocracy, and self-determination.

Americans' deep mistrust of the poor similarly has deep historical precedent, as does the tendency to whitewash history of its enduring themes of subjugating and eliminating other races and ethnicities. We carry these foundations with us today in The Myth of equal opportunity, self-determination, and post-racism. As aspirations, they could serve us well—although one can go too far in lauding the ideal of individual accomplishment.[18] As descriptions of reality, or determinants of social policy, they are hopelessly misguided.

Common Ground

Both adherents of The Myth and those who recognize its falsehoods are likely aware to some extent of the struggles faced by low-income people and minorities. Where adherents and opponents differ is in their assessments of how poor people got that way and what to do about it. Likely points of agreement include:

- Hard work matters. There are very few who believe that economic success should be attained without individual effort. Whether people agree that hard work is *sufficient* for success is another issue.
- Capitalism on the whole can be a great economic system. The alternative—state control of all economic activity—has been shown to work poorly in many countries. Across both parties, most agree on this point.[19]
- Related to the previous point, there are obvious advantages to allowing markets and market signals to allocate scarce resources in many, perhaps most, circumstances.
- There is too much inequality in the United States. As noted above, a 2019 Pew survey found that 61 percent of respondents felt there is "too much economic inequality in the country these days."[20]

It is a good sign that the nation largely agrees on that last point. On what to do about it, not so much.

Finally, adherents to both narratives almost surely *aspire* to live in an economy in which there is equal opportunity to succeed, given effort. They differ on how close we are to achieving that aspiration and on whether or how we can improve.

*   *   *

Frankly, I find The Myth, which to a large extent accepts the current economic setup as it exists, dismaying. To my eye, it simply cannot be right that a country as affluent and wealthy as ours leaves so many hopelessly behind, without any real opportunity to succeed. A narrative that accepts that, to any degree, seems cold-hearted, mean-spirited. Our country should be at the very least embarrassed by the results, which I detail below.

Seeing The Myth for what it is makes clear that the wealthy and powerful have constructed virtually all of this. But our fate, in the aggregate, is not out of our control, even though for many individuals it largely is. It will be no small task to right this ship, and to refit it to more closely resemble the vessel of opportunity we aspire to. But as other countries have shown, and as *some* of our history suggests, we are capable of it. We abolished slavery. We offered the Marshall Plan to rebuild countries, including our former enemies, in the wake of World War II. We provided tremendous aid to Indonesia after the 2004 tsunami that killed 125,000 within one-half hour and devastated that country and several others. We need now to turn to our own citizens with that same sense of generosity, urgency, and humanity.

Doing so will require a change in narrative. A first step in this battle is laying bare the many facts that contradict The Myth.

II The Facts

Few things say, "The United States economy is broken" more than the idea that while we're in a global pandemic—with nearly 600,000 Americans dead, almost 10 million jobs lost, and the population of unhoused people higher for the fourth year in a row—there's at least one billionaire somewhere going, "2020 was a great year!"

—W. Kamau Bell (2021)[1]

So how broken are we?

Writ large, our economy is advanced and prosperous, a world-leader. Our national income per capita is high, the level of efficiency with which we produce goods and services is among the highest globally, our higher education system draws thousands of international students annually, and we routinely dream up medical, IT, and manufacturing innovations.[2] All of this national success is reflected in our world-leading amassed wealth.[3]

But what lies beneath those aggregate indicators is far less appealing. Three critical facets of brokenness merit close attention:

1. The highly unequal distribution of income across the entire population and across races and ethnicities and the prevalence of unsustainably low incomes. Income inequality has garnered much attention in the popular and academic media, so my depiction of brokenness would be incomplete without a presentation of the basic facts. I also want to augment the discussion of income beyond inequality—the *difference* between higher and lower incomes—to include concern about the *absolute* size of incomes. In particular, I will focus on whether the poorest can afford basic household needs. While official poverty measures serve as a benchmark to some extent, as I will show, the official thresholds set the bar

well below any reasonable estimate of the cost of providing basic necessities in low-to-moderate-cost communities in the United States. And government assistance to low-income households does not generally provide enough aid to make the needed difference.

2. The even more unequal distribution of wealth across the entire population and across races and ethnicities. Household wealth—defined as the difference between a person's or household's assets (both financial assets like savings accounts and non-financial assets like homes and cars) and its debt—is at once a powerful measure of multigenerational economic success and a fundamental source of stability and opportunity looking forward. The distribution of wealth holdings measures how equal access is to the benefits that wealth provides. These benefits are manifold: wealth buffers families from fluctuations in income (job loss or hours reduction) or spending (unexpected bills, such as for health expenses or home or auto maintenance); wealth provides resources for post-retirement living; wealth provides access to investments in education, homeownership, or starting a business, all of which can contribute further to the accumulation of wealth over time.

3. The distressing characteristics of work in lower-wage jobs. The characteristics of low-wage work matter to millions of people who struggle to make ends meet—not only because their wages are low but also because they lack benefits, are forced to work unpredictable schedules, or struggle to pay for costly child care of variable quality, simply so that they can work in the first place. Moreover, the influence that low-wage workers have over their working conditions—their "voice"—is minimal. The earlier history of our economy shows that not only *could* we conceive of and implement a different set of arrangements for low-wage work, in fact we *did* so for a good part of the twentieth century.

I focus on these three facets of brokenness because they highlight some of the most glaring problems in our economy, because they speak to the suffering of large swaths of the population, and because they can be shown to be the product of conscious decisions on the part of government policymakers and private firms, guided in part by their prevailing narratives.

To be sure, many authors have drawn attention to individual components of this overall picture, and many of us are now more aware of these defects than we were a couple of decades ago. But I compile the relevant data and the results of these researchers' work here to demonstrate the breadth and pervasiveness of brokenness, to ensure that no one reading this book can remain ignorant of these facts, and to motivate the discussion that links these outcomes to the widespread narratives that both excuse and perpetuate them.

These three signs of brokenness should be sufficient to make the argument that our economy needs help. Even so, a host of other indicators of brokenness—poor access to housing, education, health care, financial markets—bolster the argument. The overall picture is chilling. It is difficult to avoid the conclusion that we have become terribly lost somewhere along the way—not because we failed to consult a map, but because the map we have used grossly misrepresents the terrain we travel.

4 How Broken Are We? Low (and Unequal) Incomes

I begin by relaying the voices of three individuals whose personal stories vividly illustrate life among those with low incomes.

Ashley T., a Hispanic woman, lives with her husband and one-year-old son in a suburb of Boston. After coming to the United States and attending school here, family circumstances necessitated that she move back to her home country, the Dominican Republic, where she completed high school and obtained a bachelor's degree in business administration. She returned to Massachusetts upon graduation. Finding jobs was difficult at first, as her college diploma was not recognized by some US employers. Ashley found a teller-training program through a community organization and landed a job at a prominent regional bank. She now works for that same community organization, counseling low-income residents on basic financial matters, including foreclosure avoidance. Her employer offers scheduling flexibility, which is important to her family as they raise their son.

Ashley's husband works in construction, and his earnings fluctuate throughout the year depending on the season and the availability of work. Together, their earnings put them near median household income for the US. But without her husband's income, they could not make ends meet. Ashley says, "If I were a single mother, right? I don't know if we'd be able to make it. We would only have enough to cover childcare—not the mortgage or other expenses." The volatility of her husband's income is a serious concern. Both Ashley and her husband contracted COVID during the pandemic; this meant her husband could not work. They applied for the Supplemental Nutritional Assistance Program (SNAP, commonly known as food stamps) but did not qualify, because their normal combined income was too high.

Ashley and her husband have been able to save six months' worth of income to buffer her husband's income fluctuations. They recently purchased a multifamily house and have a tenant whose rent offsets a considerable portion of their mortgage expenses. Despite their tight financial circumstances, they routinely send money to relatives in the Dominican Republic. Apart from vulnerability to decreases in her husband's income, and swollen credit card balances associated with move-in expenses, Ashley says they are "in a good place." They plan to send their son to study in the Dominican Republic—it is much less expensive there, and Ashley feels their early education system is better.[1]

Ann J. of Boston is a Black married mother of four who has a good job as a high school teacher in the city public school system. But her husband lost his job during the pandemic and since then has been in and out of work, "so it has been a struggle for the last couple of years." Her mortgage lender provided some relief from payments during the pandemic, but that aid has ended. When her husband can find work, they do well—they are "able to catch up on [their] payments." But increasing prices of gasoline and food— "the sticker shock of groceries lately, it's just been incredible"—have further stretched their limited resources. That second income is critical to their family's stability.[2]

On the very low end of the low-income spectrum is Pam A., a white mother of three mixed-race children (Cambodian and Vietnamese), who lives in a northern suburb of Boston. She was evicted from her previous residence in August 2021 but managed to avoid a spell of homelessness by negotiating with her landlord for a reprieve while she found a new place to live. Now, after having been on a waiting list for fifteen years, she has a state housing voucher that covers most of her rent. She also qualifies for federal food assistance via SNAP. She had received family income supplements earlier in her life but cannot any longer, as her time on the program has exceeded the legislated limit.

Pam works twenty-five hours per month as the coordinator for a diaper bank. While she has an associate's degree and legal training, she has had difficulty finding work and is often told that she's "overqualified" for retail jobs. She volunteers for a nonprofit, most recently working on a voter-registration drive. Her life has been tremendously complicated by several bouts with cancer. Treatment is ongoing, and her various appointments consume a significant fraction of her time. She regularly wrangles the state's Medicaid Health Insurance system to obtain payment for her treatments. She had been working as a teacher at a local historic site but, at the time of our interview, she had been on furlough since the onset of the pandemic and was hoping to be recalled soon.

That recall is critical, as her current monthly income is about $300 against at least $900 of bills. She owes $1,000 on her heating bill and can't pay her electric bill. If her heat or electricity are cut off, she may lose her housing voucher. Describing her overall economic situation, she says:

> I'm scared s__less. I didn't qualify for fuel assistance. I owe $1,000. I don't know if my heat's gonna be shut off . . . I'm not making enough money to pay my electric. So I don't know when my electric is going to be shut off. I don't know if I can keep paying my student loans. I don't know if I'm going to be able to make car payments."[3]

She copes by making partial payments on as many bills as she can, bargain hunting at the grocery store with SNAP funds, and relying on food pantries.

None of these life stories inspires confidence in our economic system. Ashley's and Ann's families earn just enough—absent any disruptions—to make ends meet. They are one illness or unemployment spell from serious economic hardship. Pam's family is not close to a sustainable living, despite receiving government aid for housing and food. As the data below will demonstrate, these examples reflect the range of experience of *tens of millions* of low-income people in the United States. They are working, barely making it or not, and their prospects for a more stable existence are tenuous.

*   *   *

The startlingly unequal distribution of income across the US economy is well-documented in recent and widely cited research from scholars Thomas Piketty, Emmanuel Saez, and Gabriel Zucman and in earlier research extending back at least to the 1950s.[4]

The US economy, in the course of producing and selling goods and providing services to domestic and foreign purchasers, generates about $21 trillion of personal income. Roughly 62 percent of that income ($13 trillion) represents earnings of workers, 9 percent ($1.9 trillion) is paid to business owners, 14 percent ($3 trillion) is paid to owners of interest-bearing assets and stocks in the form of interest and dividends, and 19 percent ($3.9 trillion) is paid to individuals in the form of government benefits such as Social Security, Medicare, and unemployment insurance.[5] Those are the economy-wide numbers, which sound impressive. But how many people ultimately receive the aggregate income generated in our economy, and how much of it do they get?

The income generated by the US economy flows quite disproportionately to the highest-income families. The top 1 percent of US earners in 2019 were paid an average of $1.1 million. That's twenty-two times the average income of those in the bottom 90 percent. Those in the rarified atmosphere of the top one-tenth of one percent averaged $4.7 million, about ninety-five times the average incomes earned by the bottom 90 percent.[6]

So top incomes in the United States are really high. But there are, by definition, far fewer people in the top 1 percent than the bottom 90 percent. So *how much* of all US income goes to the highest earners?

Figure 4.1 depicts the distribution national income. The overall income splits into four categories: that flowing to the bottom 50 percent of

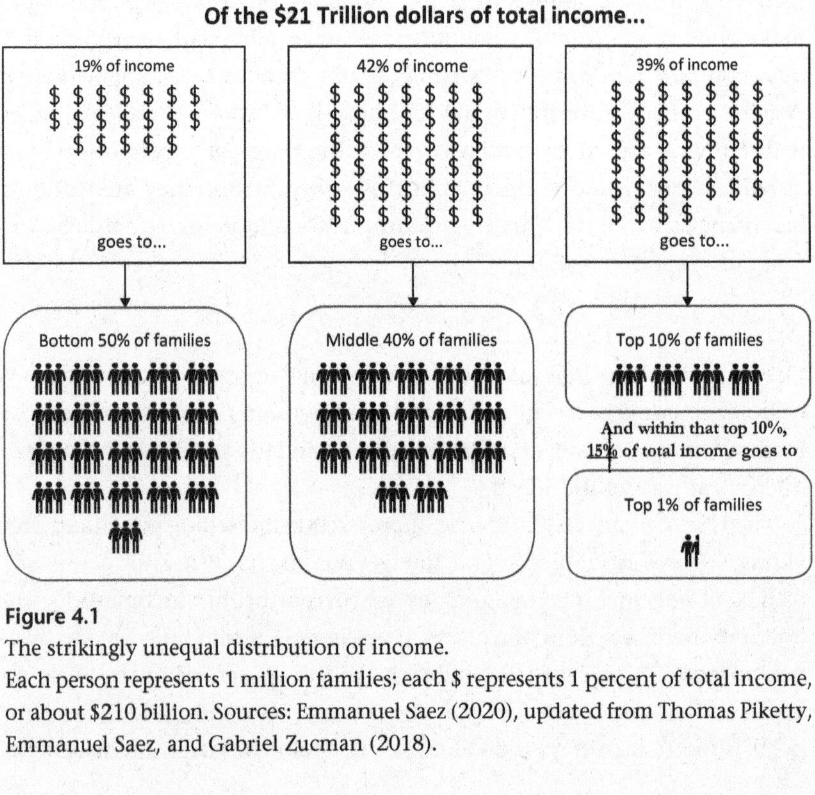

Of the $21 Trillion dollars of total income...

Figure 4.1
The strikingly unequal distribution of income.
Each person represents 1 million families; each $ represents 1 percent of total income, or about $210 billion. Sources: Emmanuel Saez (2020), updated from Thomas Piketty, Emmanuel Saez, and Gabriel Zucman (2018).

households, to the middle 40 percent, the top 10 percent, and the top one percent, broken out from the rest of the top 10 percent. The dollar signs represent shares of total personal income, with each dollar representing 1 percent of total income. Each person represents about one million households, out of the roughly 125 million in the United States.

What the figure shows is clear: lots of dollars going to few households, and few dollars going to lots of households. Distressingly, households in the bottom 50 percent of the income distribution—roughly half of US residents—collect less than 20 percent of all the income generated in the economy. Just over 40 percent of income goes to the middle 40 percent of households, so in this segment, the income distribution does not appear out of kilter. Almost 40 percent of all income goes to the top 10 percent of earners. About 15 percent of national income accrues to those in the top 1 percent of the income distribution. Earners in the top one-tenth of one percent of households—just over 100,000 households, not shown in the figure—receive 6.4 percent of all the income generated in the economy. Thus the very rich are collecting a hugely disproportionate share of the total income. And their share has been rising: it is today about twice what it was fifty years ago.[7]

One ought not expect the distribution of incomes to be completely equal. Such a "flat" income distribution would probably not reflect reasonable compensation for those of different skill or education levels, nor would it provide the incentive to obtain skills through education or training. But the degree of US inequality is likely far beyond what is required to compensate high-income workers fairly. And such inequality is far greater than that in every other economically advanced country.[8]

Even though the number of families who earn the most is of course small, the huge differences in their incomes imply that shifting income from the (far fewer) top earners to the (far more numerous) lower earners would be no small matter. A quick calculation provides a reference point: if we reduced the top 1 percent of incomes from twenty-two times the lowest 90 percent to only ten times, this would shift approximately $1.6 trillion to lower-income families, or roughly $10,000 per family. For a family earning $30,000 per year or less, that would be a life-changing transfer. If the income of the top 0.1 percent dropped from ninety-five times average to forty times, it would shift about $600 billion to lower-income families, or roughly $3,600 per family. That would also make a significant difference, especially if the shift were repeated each year. Of course, this ignores the possibility that shifting income in this way might change the way people choose to earn, save, or report their income. Redistribution is a daunting political challenge. But the point here is that there is more than enough money in the economy to meet everyone's basic needs while still paying a premium for certain types of economic activity.

While the huge differences between high and low incomes are striking, even more distressing is how low the lowest incomes are. One way to gauge how low incomes are is to compare a household's income to the poverty line, a measure originally defined as a multiple of a subsistence food budget, adjusted for the rising cost of living.[9] The official Federal poverty line for 2021 for a family of four is $27,750. The poverty line does not vary geographically.[10] Over 11 percent of all individuals (38 million) live in households that fell below the poverty line in 2021. Just over eight percent of non-Hispanic whites (15.8 million people) fell below the poverty line in 2020, as did 19.5 percent of Blacks (8.6 million people), 17.1 percent of Hispanics (10.7 million people), and 9.3 percent of Asians (1.9 million people).[11] Individuals living in a household with a single female head (no spouse present) are roughly *twice as likely* to fall below the poverty line, although this varies by race and ethnicity. Almost one-third of Blacks living in families headed by a single female lived below the poverty line in 2021 (about 4.7 million people).[12] The poverty rate likely fell with the payment of stimulus checks, the child tax credit, and the receipt of generous unemployment benefits. However, all of these benefits had expired by the end of 2021, leaving the poverty rate to rise again.[13]

The fact that 38 million Americans live below the official poverty level is staggering.[14] And it is even more shocking when we recognize that the poverty line reflects a level of income that is so low that it is simply unsustainable for many families. As a more realistic point of reference, consider estimated family budgets for a two-adult, two-child family in low-, low-medium-, and moderate-cost areas. The budget includes the costs of housing, food, childcare, transportation, health care, other necessities, and taxes. In low-cost Grenada County, Mississippi, that annual family budget totals $60,603. In Clinton County, Pennsylvania, the budget is $77,915. And in Campbell County, Wyoming, the annual family budget is $95,329.[15] Never mind high-cost areas such as New York, California, or Florida, where annual budgets rise as high as $160,000. Those at the poverty line need at least $35,000 of additional income to meet basic needs even in low-cost communities.

The obvious conclusion to draw from these benchmarks is that annual income at or near the poverty level does not come close to covering basic expenditures.[16] One can adjust these budgets to better reflect some of the realities of low-income families—for example one can exclude taxes, as families at the lowest income levels are likely receiving refunds through the earned income tax credit (EITC) program rather than paying taxes. But no amount of frugality could scale monthly expenses of $5,000–$8,000 down to the poverty level of about $2,300, even with the benefit of tax credits. Housing costs can only be reduced by so much. Skimping on food implies reducing quality and quantity, both of which can have long-term health effects. For most, transportation is an essential complement to working.

Aside from the EITC, there are other government subsidies and transfers that can defray costs for the lowest-income families. The Supplemental Poverty Measure (SPM) attempts to capture the value of these subsidies and transfers by factoring in non-cash as well as cash payments from the government. The SPM also includes the net contribution of paying taxes or receiving funds through the EITC. The value of the EITC is sizable—for a single-headed family with two children and adjusted gross income of $30,000, the estimated EITC benefit is about $3,700.[17] Figure 4.2 examines

Figure 4.2
Fraction of families earning below indicated income levels, with location-specific family budget estimates. SPM Total Resources, 2021.

the fraction of families earning below specified levels of income, including the family budget estimates just discussed.

As figure 4.2 shows, even with an augmented income measure like the SPM, a sizable fraction of the population earns very low incomes, all in. More than a third of families earned $50,000 or less in 2021, a figure that falls well short of estimated annual budgets even in low-cost communities. About one-fifth of all families earned $30,000 or less, just a shade above the official poverty level for a family of four.[18] A key conclusion from these data: while government programs absolutely help families, they often do not raise incomes to a sustainable level.[19]

It should be noted that low annual wages are not primarily the result of working less than a full week. The Current Population Survey finds that low-income workers typically work full weeks. Among workers in households with incomes below $50,000 annually, the median response for both "usual hours worked" (that is, average hours per week, in the year prior to the survey year) and "actual hours worked" (that is, hours worked in the week prior to responding to the survey) is forty.[20]

The bottom line is that a disheartening number of people live with a crushingly low level of income, even after accounting for government support. Given any reasonable reckoning of basic family expenses, tens of millions are working full time and barely making it—or not—even with government supports. That should not be an acceptable outcome.

Racial and Ethnic Income Inequality

It should come as no surprise that people of color earn less than whites on average. Figure 4.3 illustrates the disparities using the supplemental poverty measure. Incomes for the lowest 10 and 25 percent of earners are low in an absolute sense, at $14,000–$32,000 per year for Black and Hispanic families. In relative terms, Black family income is about 70 percent of white family income, and Hispanic family income is about 80 percent of white family income.[21]

Even when income is measured according to the more generous SPM, half of Black and Hispanic families have less than $50,000 per year in total income; the same median benchmark for white families is $67,000 according to this income measure. Low incomes are acutely low for Blacks and Hispanics, putting a sustainable life out of reach for millions.

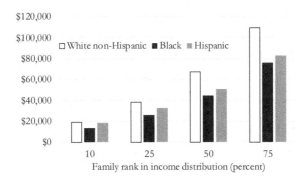

Figure 4.3
Family income by race and ethnicity, based on SPM. Source: SPM Total Resources, 2021.

On Low Incomes and the Current Safety Net

In the data presented above, a number of government programs, paid in cash and in-kind, are included in the measures of household income, boosting income compared to what it would be without such government aids. These include food support (SNAP), housing assistance, tax assistance through the EITC, and dependent support, which these days is provided through the Temporary Assistance for Needy Families program (TANF). Together, these programs and a number of others comprise the household safety net, which is meant to prevent families from unnecessary suffering. In many cases, they literally help families to survive.

Many people hold factually inaccurate views of the safety net. Some still believe Ronald Reagan's 1976 description of the supposedly typical "welfare queen" who fraudulently collected benefits from various government programs.[22] As Josh Levin documents in a 2013 *Slate* article, Reagan intentionally employed this narrative to heighten the perception of fraud, in the wake of an eightfold increase in investigations across the country. But in reality, fraud was not rampant, and welfare payments were not on the rise. Instead, investigations rose because states had newly criminalized overpayments that had previously been resolved as a routine administrative matter.[23] This is a glaring example of the use of The Myth—distrust of the poor, compounded by institutionalized racism—to argue for dismantling much-needed economic supports.

So what does the safety net actually look like today? Benefits are overwhelmingly *not* provided as unrestricted cash payments but instead as restricted payments or in-kind services delivered. And where aid takes the form of cash or cash-like payments (for example, SNAP and TANF), it comes with strong work requirements. SNAP is for those aged 16–59 and includes a requirement to register for work, participate in SNAP employment training or workfare as determined by the state SNAP agency, take a suitable job if offered, and not voluntarily quit a job or reduce work hours below thirty per week "without a good reason."[24] TANF combines state and federal rules. The federal government specifies that half of all TANF families must include a work-eligible individual, and at least 90 percent of two-parent TANF families must have two work-eligible individuals in work or work-related activities for a minimum number of hours each month. Two-parent households must work an average of at least thirty-five hours per week, more if they receive federal childcare subsidies. Many additional requirements apply, including income and asset limits and limits on the number of weeks one can spend on job-search or "job-readiness" activities. With some exceptions, adults aged eighteen to fifty are limited to three months of benefits out of every three-year period, unless they are working or in a training program.[25]

SNAP benefits may be used only for specific food items. They cannot be spent on a number of common grocery items such as beer, wine, liquor, tobacco, vitamins, medicine, "foods that are hot at the point of sale," pet food, cleaning supplies, paper products, hygiene items, and cosmetics.[26] The benefit is usually issued as a restricted debit card rather than cash. TANF is available to US citizens and legal aliens with a child younger than eighteen, or who are pregnant, or who are themselves eighteen years old or younger and the head of household.

The work requirements for these programs were a central feature of the Personal Responsibility and Work Opportunity Reconciliation Act of 1996, the Clinton-era welfare reform whose title demonstrates its focus on ensuring that welfare recipients are working.[27] Most aid programs are now administered as block grants from the federal government to the state governments so that, with some restrictions, states have leeway in how they administer the programs and how much they spend on benefits.

Many families who are eligible for TANF often cannot take advantage of the program. Only one-fifth of families with children in poverty received

TANF benefits in 2020, down from 68 percent in 1996.[28] The fraction of eligible children who received TANF benefits in 2019, the most recent data available, was also about one-fifth. That rate had been as high as 80 percent in the 1970s under TANF's predecessor, known as Aid to Families with Dependent Children. The child participation rate declined in the fifteen years following the implementation of TANF in 1996, and has been fairly steady since.[29]

Why has participation been so low? Barriers to TANF participation appear to be largely structural, and there are many. They include low applicant acceptance rates; the pitifully low benefits paid by TANF in many states, which disincentivizes participation; the extremely low income thresholds in some states, which shrinks the pool of eligible applicants; lack of federal accountability for serving families in need; the administrative burden associated with applying and remaining eligible for benefits; the stigma that attaches to recipients; and the often-stringent asset limits for participants, which also limit participation.[30] As an example, in Mississippi, the acceptance rate for applicants in 2017 was an abysmal 1.42 percent, the current maximum monthly benefit for a family of three is a paltry $260, and the monthly income threshold for a family of three is $680—any family of three earning more is ineligible.[31] TANF has been implemented so as to drastically ration aid to the poor, which especially affects families of color.

In contrast, the participation rate for SNAP is much higher. Four of five eligible individuals received benefits in 2018, including essentially 100 percent of children. Both of these SNAP participation rates have risen dramatically since the early 2000s.[32] Why the increase? Improved uptake is directly traceable to federal actions to improve access by reducing administrative burdens, in sharp contrast to TANF. Specific changes included restoring benefits to most legal immigrants, simplifying the treatment of income, reducing participants' income-reporting burden, and allocating funds to improve outreach to eligible people.[33] More importantly, the contrast between TANF and SNAP participation rates highlights the role that policy choices, rather than individual decisions, play in the effectiveness of the safety net.

*   *   *

Slashing welfare spending has been on the Congressional docket, on and off, for decades, in part as a means of reducing the size of the federal budget. But contrary to popular belief, apart from Medicare, Social Security,

Medicaid, and Disability Insurance, none of the safety net programs are hulking behemoths. In fact, none accounts for more than about 3 percent of federal outlays, as figure 4.4 indicates.[34] The most recent data, shown in figure 4.4, are distorted by the COVID pandemic in two ways. First, unemployment compensation swelled far beyond its normal level in response to the COVID-induced rise in unemployment. Second, COVID-specific stimulus payments that sought to mitigate the effects of the economic downturn, the third-largest payment in the figure, were explicitly temporary. Indeed, expenditures on both categories diminished or were phased out entirely as COVID-specific programs were terminated.

In summing up the state of the current safety net in the United States, economist Melissa Kearney suggests, "If policymakers have dual goals of reducing federal government spending and reducing cash support for nonworking individuals to increase employment rates, a focus on welfare programs that provide income support to low-income families is misplaced. Those programs constitute a tiny share of federal spending and already have stringent work requirements."[35] It turns out "safety net" is a bit of a misnomer. The system provides little safety, and the net doesn't "catch" many people, saving them from economic freefall.

Survival

It should by now be clear that for far too many Americans, household resources are simply inadequate to pay for necessities, even after accounting for contributions from the tax system and the safety net. How then do these families survive?

First, they cut corners, decreasing the quality of food purchased, making clothing last longer, using diapers longer, skipping preventive medical care, and shuffling bill payments, as Pam A.'s story demonstrates. But these short-term cutbacks imply long-term costs in terms of health and financial wellbeing.

Second, they take on debt. Janet from Boston, a Hispanic woman whose budget is "very tight," had twelve credit cards at one point. After attending financial-counseling sessions, she was able to "use tax refunds and stimulus checks to pay down credit cards—now balances are not so bad, and monthly payments are manageable." She noted that her credit card debt

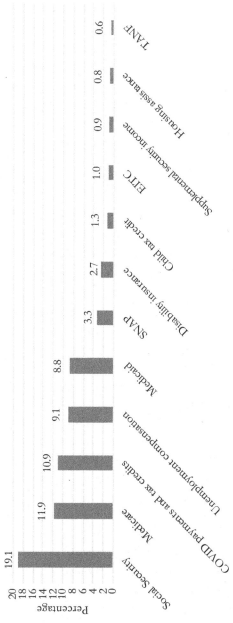

Figure 4.4
Federal government outlays for payments to individuals, 2021. Percentage of total federal government spending. Source: Office of Management and Budget (2022).

escalated because "it was the only way to pay for basics . . . she had to use them to make it."[36]

The family networks that many middle-class households fall back on for support in times of financial stress are largely unavailable to the residents I spoke to. Carlos from Lawrence, a northern suburb of Boston, was born in the Dominican Republic. His family "didn't have a lot," but "we were happy, we were stable." He learned at an early age the importance of work, and his earnings as a child helped to support the household. Now in his fifties and a naturalized US citizen, he has achieved some financial stability. When I asked him if he had received help from his family during the leaner years, he said simply, "No." And could he expect an inheritance or other money from his extended family? "I haven't thought of it," he said. It's just too unlikely.[37]

Tasha from Lynn, another town north of Boston with a large poor and minority population, is a single mother of two children. As a child, she lived in a number of different family situations. At age two, she was placed in foster care after the state of Massachusetts determined that her blind mother could not care for her and her three siblings. After that, she and her siblings lived for five years with their aunt. Then, between the ages of sixteen and nineteen, she lived with another foster family, while her now-grown siblings were dispersed to other residences. Due to those years of moving around and living with different parental figures, Tasha says, "I lost a part of my childhood." She graduated from high school, worked while in college, found an affordable room in an all-women's home, earned her associate's degree in education, and worked as a preschool teacher for thirteen years. Tasha told me that she has never received assistance from her family. Indeed, she sometimes will offer assistance to her relatives if they really need it: "If they need $10 or something, I'll give them something, if I have it."[38]

Ashley T., whom you met earlier, similarly does not receive assistance from her family. "They are all in the Dominican Republic," she says. "I can't count on them, in fact I send money to them."[39]

Pedro A. is a Hispanic man who grew up in the Dominican Republic and now lives in a Boston suburb. He was active in the church as a child, an experience that "shaped me as the person I am today." Asked about his current economic circumstances, he says that although he abstains from many purchases and "doesn't enjoy a lot of things," he still feels pinched at the end of each month. "The cost of living is too high, and I don't make enough," he says. But his faith buoys him. "I have not lost my hope that it will get better, and I will achieve those things I need to achieve," he said. When asked if he receives any family assistance, he replied, simply, "No."[40] If anything, for these households, extended family represents an additional drain on resources, not a source of stability.

One might infer that households in the lowest one-fourth of incomes are less burdened by debt because, for them, the ratio of outstanding debt to household income is lower than for those in higher incomes. But this is deceptive. Low-income households have less debt because these individuals and families often cannot afford to own homes, so they are less likely to have a mortgage. Of course, that also means that the value of a home does not appear as an asset on their balance sheet. And lower-income households do take on debt: to pay for cars and education, for example. For these debt categories, low-income households' debt load is much higher than that of higher-income households. For example, among lower-income people with education loans, that debt represents 100 percent of their annual income, versus about 50 percent or lower for people in higher-income categories. Among low-income people who own their homes, debt loads are about twice as high, relative to income, as those of higher-income homeowners.[41] Low household income plus heavier reliance on debt equals more economic instability.

*   *   *

The simple conclusion from the income data is this: income inequality is huge. Top earners take home large multiples of the average worker's pay. More distressing, low-income workers lack the resources—even after including government payments and transfers—to pay for basic necessities. Race- and ethnicity-based inequality adds another layer of significant disparity. As we will see below, no matter the measure, the magnitude of these disparities in household income is multiplied when we turn to household wealth.

5 How Broken Are We? The Distribution of Wealth

While income inequality has received far more attention, historians, sociologists, economists, and policymakers are increasingly focusing on wealth inequality. And with good reason: the best available statistics on the distribution of wealth in the United States show enormous concentration of wealth at the very top of the distribution and gaping disparities between the accumulated wealth held by white families and most others.

Most wealth studies focus on differences in families' net worth. Net worth is defined as the difference between all assets and all debts. Total assets include financial assets such as checking and savings accounts, retirement accounts, stocks, and bond holdings and nonfinancial assets such as homes, cars, and durable consumer goods. Debt includes mortgages, education loans, auto loans, and credit card balances. If the value of a family's assets is greater than the value of their debt, they have positive net worth. Many lower-income families' debt exceeds their assets. They have negative net worth.

Pedro A., whom you met a few pages ago, earns $16 an hour as a parking clerk for a city near his home. His wife earns some money—"very little," he said—yet they cannot pay all their bills each month. As to how they cope with the mismatch of income and expenses, "It's difficult." Even as they "abstain" from purchases, Pedro feels "like he has a rope at the end of his neck" at the end of each month. When I asked Pedro whether he had any money set aside to buffer against the ups and downs of income or hours worked, he replied with a chuckle, "Wouldn't that be nice?"[1]

Rosada S. has been in the United States for nine years, the last five in a city north of Boston. She and her husband have no savings, in part due to difficulties brought on by the pandemic. Her husband was fired from his job because he was unable to work after contracting COVID. He was out of work for eleven months, which put an end to their savings plan. "We had a little saved, but we had to spend it all when he was unemployed," Rosada told me.[2] Janet from Boston, whom you met earlier, told me that she had an "emergency fund" to buffer against unexpected expenses, but it was emptied when she had to pay for a $2,500 car repair.[3]

Wealth generally reflects a long family history of economic success or failure. Except in rare circumstances, wealth is accumulated across generations through stable educational attainment, moderate-to-high-income employment, stable homeownership, successful business ownership, and, critically, participation in a host of government programs that have provided wealth-building opportunities to white families. Families that benefitted from government land grants, educational and housing assistance, unemployment insurance, and the like began their dynastic wealth building earlier in their family's history than those (largely families of color) that could not. Families that have experienced success in business, homeownership, and career progression over multiple generations have the chance to build substantial wealth and pass it down across generations.

Families with liquid savings—savings that can be readily converted to cash, without long time lags and significant transaction fees (checking accounts are liquid; housing is illiquid)—are better able to buffer themselves from unexpected disruptions in income or hours, or unexpected spending shocks. The above stories of Pedro, Rosada, and Janet testify to the importance of savings buffers. Without a savings buffer, the path to education can be disrupted, housing lost, and businesses shuttered.[4] The Federal Reserve's Survey of Household Economics and Decisionmaking showed in 2021 that almost one-third of families could not easily come up with $400 in cash or its equivalent in case of an emergency. For Blacks, this percentage rises to 52 percent, and for Hispanics 46 percent. The one-third who could not come up with the cash would pay for the emergency expense by borrowing on a credit card and paying off over time (14 percent); borrowing from family or friends (8 percent); selling something (6 percent); borrowing from a bank (2 percent); or using a payday loan, deposit advance, or overdraft (1 percent).[5] Buffers matter because economic life is uncertain, and few go through life without a number of significant disruptions.

Looking first at the overall population, wealth holdings are highly concentrated among the wealthiest in the economy. Data from the Federal Reserve's Survey of Consumer Finances (SCF) are shown in figure 5.1.

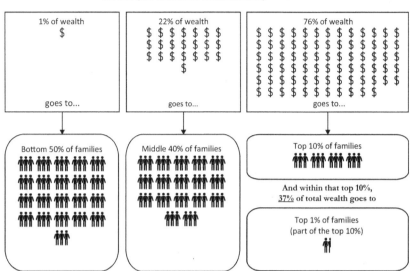

Of the $95 trillion of total wealth,

Figure 5.1

The incredibly unequal distribution of wealth.

Each person represents 1 million families; each $ represents 1 percent of total wealth, or approximately 1 trillion dollars. Source: Survey of Consumer Finances 2019 public microdata, author's calculations.

The figure shows clearly the lopsided concentration of wealth in the upper portion of the wealth distribution. In 2019, the most recent survey year, the top 10 percent of wealth holders held more than 76 percent of aggregate wealth; the bottom 50 percent held just over 1 percent. While the degree of income inequality is disheartening, the magnitude of wealth inequality is jaw-dropping.

This picture changes a bit if we add two other sources of wealth to the standard accounting to derive a more comprehensive wealth aggregate. Researchers John Sabelhaus, Jeff Thompson, and Alice Volz advocate a combined wealth measure that adds the value today of future social security earnings, which are more evenly distributed than are other forms of wealth; and the value today of future defined-benefit pension payments, which are available not only to some highly compensated private workers but also to some public sector workers, many of whom earn mid-level incomes.[6] While these future payment streams share some features with other components of household wealth—they represent claims on future payments, as stocks and bonds do—they are qualitatively different in other respects. In particular, these forms of wealth represent claims to *distant and uncertain future income* and as such are not readily convertible to cash and cannot be borrowed against (Social Security not at all; some pensions to a limited extent). One cannot say at age thirty or forty or even fifty what one's Social Security income will be, as it depends on earnings throughout working life. Future defined-benefit pension earnings are similarly uncertain, as they depend on the length of an employee's tenure with a company and the employee's earnings during their time with the company. These sources of future income should thus be treated with care, as they do not provide the same kind of buffering and access to economic opportunity as savings or investment accounts.

Simple economic models would suggest that households form sophisticated expectations of future Social Security or pension income. These abstractions assume that the promise of (uncertain) future Social Security or pension income means these households need to save less today and thus can consume more. But that assumption is a bit heroic. Studies find that a large number of pension holders seem not to be aware of the specific benefits their pensions offer—how much future income these assets will provide them.[7] One of my interviewees, when asked about her retirement benefit, said, "I don't think I have a 401k. I'm pretty sure I don't. I think I do have a pension, or some retirement plan through the city . . . I never actually looked into the benefits."[8] If pension holders do not know the benefits they can expect to receive, then it is difficult to see how they could alter their behavior today in response to a benefit whose financial implications they don't understand.

Whether measured conventionally or by combined wealth, the preponderance of wealth is held by a very few in the United States. Because wealth equals opportunity—for housing, education, business formation, economic stability—this inequity provides a concrete sign of the dramatic inequity with which we distribute opportunity.

The Racial/Ethnic Distribution of Wealth

In the mid-2010s, Darrick Hamilton came to the Federal Reserve Bank of Boston to present his work with William Darity Jr. on the causes of racial and ethnic wealth gaps. As we gathered in the back conference room on the ninth floor of the iconic Fed building, I was among the skeptics in the audience. Many of us had heard about the wealth gap—it had existed for decades and had been highlighted by a number of economists, notably Tom Shapiro and his colleagues at Brandeis.[9] But as for the sources of these gaps, I found it difficult to let go of my own narrative about the line of causation, about the importance of income and accumulated savings in determining wealth. When Darrick suggested that income and savings patterns do *not* explain the gaps, I pushed back.[10] I did not conduct a survey, but I can be fairly sure that most Fed economists at that time would have agreed with me: surely the fact that white families earned more than families of color implied that they saved more. Over time, that difference in accumulated savings should explain the wealth gap. Therefore eliminating the income gap would close the wealth gap.

I now believe I was wrong, as were the many economists who thought the same way. While I knew of some of the broken promises in the wake of the Civil War, like many others at the time, and many still today, I was ignorant of the litany of systemic institutional factors that Darity, Hamilton, and others had been uncovering as the ultimate causes of these vast wealth disparities. In ensuing interactions, Darity, Hamilton, Shapiro, and their students and colleagues helped the Boston Fed to understand the huge and long-lasting impacts of these racial inequities, reshaping our attitudes and ultimately affecting views across the Federal Reserve System. That transformation in thinking continues to this day.

If you were dismayed by the disparities in incomes across race and ethnicity, you will be gobsmacked by the huge racial and ethnic disparities in accumulated wealth. The top panel of figure 5.2 displays the median family net worth for whites (the white bars), Blacks (the black bars), and Hispanics (the gray bars), in thousands of 2019 dollars, over the past thirty years.

Nearly 165 years after the end of the Civil War and the Emancipation Proclamation, more than a century after the first significant influxes of Hispanics from Mexico, the Caribbean, and South America, net worth across racial and ethnic categories has not come close to equalizing. This lack of progress derives from the combination of two key features of wealth accumulation. First, wealth is typically accumulated across many generations. Second, across many generations, institutional racism has erected barriers to wealth accumulation for families of color, while providing numerous

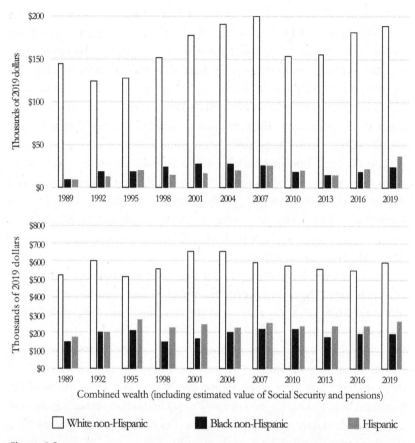

White non-Hispanic   Black non-Hispanic   Hispanic

Figure 5.2
Top panel: Median family net worth, thousands of 2019 dollars. Survey of Consumer Finances. Bottom panel: Median family net worth—"Combined" wealth, including estimates of Social Security and pension wealth, from Sabelhaus, Thompson and Volz, thousands of 2019 dollars.

boosts to wealth accumulation for white families. This is a divide a long time in the making, which has taken constant care and feeding to maintain.

Black and Hispanic net worth relative to white net worth has, by the conventional measure, hovered around 10–15 percent for decades. According to the broader measure incorporating non-marketable wealth, depicted in the bottom panel of the figure, Black and Hispanic wealth has remained stable at 30–40 percent of white net worth. Adding the arguably more ephemeral asset categories of future Social Security and pension earnings still does not close the wealth gap.[11]

The SCF from which the baseline data are derived does not survey a large enough sample to provide accurate information on additional demographic categories or on differences in wealth gaps across major cities. To be sure, the Hispanic demographics in Miami differ from those in Boston, with the representation of Cubans and Puerto Ricans higher in Miami and Dominicans more prevalent in Boston. The representation of Asian and Indigenous people in different regions also varies significantly.

To gather more nuanced data across these demographic groups and geographies, the National Asset Scorecard for Communities of Color (NASCC) conducted surveys in five major metropolitan areas around the country between 2014–2017: Boston; Los Angeles; Washington, DC; Miami; and Tulsa. Table 5.1 summarizes the results.[12]

One pattern is consistent across all of these demographic groups and cities: white families possess net worth that is many times that of their counterparts, with the exception of some Asian populations, notably Chinese, Japanese, and some Koreans. Most others report net worth in the *single-digit percentages* of their white counterparts. Indigenous people in the Tulsa metro area report a variety of experiences. All have far less wealth than white families, but the Cherokee and Creek tribes fare better than others. These staggering findings have been uniformly replicated across similar studies to date. It would be difficult if not impossible to employ a narrative to conveniently explain away these gaping inequities: Free markets require this? These people should have worked harder?

It may be surprising to some that the same demographic subgroups do not have the same wealth experience in all cities. Note, for example, that Korean respondents in the nation's capital have accrued wealth that is statistically indistinguishable, on average, from that of white families. But in Los Angeles, their wealth is a small fraction of that of white families. These data are helpful in highlighting the similarities and differences in the experiences of families across demographic subgroups and locations. In thinking about what policies and programs might be most effective in closing yawning wealth gaps, we do well to account for the range of effects that varying histories of discrimination have produced.

Differences in age, educational attainment, and homeownership could account for some of the differences observed in household net worth.

Table 5.1

Household median net worth by race and ethnicity, broken out by metro area

Race/Ethnicity	Median net worth (percent of white net worth, statistical significance[a])				
	Boston	DC	LA	Miami	Tulsa
White	100	100	100	100	100
US Black	0***	1***	1**	4*	6***
Caribbean Black	4.8**			11	
African Black		1***	20		
Puerto Rican	1***			(4)	
Dominican	0.0***				
Cuban				21	
South American				1	
Mexican			1**		4.8***
Other Hispanic	1***	5***		9.8	
Chinese		77	115		
Japanese			167		
Korean		175	7**		
Vietnamese		149	17*		
Filipino			69		
Asian Indian		202	130		
Cherokee, tribal enrolled					52
Muscogee, tribal enrolled					29*
Other, tribal enrolled					5
American Indian, no tribal enrollment					3**

[a]Asterisks indicate the degree of statistical confidence in the differences from white net worth. Statistical confidence in differences is strong (***), moderate (**) or weak (*). Where there are no asterisks, one cannot have much confidence that the indicated percentage differs from White net worth (always 100 percent by definition).

Source: NASCC Color of Wealth Studies.

Because households on average accumulate debt early in their lives, and accumulate assets later on, younger households will tend to have lower net worth than older households.

One might hope that equalizing education or homeownership across races and ethnicities would equalize net worth, but the data suggest that this is not the case.[13] Darity and coauthors find that equalizing outcomes in terms of income, employment, education, homeownership, and so on *will not* equalize outcomes in terms of net worth. Figure 5.3 shows how household net worth varies with educational attainment and race.[14]

This chart shows that the median net worth of a white household whose head of household has not received a high school diploma exceeds that of a Black household whose head holds a college degree. That is not an error in the data!

These snapshots from one point in a person's life cannot capture the effects of educational attainment, training, and job experience on wealth accumulation over a lifetime. Using a more comprehensive measure, John Sabelhaus and Jeff Thompson find that, if we were able to equalize earnings over a full working life, we might come closer to equalizing wealth than figure 5.3 suggests. But the policy implications of this research are less hopeful.[15] How long would it take to close lifetime earnings gaps? Improving educational attainment across racial and ethnic groups and providing additional training and access to stable employment in remunerative sectors would surely take a generation or more. Researchers at the Federal Reserve Bank of Cleveland estimate that, once earnings gaps are closed,

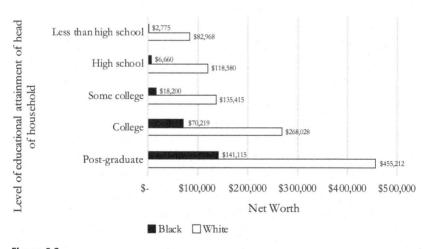

Figure 5.3
Education does not explain the wealth gap.

closing the wealth gap through accumulated savings would take *more than three-quarters of a century*. Adding the time required to close the earnings gap, it would almost surely take more than a century to equalize wealth through this channel.[16]

What these exercises emphasize is that it takes *generations* for improvements in human capital to build wealth. To close wealth gaps within an acceptable timeframe, we will need to do more than equalize educational attainment and income.

What about equalizing homeownership—would that close the wealth gap? Homeownership has proven a powerful means of accumulating wealth for white households. In the 2019 SCF data, nearly three-quarters of white respondents were homeowners. But homeownership has proven less beneficial to households of color, in part due to lower homeownership rates and in part due to lower accumulated home equity among those who own homes. The homeownership rates for Black and Hispanic SCF respondents were 45 and 48 percent respectively. On average white homeowners had accumulated $240,000 of equity, as opposed to $117,000 for Black families and $147,000 for Hispanic households. Darity and colleagues find that Black homeowners have accumulated less than half the net worth of white counterparts.[17] Homeownership by itself does not close the wealth gap.

If not homeownership, then perhaps entrepreneurship is a pathway to wealth accumulation for people of color. Yet the history of entrepreneurship has not been an unmitigated success in this regard. A study by the National Community Reinvestment Coalition finds that, although Black business ownership increased between 1992 and 2012, total revenue generated by all Black-owned businesses fell during that period, and Black median income did not increase with entrepreneurship. The study also finds that Black-owned businesses tend to operate in markets where incomes and revenues are lower; with lesser access to capital from financial institutions; and, not surprisingly, with much lower owner wealth at start-up.[18] Scholars at the Brookings Institution found that highly rated businesses in Black-majority neighborhoods earn less revenue than similarly rated businesses outside of Black neighborhoods.[19] Like homeownership, entrepreneurship has failed to provide a reliable path to wealth accumulation.

What this research suggests is that wealth disparities are not well explained by differences in education, employment, homeownership, or entrepreneurship. Instead, they derive from centuries of systemic discrimination against families of color, denying them opportunities to accumulate wealth that have been generously provided to white families.

Is Brokenness Just a Passing Phase? How Common Is Escape from Low Income and Low Wealth?

Pedro A., whom you met earlier, hopes "to evolve in my career." He knows that English-language training and additional skills would allow him to raise his income. But right now, he "can't afford to get more schooling or training." Every hour spent in training is an hour of wages lost, in addition to the cost of the training, and, when we spoke, he was looking for another job on weekends just to make ends meet. He believes that he and his wife's low earnings, despite more-than-full-time work, "makes a kind of trap." How can he take the time to get the training he needs to advance? How is it possible to achieve economic mobility when caught in this trap?

While it is undeniable that absolute income levels are hopelessly low for millions, this might be less discouraging if, on average, individuals and households were able to move up the income distribution over time. Sadly, the evidence suggests that is not the case.

To begin with, there has been little improvement in the inflation-adjusted incomes of those in the lower portions of the income distribution. Census Bureau data from 1967 to the present show that, especially since 1990, progress in incomes for the lowest 20 percent of the income distribution has been scant.[20] After adjusting for inflation, growth in income exceeded inflation by less than one-quarter of 1 percent annually from 1990 to 2020. Incomes *fell* for the twenty years between 2000 and 2020. The picture is barely better for the second-lowest 20 percent of incomes.

These data paint a desperate picture, although they don't tell us how likely it is for *individual households* to improve their income over time. This is the subject of a substantial literature on income mobility. One simple way of describing mobility is to follow families' incomes over time and calculate the percentage of families in, say, the lowest quintile that move into one of the higher quintiles over the course of some specified period. Table 5.2 shows the probability that a US family would make such a jump, for the period of 2003–2013.[21] The bold entries in the table represent the probability of staying in the same quintile—always the most likely outcome. The other entries show the probability of moving from an original

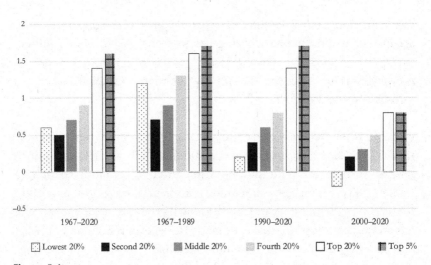

Figure 5.4
Progress in inflation-adjusted incomes by income quintiles. Annualized rates of change, 1967–2020.

Table 5.2
Probability of moving up or down in the income distribution (percent)

| | Quintile 10 years later | | | | |
Original quintile	1	2	3	4	5
1	**64**	24	8	3	1
2	23	**45**	24	7	2
3	8	29	**46**	23	4
4	4	7	18	**54**	18
5	3	4	6	16	**72**

quintile into another quintile ten years later. For example, the first entry, 64 percent, implies that the likelihood of staying in the lowest quintile is high: 64 percent remained in this quintile after ten years, and only 36 percent moved up. Most of those who moved went to the second-lowest quintile. Only 4 percent reached the top 40 percent of the income distribution. The rags-to-riches story rarely materializes in real life. Meanwhile, those in the top quintile rarely dropped below the second-highest quintile over this ten-year span. Bhashkar Mazumder estimates that, given the meager rates

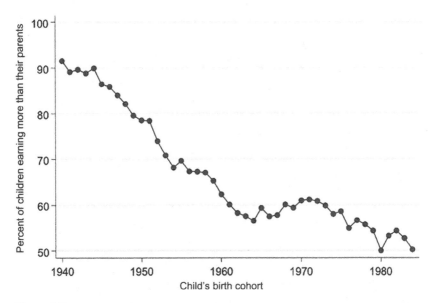

Figure 5.5
Mean rate of absolute mobility by cohort.

of progress in incomes we have seen, it would take 125 to 150 years for a family of four at the poverty level to increase their income to the national average—an extremely low rate of economic mobility.[22]

Another measure of intergenerational mobility asks what fraction of individuals in the population earns an income greater than their parents did. Research by Raj Chetty and his coauthors suggests that mobility in the United States by this measure has fallen significantly, with the fraction of children earning more than their parents declining from about 90 percent in 1940 to about 50 percent today, as shown in figure 5.5.[23]

Sadly, the data on wealth mobility are even less encouraging than those for income mobility. Typical analyses of wealth mobility show that it is quite unlikely for those in low strata to move at all, and, if they do, they are unlikely to move far.[24] Mobility also has not improved in recent years. Researchers Daniel Carroll and Nicholas Hoffman conclude, "Panel data from the past 30 years show a decline in wealth mobility across several measures. It appears that families are less likely to change wealth quintiles over time, while those that do move are less likely to move very far."[25]

Wealth mobility varies significantly by race. A study by sociologists Fabian Pfeffer and Alexandra Killewald shows that only 5 percent of Black children born in the middle quintile of the wealth distribution will attain the top quintile by adulthood, compared to 16 percent of white children in the same circumstances. For Black children in the middle quintile, the likelihood of attaining the second-highest quintile is half that of white children born in the middle quintile. The odds of a Black child dropping from the middle quintile to the bottom is 39 percent, compared to 16 percent for a similarly situated white child. The odds are equally skewed for children who start in the *top* quintile of wealth—Black children are much more likely to fall out of that quintile than are white children.[26]

So wealth mobility is low, and it has gotten worse over time. It is worse for Black children than for their white counterparts. One reason mobility has declined may be that the top wealth deciles keep getting higher and higher. Put differently, the rungs of the wealth ladder have gotten farther apart and thus harder to climb, especially toward the top of the ladder.

The conclusions I draw from these data on mobility are twofold. First, the lowest incomes have barely kept pace with inflation over the past thirty years, losing ground relative to the rise in the cost of living for much of that period. So low incomes are *not* getting better over time, and it is highly unusual for low-income households to join the ranks of middle- and high-income families. Second, wealth mobility is rare, even over long periods of time. Once again, what we had hoped to be a land of opportunity appears not to be. That land would be a great one in which to live, which is a way of saying that equal opportunity remains an aspiration, not yet a reality, in our country.

6 Broken Work: The Prevalence and Characteristics of "Low-Quality" Jobs

> The system is broken, it's been broken for a long time. Racism is affecting the system. Greed is affecting the system. . . . All these corporations are raking in billions. . . . We all need a livable wage.
>
> —Ann J., Dorchester, Massachusetts[1]

In the fall of 2017, the Regional and Community Outreach department of the Boston Fed began a project to document the characteristics of low-wage jobs and understand why these characteristics prevailed. I gravitated to this topic, as it delved into evidence that challenged conventional views of how labor markets work. My role in the project was in part to lend economic rigor to the analyses, but it was also to learn more about how our economic systems had conspired to produce a constellation of jobs that feature not only low wages but also poor working conditions in general. The more I read and discussed, the more dismayed I became that our economy accepts working conditions echoing those of the pre-union late nineteenth and early twentieth centuries.

Adherents of The Myth explain the characteristics of work as necessary outcomes in efficient, free markets. If low-income jobs have become onerous or oppressive, then this must be the way free-market capitalism is supposed to work in the face of technological advance that replaces low-skilled workers with automation, and given free trade that inexorably directs manufacturing and other lower-skilled jobs abroad. Indeed, the forces of automation and globalization have put pressures on the United States and other developed economies. But as we'll see later, other developed economies have responded in ways that more effectively limit economic disparities, even if they have not been completely immune.

The question is why our economy has responded to the pressures of automation and offshoring as it has—not by educating and training our workforce to meet new economic realities but by relegating an increasing fraction of our workforce to dismal jobs. What was going on from the perspectives of business and society that made poor working conditions acceptable? Were businesses powerless in responding to market conditions, or did they make choices, individually and jointly, which led to declining workplace standards?

As Rick Wartzman and Steven Greenhouse demonstrate, the US workplace was not always structured in the way it is today.[2] The prevalence of unions that countered employers' power in the workplace, the extent of on-the-job training, the responsibility that employers appeared to feel for their employees' welfare—all this has changed over the past fifty years.

That same fall as the Boston Fed began its low wage–jobs project, I participated in a Fed conference on community development. I was fortunate to introduce Wartzman, the author of *The End of Loyalty: The Rise and Fall of Good Jobs in America*, at the conference. Between reading the book and discussing Rick's work with him, I was struck by two observations. First, a stunning share of the working population earns pitifully low wages, with correspondingly poor benefits, and supplements their income with much-needed government support. Second, I could find nothing in economic theory that tells us that a well-functioning, successful, and rich market-based economy requires a sizable chunk of its population to live in crushing poverty. Others have focused on lack of education, training, and work experience as explanations for high poverty rates, and it is true that fixing these must be a part of the solution. But Wartzman focused on the rise and fall of benevolent corporate practices after World War II—the employer side of the equation that determines outcomes for workers. My exposure to Wartzman's work helped to kindle my interest in writing this book.

This chapter turns to the plight of low-income working households, and in particular, to the characteristics of lower-wage jobs. To summarize, there are many workers laboring in one or more of these jobs. The jobs generally offer low wages, relatively poor health and retirement benefits, low likelihood of advancement, unpredictable work schedules, and poor "worker voice"—the ability for workers to have a say in their working conditions. As Zeynep Ton puts it, millions of jobs in retail, hospitality, food service, day care, and other sectors "are lousy and have been for decades."[3]

By Ton's estimate, "almost one-fifth of American workers have bad jobs. They endure low wages, poor benefits, schedules that change with little—if any—notice, and few opportunities for advancement."[4] It has not always been this way, and the change is quite plausibly related to the maximize-shareholder-value dictum that Milton Friedman so forcefully espoused.[5] The bottom line here is that tens of millions of US workers labor for low wages in poor working conditions and in many cases must turn to government assistance for food and housing to survive, and for childcare to *enable them to work* in the first place.

A large and rising share of the US workforce works in service-sector jobs, many of which offer low and stagnant wages.[6] Retail salespeople, for instance, garnered median weekly earnings of $745 in 2021. For women in retail jobs, the number drops to $635.[7]

In many low-wage jobs, whether in the service sector or otherwise, the full constellation of job characteristics is dismaying. As summarized in the chart below, health benefits, retirement benefits, and leave provisions differ significantly from the lowest- to the highest-paid jobs. US workers in the lowest 25 percent of the wage distribution are about half as likely as those in the highest 25 percent to receive these benefits from their employers, and those in the lowest 10 percent of the wage distribution are about one-third as likely to receive the benefits.[8] A 2016 study found that 39 percent of employees did not have access to a single paid sick day.[9] Black and Hispanic

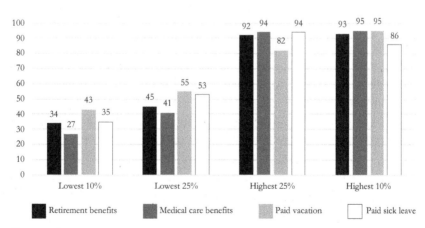

Figure 6.1
Percentage of employees with access to employee benefits by wage percentiles.

workers are even less likely than the average to be granted paid sick leave. The provision of defined-benefit pensions is not broken out in these data, but access has declined across the board. Such pensions are now offered to about 15 percent of the private-industry workforce, a drop of almost 60 percent since the 1990s.[10]

The data on work schedules are softer, but studies indicate that between 20 and 60 percent of people employed in the retail and service sectors are affected by unpredictable scheduling.[11] Industry-specific studies suggest that roughly half of workers in the retail and restaurant sectors received less than one week's notice of schedule changes.[12] Elaine Zundl and coauthors find that scheduling uncertainty appears to have survived the pandemic quite well.[13]

Other aspects of low-wage workers' working conditions make life a constant struggle. Childcare is of course an essential complement to work for households with children. But the high cost and variable quality of childcare force households in lower income brackets into impossible decisions. In 2018, annual household expenditures on full-time childcare for two children averaged $18,442 in the South and $26,102 in the East.[14]

These figures represent the sticker price for childcare and do not reflect funds households receive from state childcare assistance programs, which vary substantially in their generosity.[15] But even with benefits, out-of-pocket childcare expenses demand a sizable fraction of family income and are a huge burden for low-income households. Using data from the Survey of Income and Program Participation, Rasheed Malik finds that childcare payments absorb 10 percent of income across *all* working households with children under the age of five. The share falls with age and greater educational attainment but varies little across racial and ethnic categories. However, the share of income devoted to childcare payments for households with income less than twice the poverty level—about $55,000 for a family of four—rises to 35 percent. So even with government subsidies, childcare is clearly unaffordable for lower-income households. While a good number of households under this low-income cutoff do not pay childcare expenses, roughly 20 percent of the 5 million households paying for childcare (or about 1.1 million households) are in this low-income bracket.[16]

Given these high costs, lower-income households must often choose less costly childcare options, which usually means lower-quality childcare. Expecting households to make such trade-offs is cruel. In sum, the real burden that childcare places on workers in the lower income strata is staggering.

These statistics quantify key characteristics of "bad jobs." White, upper-income workers would never consider a job opportunity with low wages, poor or nonexistent health care benefits, no paid vacation or sick leave, few or no retirement benefits, and work hours that are scattered throughout the week and subject to frequent change with little notice. But this is the reality for tens of millions of workers.

A Shift in Workplace Norms

The prevailing features of the employer-employee contract for lower-wage jobs, whether formal legal requirements or informal workplace norms, have shifted profoundly over the past fifty years or so. From the 1920s through the 1960s, employer-employee relationships were marked by stability and security. A central element in the change of norms has been the increasing use of third-party contractors to provide services that were once performed by directly employed staff—cleaning, food services, accounting, building maintenance. Respondents to a Pew survey ranked the increased use of contractors and temporary employees third among the "biggest harms to U.S. workers" behind increased outsourcing of jobs and "more foreign-made products being sold in the U.S."[17] Why does this matter?

From the employer's perspective, putting cleaning, food services and maintenance out for competitive bidding is a strategy to reduce costs. Whoever charges the least is likely to win the contract. Contractors also handle tasks that are not part of an organization's core competence, allowing it to focus on its central mission. But outsourcing of this kind means that the worker is at arm's length from the people who manage the organization they are working for, if not the company that legally employs them. Benefits and work conditions are no longer the responsibility of the outsourcing organization; they are the responsibility of the contracting firm. And career ladders that once promised the opportunity to rise from a low-skilled job to a higher-skilled and higher-paying job within the organization, are eliminated.

Along these lines, Neil Irwin contrasts the experience of two female janitorial workers, one at Eastman Kodak in the 1980s and one at Apple headquarters in the 2010s.[18] On an inflation-adjusted basis, their salaries are about the same. But "that's where the similarities end." The Kodak employee had four weeks of paid vacation, tuition reimbursement, an annual bonus, and mobility within Kodak. The Apple employee hasn't taken vacation in two years, receives no bonus, and has no chance of transfer within Apple. The Kodak employee finished her college degree, was promoted into a professional-track IT job, and went on to become the company's chief technology officer.

In addition to contracting out many low-wage jobs, firms have gradually pared back the generosity of benefits, especially at the lower end of the wage scale. Employer-funded defined-benefit retirement plans—the classic pensions of the 1950s and 1960s—are a rarity today. Where employers offer retirement plans, they are far more likely to be 401k or other defined-contribution plans. These plans offer workers certain tax advantages—and in many cases matching employer contributions—as a means of building retirement resources. This change entails two major shifts in planning for retirement. First, unlike defined-benefit pensions, which provide a sum at retirement that depends on known determinants, such as job tenure and ending salary, 401k and other defined-contribution plans provide less-certain funds. Retirement resources available from a 401k plan will depend on the gains—or losses—accrued by investments over the years between enrolling in the plan and drawing payments. And second, those returns depend on the investment decisions of the worker. The employee decides both *how much to invest* and what to invest in. In defined-benefit plans, investment professionals decide how to invest pension funds, and the company decides how much to invest in order to provide promised retirement benefits for its employees. Under a defined-benefit plan, the employer has to make up any shortfall between realized investment gains on its pension assets and the retirement payments it promises to its employees. With 401k plans, the employee bears all of that risk. If they don't save enough, if they make poor investment choices, or if they have the bad luck to retire after a period of low investment returns, they have to work longer or spend less in retirement.

Cost-shifting of health plans has been progressing for decades. Both insurance premiums and out-of-pocket costs have been rising much faster than wages. Although the share of premiums paid by employers has held fairly steady at about 70 percent since 1999,[19] a Peterson-Kaiser Family Foundation analysis shows the combined cost of premiums and out-of-pocket expenses for households grew almost 70 percent from 2008 to 2018, even as wages on average grew about 25 percent.[20] That is to say that employer-sponsored health plans now feature less coverage per dollar of premium paid and rising out-of-pocket costs, thereby shifting costs to the employee. Given the slower growth in wages at the low end of the wage spectrum, this rise in health care costs places a greater burden on those lower-wage workers who have access to employer-provided health insurance—a dwindling number, as documented above. And low-wage workers with insurance tend to pay a higher percentage of premiums. At firms with large numbers of low-wage workers, those employees with family coverage pay, on average, 41 percent of the cost of premiums, as compared to 30 percent at other firms.[21]

These changes did not happen by accident. They were instead the result of decisions by countless companies that have adopted the shareholder-first business model, necessitating ruthless cost cutting with little regard for the consequences for workers. As Irwin and Wartzman write, this strategy has improved efficiency and gained profits for firms and their shareholders, but it also contributes to the hopeless situations that many working poor face.

Recent data suggest that workers are beginning to reach their breaking point. In late 2021, "quits"—voluntary departures from employment—reached a record high of 3 percent of those employed.[22] Massive voluntary departures imply rising confidence among employed workers that they can readily find another job, presumably with better wages, benefits, and work conditions. Time will tell if quitting produces those outcomes for workers, but there are some promising signs. Paul Krugman notes that, coincident with the rise in quitting, employers "aren't just whining about labor shortages," as has been the norm historically. They have increased pay for leisure and hospitality workers: by April 2022, average hourly earnings for these workers stood 18 percent above February 2020 levels.[23]

7 The Rest of the Story: More Signs of Brokenness

Low income, vastly unequal wealth, and poor working conditions at low-wage jobs are three of the most obvious signs of brokenness. But, sadly, the complete list of brokenness indicators is longer.

The Distribution of Housing

Many of us, particularly those like me who are white, well-educated, and economically privileged, take for granted that we will be able to afford safe, stable housing. But as the above data on income relative to budgets suggests, good housing is out of reach for many. Matthew Desmond's compelling work on the instability of housing for low-income households provides firsthand evidence of the precarious housing reality for too many in the United States.[1] As Desmond's examples make clear, housing is a prerequisite for a stable and secure economic life. Constant disruptions to one's place of residence make working, child-rearing, and health care grueling struggles.[2]

Between 2000 and 2016, roughly one of every forty renting households were evicted each year. For example, in 2016, there were 2.4 million eviction filings, resulting in just under 900,000 evictions. To put this in perspective, the number of households under threat of eviction each year is roughly equal to the number of foreclosures that were completed nationally in 2010 at the peak of the financial crisis. Evictions are thus an annual, ongoing financial crisis for low-income renters.[3]

Evictions rose at the onset of the COVID-19 pandemic in many states. In general, the institution of eviction moratoriums at the federal and state levels stabilized eviction rates, but in the months following the lifting of many of these moratoria, evictions have again trended upward.[4]

The statistics on housing affordability are equally sobering. Almost 60 percent of all households—both renters and owners—earning less than $20,000 paid housing costs in excess of 50 percent of their household income in 2021. The percentages are higher for Black and Hispanic households. Forty-one percent of Hispanics in this income range pay 100 percent or more of their household income for housing. Government transfers can partly make up the difference between their income and their housing needs, to say nothing of everything else they can't afford. In the next higher income range ($20,000–$30,000 per year), most Blacks and Hispanics still pay 40 percent or more of their household income for housing. The share of income going to housing costs is no better for low-income *renters* of color: More than one-third of Black and 42 percent of Hispanic renters pay 100 percent or more of their household income for housing.[5]

For those in lower income categories who have rental housing, the quality of their residences is often poor. According to the 2021 American Housing Survey, 11 percent of those households in the $0–20,000 income range and 9 percent of those in the $20,000–30,000 lived in "severely" or "moderately" inadequate housing. Across all income categories, Blacks and Hispanics are 25 to 35 percent more likely than whites to live with inadequate rental housing. Inadequacies range from problems with plumbing, heating, and electrical infrastructure to maintenance, pest infestations, and holes in floors.[6]

It could be, and sometimes is, worse: more than 500,000 Americans were homeless in 2020. At least, as far as we know. That number is likely an undercount, given the difficulties in finding people without fixed residences. The data we have indicate that roughly 40 percent of homeless people were living on the streets in 2020; the remainder lived in temporary housing. Blacks (39 percent) and Hispanics (22 percent) are disproportionately represented among the homeless.[7]

These data make it abundantly clear that access to housing is a significant challenge for low-income households. Recall the typical household budgets discussed earlier. These households are not close to "making ends meet," given the other expenditures they must make on food, clothing, childcare, health care, and transportation. Housing costs pose a constant strain on their meager resources.

Housing stress also differs across race and ethnicity. The data above cannot parse the underlying reasons for these differences, but the historical and economic record on systemic discrimination in housing is clear. From government redlining of communities—agents literally outlined in red communities of color whose residents were deemed unacceptably high risks for mortgage lenders—to covenants that explicitly prohibited people of color from living in certain neighborhoods to significantly unequal access to mortgage credit in the post-redlining era, people of color have long been denied the opportunity to live in safe housing.[8]

The brevity of this summary is in no way meant to diminish the importance of safe, stable housing. Those who cannot afford safe, stable housing will have great difficulty achieving economic success. Housing is foundational. It is not readily available to all households, as it should be.

Uneven Access to Health Care

Income, race, and ethnicity are associated with distinctly different health outcomes, according to the most recent data. In general, lower-income families and families of color have poorer access to important health care benefits, and Black families experience higher death rates, higher maternal mortality, more frequent ER visits, and lower life expectancy than their white and Hispanic counterparts.[9] Anne Case and Angus Deaton's findings suggest that for some poorer and less-educated white families, the grind of living in poverty has caught up in recent decades with their health, triggering a raft of "deaths of despair."[10] Consistent with these findings, Alan Auerbach and colleagues find that those born in 1960 and now in the top 20 percent of lifetime incomes can expect to live *thirteen years* longer than those born in the same year and now in the bottom 20 percent of lifetime incomes—a gap that has grown by almost eight years as compared to the cohort born thirty years earlier.[11]

Medicaid, which is designed to provide health insurance for poorer families, has been rationed in some states, despite the federally funded Medicaid expansion that is part of the Affordable Care Act. Eleven states have not adopted the expansion, and many of those rank among the lowest-income states on a per capita basis.[12] For ideological reasons, these states have refused federal funds to provide medical care to their poorest residents.

Patterns in US health outcomes are not replicated in other developed economies, which show stable or declining mortality rates across demographic groups. Only the US system, which leaves both whites and people of color in desperate economic circumstances for decades, is seeing reduced longevity.

Overall, the differences in health outcomes provide another clear sign that all is not well in our economy. Access and outcomes vary a lot. The basic level of security that good health care should provide is simply out of reach for so many families.

Broken Schoolhouses

In the early twentieth century, the United States embarked on a nationwide project to bring secondary school education to every youth, well in advance of most other Western nations. In 1910, 9 percent of eighteen-year-olds had high school diplomas. By 1940, more than 50 percent had earned the parchment, and the rate climbed to nearly 80 percent by 1980.[13] According to many studies, the economic return to high school and higher education is substantial and has likely increased in recent decades. In other words, that century-plus-old investment has paid off.

It has paid off, that is, for those who have the good fortune to have benefited from generations of educational opportunity. Test scores, an imperfect but still informative measure of school performance, show significant and persistent gaps across races and ethnicities. As an example, Massachusetts, a state with very high per-pupil expenditures and very high overall educational performance, still exhibits a 25-to-30-percentage point gap in reading for Black and Hispanic pupils relative to whites, measured at the fourth- and eighth-grade levels. The gap is even higher for math scores, at both grade levels.[14]

The same gaps are evident in SAT scores, with the average white student's SAT math score 93 points above the average Black student's. The College Board's college-readiness benchmarks for math scores reveal a 30—40 percent gap between white students on the one hand and Hispanic and Black students on the other.[15] Data from the US Department of Education find a *growing* performance gap between economically disadvantaged and other students for the years 2011–2019, both for math and for reading.[16] Importantly, as Andre Perry cautions, "Standardized tests are better proxies for how many opportunities a student has been afforded than they are predictors for students' potential." Like household wealth, performance on standardized tests reflects the cumulative effect of decades of generational opportunities—or lack thereof.[17]

High school graduation rates vary by race, ethnicity, and income status, for all states. Figure 7.1 displays the US averages and documents the 8–10 percentage point gaps between Black, Hispanic, and low-income students relative to their white counterparts. There is significant variation across states and other counted territories, with the lowest overall graduation rates in Washington, DC, and New Mexico. The luck of geography matters to educational attainment.[18]

There remains significant debate about how best to address these gaps in educational attainment. One possibility is that more spending will make a difference. The highest spenders—Washington, DC, New York, New Jersey, Vermont, and Wyoming—all invest more than $20,000 annually per pupil. The lowest—Arizona, Idaho, Mississippi, North Carolina, Oklahoma, and Utah—spend less than $10,000 per pupil.[19] Would equalizing spending help to close educational-attainment gaps? The simple correlations between education spending and outcomes are far from perfect, likely because so many other factors also contribute to education outcomes. As a consequence, this is an active area of study that aims to disentangle complex webs of

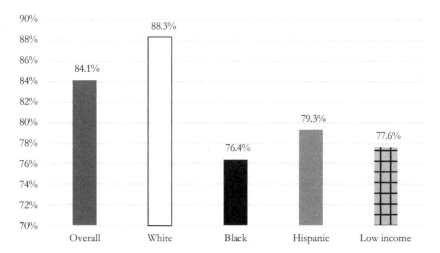

Figure 7.1
Graduation rates by race, ethnicity, and income, 2015–2016.

causation. But the best research to date indicates that spending does make a difference with respect to long-term outcomes.[20]

Whether or not spending is the solution, we need to level the educational playing field. Attaining a good secondary school education should not be left to the luck of the draw, depending on the color of your skin and which neighborhood you happen to grow up in.

A Broken Prison System

Another area of dysfunction is our ill-conceived, overused, discriminatory, and often profit-focused prison system. This problem has been thoroughly researched, but I want to ensure that all readers of this book are aware of the key features of our nation's prison system.

First, we are not in good company when it comes to the size of our prison population, which currently numbers more than 2 million. When we include those in the US who are on parole or on probation, the count more than triples.[21] Data for 2021 (figure 7.2) show that the United States is the global leader in prisoners per capita. There are no other high-income nations anywhere near us in the rankings. Our numbers significantly exceed those of countries that Americans think of as punitive, such as Rwanda, Cuba, and the Russian Federation. China and Iran don't even make the top-thirty list, although this could reflect political manipulation of official statistics. Germany has one-tenth the incarceration rate of the US, France one-seventh the rate, and Italy one-eighth.[22] Something has gone terribly wrong here.

How did this happen? Michelle Alexander's groundbreaking work on the systematic incarceration of young Black men makes clear that this was an intended outcome of the "War on Drugs" declared in 1982, which culminated in a seven-fold increase in the US prison population, with drug-related convictions accounting for the majority of that increase.[23] Today, 38 percent of inmates are Black and 30 percent are Hispanic, well in excess of their representation in the general population. Forty-five percent of those currently incarcerated were convicted of drug offenses, more than twice the share of any other crime category.[24]

While most of the drug offenses for which people are convicted are minor, the lifetime implications are not.[25] As Alexander documents, lives

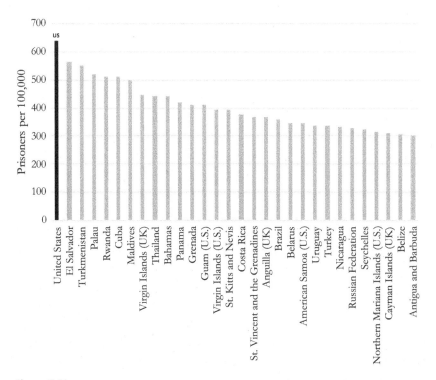

Figure 7.2
Prisoners per 100,000 residents.

can be forever changed by conviction for a minor drug offense. Offenders can lose eligibility for food stamps, often lose the right to vote (the restrictions vary by state), and may be evicted from public housing and lose their jobs. It doesn't matter whether the conviction came at trial or via plea bargaining. Criminal background checks make it difficult for offenders to find jobs. In recognition of this hardship, some states have enacted legislation to limit or prohibit the use of criminal background checks in hiring decisions.

It is thus not hard to imagine how incarceration even for a relatively minor offense can spiral into a lifetime of poor employment or unemployment, poverty, and homelessness, with restricted access to the public supports that help needy people survive. These choices that we as a nation have made have had a profound influence on the economic and social outcomes for millions of adults, largely Black men. It cannot be right, yet it persists to this day.

Who's Running This Economy? A Broken Pattern of Firm Ownership and Control

The representation of women and minorities on boards of directors in the United States is woefully low. Some companies have made progress as boards turn over, but as of 2020 the composition of boards still looks lop-sidedly white and male. A recent Deloitte report on *Fortune* 500 companies shows women filling only 26.5 percent of board seats, racial and ethnic minorities 17.5 percent, and Blacks and Hispanics under-represented at 8.7 and 4.1 percent, respectively. Minority women make up less than 6 percent of board members among these large companies. Companies are still run mostly by men, and mostly by white members.[26] These numbers have improved, but only very gradually, since the study began in 2004. And the picture does not improve if we expand our data set: among the 3,000 largest publicly traded companies, ethnic and racial minorities made up 17 percent of directors in 2021.[27]

Demographic representation is no better when we examine top executives at US firms. A 2020 Stanford Business School study finds that only one-quarter of C-suite positions in *Fortune* 100 companies are held by women, and women are underrepresented in C-suite positions that are typical feeders for the CEO position—that is, in jobs that are thought of as "profit centers," as opposed to, say, heads of human resources and general counsels. Eight percent of these companies' CEOs are women, up from 2 percent in 2008. Racial and ethnic diversity looks worse. Nine percent of CEOs are ethnic minorities, up from 4 percent in 2008. Only four CFOs are people of color, and only 16 percent of all C-suite positions are held by people of color.[28] It's fairly clear that women and minorities do not have equal opportunity when it comes to running our economy's companies, either as directors or as top executives.

Entrepreneurship among people of color remains a challenge as well. The Census Bureau's most recent Annual Business Survey, covering 2019, finds huge disparities by gender, race, and ethnicity. To begin with, ownership is disproportionately male and white: 61 percent of owners are men and 81 percent are white. White male owners also take in disproportionate revenue, employ a disproportionate share of the workforce, and distribute a disproportionate amount of America's payroll (see figure 7.3).[29] Recent research by the National Community Reinvestment Coalition reports that

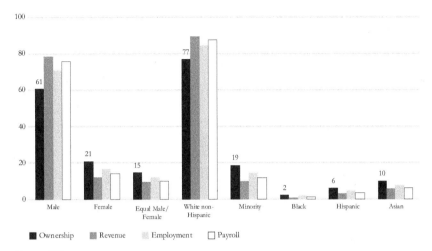

Figure 7.3
Business ownership, revenue, employment, and payroll by gender, race, and ethnicity (2019).

Black-owned businesses are more likely to operate in the South where incomes are lower, in sectors associated with lower revenue generation and profitability, with less family wealth to bring to the business, and less ready access to financial capital.[30]

In sum, the answer to the question "Who's running this economy?" is "affluent white men," who most often come from advantaged backgrounds.

Broken Banks and Financial Markets

The banking system does not serve all populations equally. The Federal Reserve's "Report on the Economic Well-Being of U.S. Households in 2021" shows that the probability of being unbanked (households with no checking, savings, or money market account) or underbanked (households with a bank account but also using payday loans, pawn shops, check-cashing services, and so on) varies considerably by income, race, and ethnicity.[31] People with household income under $25,000, lower educational attainment, and Blacks and Hispanics all show much lower connection to the banking system.

Access to credit—the ability to borrow for homeownership, auto ownership, education—is similarly divergent across racial and ethnic categories. A

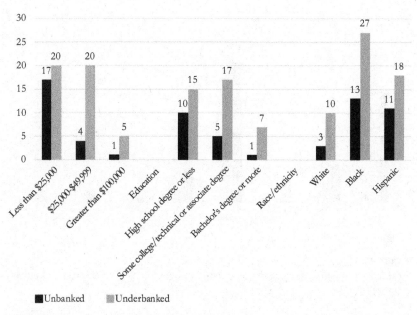

Figure 7.4
Unbanked and underbanked households by income, education, and race/ethnicity.

landmark study by economists at the Boston Fed found significant evidence of discrimination in mortgage lending in the early 1990s.[32] That study used all of the information about borrowers that was available to loan officers to estimate the probability of rejection for a mortgage application. The study found that after controlling for *everything* that was recorded in the loan file, the probability of rejection was still significantly affected by the race and ethnicity of the applicant. A follow-up study has not been conducted—most of the data are no longer held by institutions regulated by the Federal Reserve—so we do not know if this behavior has changed over the past thirty years.

Researchers at the Federal Reserve Bank of New York produce a Credit Insecurity Index, which combines credit-access and credit-stress data. Credit stresses include exceeding credit limits, subprime credit scores, and consistently delinquent payment history. The most recent data, from 2020, reveal significant geographic differences in credit insecurity, which tend to persist over time. States with the most insecure counties cluster in the mid-South, Southeast, and parts of the Southwest. The map in figure 7.5, using data from the fourth quarter of 2018, shows the same pattern.[33]

Map of Credit Insecurity Index Scores by County as of 2018 Q4

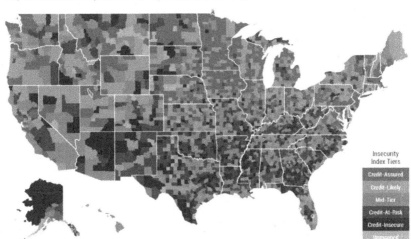

Source: FRBNY Consumer Credit Panel/Equifax

Figure 7.5

Map of Credit Insecurity Index scores by county as of 2018 Q4. The most credit-insecure counties are those in the darkest shades of gray.

The financial sector provides essential services to many households and businesses by offering a safe place to deposit earnings, by enabling transactions, and by providing loans that are essential to everyday life and business. But access to these basic services is clearly unequal across income and racial/ethnic categories, as well as across geographies. Of course, some of the geographic differences are likely explained by differences across these locations in income and accumulated wealth. But if so, why are income, wealth and credit access disparities so concentrated in these locations? What is it about our system that delivers such different results based on zip code?

III The Myth versus the Facts

You now know the prevailing narratives held by the general public, and I've presented evidence indicating how widespread adherence to these framing devices is. It seems clear that the key elements of The Myth—belief in the notion that individual effort determines success, that racism no longer influences economic outcomes, that markets must be free of government interference, and that businesses have no choice but to maximize shareholder value—run quite deep in the consciousness of most Americans. Like the force in *Star Wars*, The Myth surrounds us, penetrates us, and binds us together.[1] Actually, I'm not so sure about that last one. But the things we believe true often are not. While there is some truth to The Myth, the preponderance of the evidence shows that it is a combination of aspiration, wishful thinking, avoidance of uncomfortable facts, and willfully misused dogma. The Myth persists in spite of the facts on the ground.

8 Evidence against The Myth

Ms. P. was born into a family that fled Cambodian genocide in the late 1970s. She lost her father while her family was living in a Thai refugee camp almost forty years ago. Her family moved to the United States when she was three years old. She now lives in Lowell, Massachusetts, where she has a good job working for the city. Still, at the age of forty, she is "barely getting by," which speaks to the persistence of low income and the lack of mobility that is so evident in the data. She leads a small nonprofit on the side and is trying to start a business to "get out of this financial rut—and own my own place." So much for laziness. When I asked her if she had savings set aside, she said, "Yeah, barely. And then when I do, you know, have something in a savings account, I end up having to pull stuff out to pay for things."[1]

In talking with her siblings, she often notes, "If dad were alive, we'd have a different life." No doubt. Her father was well-educated, a doctor who could surely have augmented the income that Ms. P.'s single mother was able to provide—she spoke fluent French and Khmer but came to the United States with no command of English. That sort of luck—one's starting conditions in life—has been shown to have profound influence on outcomes much later in life.

It is not surprising that luck plays some role in determining individual outcomes. What is surprising is how large a role luck plays.

Individual Effort and the Role of Accidents of Birth

The amassed evidence on the sheer number of families and individuals who suffer poor economic outcomes constitutes prima facie evidence that effort can't be all that's required for success. It cannot be that everyone in the lower income and wealth deciles just hasn't put in enough effort to escape poverty or near-poverty. That thesis is absurd on its face. Tens of millions of US workers are struggling because they are all lazy or have all made bad choices? Indeed, this proposition is not just absurd but also deeply disrespectful to those who struggle to succeed despite their starting points and lack of opportunities.

Nor is it reasonable to assume that everyone in the upper deciles of income and wealth arrived there solely due to extraordinary effort, diligence, and brilliance. But narratives can blind us to the realities staring us in the face.[2] Loads of evidence shows that where we wind up is a product not just of effort and ability but also quite importantly a matter of *luck*.

One of the most striking bodies of such evidence is the Opportunity Atlas, a collective work of Raj Chetty, John Friedman, and Nathaniel Hendren.[3] Their data allows one to link the income of a current adult, wherever she lives, to the specific location in which she grew up. The database also collects data on race, gender, and the income of the household in which each grown adult was raised.

What emerges is striking: where you are born makes all the difference. Very local geographic effects are associated with very different outcomes for adults. Those effects are much more pronounced for people of color than they are for whites. Consider the median household income for men who grew up in low-income families in the Forest Hills and Roslindale neighborhoods of Boston, or in the Fowl River and Westfield areas of Mobile, Alabama. The two neighborhoods in each city are contiguous, their centers separated only by hundreds of yards. But the economic outcomes for men who grew up poor in these locations are likely to be miles apart.

The differences for white men are modest: median adult household income is 15 percent lower for those raised in Forest Hills versus Roslindale, and only a bit lower for those raised in Fowl River versus Westfield.[4] But the differences for Black men are huge. Adult incomes differ by 32 percent between the two neighborhoods of Boston. Mobile overall is an unlucky location in which to have been born—incomes are much lower than in Boston—but the difference between adjoining neighborhoods of Mobile is remarkable: incomes for black men who grew up in Fowl River are about *one-sixth* those of black men who grew up in Westfield. And the difference between being born Black or white in the lowest-income neighborhoods is striking. Median adult incomes of Black men born in Forest Hills are about

60 percent of those of adult white men born in the same neighborhood. In Fowl River, the figure is 20 percent.

There are no doubt reasons for these differences across very nearby neighborhoods: schools may vary in quality, for instance, and public-safety conditions can be dramatically different just a few hundred yards away.[5] But the point is that a child *has no choice over where she is born*. And yet where a child is born can have a profound influence on economic success in adulthood. That surely should be considered luck, and certainly it is from the vantage point of the child.

So individual effort is on average insufficient to overcome the bad luck of geography, unless you believe that the now-adults raised in these neighborhoods just happen to be disproportionately lazy. That's a tough assumption to sustain.

Much of the hard data documenting our broken economic system points to the role that luck plays in economic success in the United States. Children cannot choose their parents, location, family income, or wealth, and it is abundantly clear from the data that family income and wealth vary widely across families. We might worry less about accidents of birth that determine initial income and wealth and schooling if these conditions had little effect on lifetime outcomes. But the data on income and wealth mobility offered earlier, coupled with the results presented in this section, suggest that these initial conditions matter profoundly for adult outcomes. We should not as a nation dismiss these results with a narrative shrug. The world we live in is not "just the way it has to be."

Save the Deserving: Evidence from the Great Recession and Financial Crisis of 2007–2009

A reading from The Myth: If capitalism truly knows best, then it's best not to interfere with it. If unfettered markets inevitably find the best solutions to economic problems, then they should remain unfettered. The Great Recession and Financial Crisis of 2007–2009 demonstrated that those are very big ifs.

Capitalism serves in many ways as an efficient system for allocating resources—certainly better than the known alternatives. I am not advocating that the United States move to a government-controlled allocation system. The former Soviet Union's experience with that system should serve as ample warning.

But US capitalism quite clearly does not always know best. Markets have not yet provided solutions to longstanding economic problems such as chronic poverty and unequal access to education and financial services, let alone the persistent effects of racism. And while our form of capitalism works well in many respects when all is calm, it can fall apart quickly when disruptions occur.[6] And when it falls apart, it needs extensive and forceful government support, even for those in the highest income and wealth brackets and even for the largest and formerly most profitable businesses. Economic crises also make clear—often in hindsight—the risks of eroding regulations that provide some measure of protection against overly free capital markets. In some of our most recent episodes of upheaval, the priorities that our government embraces in providing support became quite clear. Sadly, those priorities reflect deep adherence to elements of The Myth.

The Great Recession and Financial Crisis of 2007–2009 demonstrated vividly how US capitalism can fail its citizens. It also showed who's first in line to receive government aid when it's required, and it's not the neediest.

I had a ringside seat to the largest economic disruption in at least a quarter-century as director of research at the Boston Fed. I learned about details of financial markets that none of us had had to worry about before they began to unravel. I vividly recall watching stock tickers to see which firms were failing each day, how far the stock market would drop, and whether the actions taken by the Fed and Congress would be sufficient to stop the skid into the abyss. Weekdays, nights, and weekends were filled with hastily convened policy meetings, as the crisis proceeded in unexpected ways and we tried to design new tools on the fly to limit the carnage. Don't ever let anyone tell you this wasn't that bad an episode: it was, and it could have been much worse. Policymakers, especially then–Fed Chairman Ben Bernanke and others at the Federal Reserve System, deserve credit for avoiding the worst.

There were two distinct but related phases of the crisis: the financial meltdown and the ensuing recession. The meltdown was rapid and severe. The short-term lending that undergirded so much financial and nonfinancial business activity began to evaporate. Markets were still as free as ever, but they weren't functioning, and there was evidently no way for them to self-correct.

Fortunately, the Federal Reserve was there to provide a floor under the freefall, by quickly ensuring that an array of financial institutions could continue to provide short-term loans to businesses. In a matter of weeks, the Fed designed programs to support the money market mutual fund industry (large investors in mortgage-related assets) and the commercial-paper market. The Fed's Term Auction Facility provided competitive multi-week loans to banks that were unable to borrow due to the liquidity crunch. These and several other programs aimed at stabilizing short-term borrowing and lending.

Which was very nice. It was certainly not a free-market solution. And it was also far from the end of the story. As short-term credit markets were being repaired, the Treasury and the Fed were engineering the rescue of the nineteen largest financial entities in the country, utilizing funds from the Troubled Asset Relief Program (TARP).

Of the $700 billion appropriated by Congress for the TARP:

- $250 billion went to the Capital Purchase Program, which provided funds to small and large banks, although the bulk went to eight of the largest financial institutions.[7] The program purchased preferred stock that paid 5 percent dividends from 2009 until 2013, at which point the dividend rate would increase to 9 percent, as an incentive for banks to buy back the preferred stock. These banks (or their purchasers/successors) ultimately repurchased all of these shares.

- $80.7 billion went to General Motors, Ford Motor Company, and Chrysler to avoid imminent bankruptcies in the auto industry. The money comprised loans and share purchases. The government recouped all but $9.3 billion of that investment.[8]

- $182 billion went to bail out AIG, through a combination of loans and preferred-share purchases. The Fed initially held $90 billion of credit extended to AIG on its balance sheet; it gradually reduced that amount to zero through sales of assets through January 2011.[9]

- $75 billion went to the Homeowner Affordability Modification Program, to help homeowners refinance or restructure their mortgages to avoid foreclosure.[10]

In all, the Treasury and the Fed put out trillions of dollars to rescue the financial services industry and a few key nonfinancial businesses. Coupled with a supervisory "stress test" of the nineteen largest banks in the spring of

2009, which provided an estimate of the funds that the largest banks might need to offset the losses likely to mount with the growing recession, these actions produced a rapid rebound in the health of the financial sector. But without the dramatic and unprecedented measures taken by the Fed and the Treasury, our world-class capitalist system would likely have collapsed in a heap of steaming mortgage-backed securities, unable to pick itself up by its financial bootstraps. What would that have meant? Many of the largest financial institutions—banks, mutual funds—would have collapsed. Everyday businesses' ability to borrow money to pay workers and finance inventories would have been cut off, resulting in layoffs and reduced orders of business inputs, with damaging ripple effects. Many more people would have lost their jobs and their homes. The imagery of the Dust Bowl and the Great Depression seems apt.

It may be that much of the rescue would not have been required if financial institutions had been prepared for the possibility of falling house prices and widespread mortgage defaults. So how prepared were the most sophisticated financial institutions for this possibility? Not well. Many continued to forecast flat housing prices even in 2007. They put in place little or no insurance against the possibility that prices would fall significantly and thus that the value of these assets would decline. Why was that? Where were the well-functioning, sophisticated, risk-savvy financial markets when we needed them most?[11]

In my view, this failure to take precautions against the ramifications of falling housing prices represented a colossal failure of financial prudence and risk management. It is nearly impossible to know when a bubble (in housing prices, in this case) is going to burst, although a number of economists and market observers suggested that housing prices might soon crash.[12] But when housing prices have already stopped rising, it takes little imagination to envision the possibility that prices will fall going forward. Put differently, if you see prices remaining flat as the most likely outcome, then surely the probability that they could fall is high. The ramifications of a significant national decline in housing prices were well-understood: big losses would result. Yet there appears to have been little interest in managing the risk that accompanied falling housing prices.

In part, the rapid and vigorous rescue of the financial system was undertaken because the financial crisis was fast-moving and difficult to predict and because the Bush and Obama administrations and the Fed reasonably saw echoes of the Great Depression in the rapidly deteriorating financial market conditions at the time. Policymakers took action because financial institutions do provide vital services to keep nonfinancial businesses running.

So the government saved Wall Street, albeit with some (well-deserved) losses. It is interesting to contrast this with what the government did for Main Street, especially for the workers and homeowners in the economy.

*   *   *

Even as the financial collapse was alleviated with hundreds of billions of dollars of taxpayer funding, the Great Recession was roaring ahead. The loss of confidence by firms witnessing the massive upheaval in financial markets, coupled with the difficulty Congress had in mustering a response to the crisis—recall that the first attempt to pass a financial rescue bill failed, with Republican opponents citing objections to government intervention—led to a dramatic pullback in hiring and a rise in firing in late 2008 and early 2009.[13] The result was a rise in the national unemployment rate from about 4.5 percent in April 2007 to a peak of 10 percent in October 2009, well after financial firms had recovered.[14]

Unlike the financial sector, employment took years to recover: the unemployment rate did not drop below 5 percent until seven years later. The economic recovery was enabled in part by significant Fed support— very low short-term interest rates and massive asset purchases that lowered longer-term interest rates and boosted a variety of other asset prices. In recognition of the persistently weak economy, the Fed chose to delay the return to normal interest rates (above 2 percent) until late 2018.[15]

In the late winter of 2009, Congress debated and ultimately passed the American Recovery and Reinvestment Act, a $787 billion bill that included a variety of stimulus measures. The largest components were an income tax credit of $400 per worker and $800 per couple (at a budgetary cost of $97 billion), Medicaid aid to states ($99 billion), aid to school districts ($54 billion), extended unemployment benefits ($64 billion), funding for transportation initiatives, including highway and bridge construction ($46 billion), and investments in green-energy technology and other energy initiatives ($34 billion).[16] It is interesting to note that, at the time, concerns were expressed about the infrastructure component of the bill, which certainly could have been much larger. But Congress was worried that appropriations that were ultimately spent a year or two later would be ill-timed, stimulating the economy when it had already fully recovered. Thus the emphasis was on "shovel-ready" projects.[17] With hindsight, the concern that infrastructure-related construction might occur too late was based on wild optimism about the rapidity of economic recovery.

While these efforts no doubt kept the crisis and recession from becoming even worse, they left millions unemployed for many years after the financial side of the crisis had effectively ended.

*   *   *

What should we learn from this pivotal economic episode? As sophisticated as it appears to be, our economy can get itself into big trouble, in an astonishing variety of ways.[18] It turns out that free markets are not self-correcting entities that are best left to their own devices. The troubles of the financial crisis arose because many market participants made ill-advised decisions and took on risk that even ex ante was foolish. When the bottom fell out, it was not possible for these institutions or the markets they traded in to save themselves. Only through government support were we able to keep the economy from slipping into the chasm of a second Great Depression. As it turns out, our capitalist economy simply cannot function without critical government supports, especially during crises, including crises of the private markets' own making.

Very closely related, most activity in our economy requires some level of regulation, contrary to the most simplistic interpretations of free markets.[19] Arguments for regulation are manifold. Regulation is needed to reduce the damage inflicted by so-called externalities—costs to society caused, but not borne, by producers. The pollution generated by manufacturing and natural-resources extraction is a classic externality: production of manufactured goods and extraction of resources causes pollution, an environmental cost that is borne by others. Taxing producers for the pollution they cause shifts that cost back to them, and reduces the amount they produce and thus limits the pollution they cause. Such taxation also incents producers to invest in less-polluting means of production to avoid the tax. Regulation is also valuable in correcting informational asymmetries, such as those that make it impossible for consumers to know all the characteristics of the food or pharmaceuticals they purchase. In the cases of financial markets, regulation limits the extent of risk-taking by financial firms. The goals of such regulation are to protect depositors' money and to minimize the likelihood that financial-sector losses will lead banks to cut off essential borrowing by nonfinancial business, increasing layoffs and turning a financial disruption into a full-blown recession. Many would agree that we had rolled back financial regulations too far in the lead-up to the crisis. The Dodd-Frank legislation of 2010 imposed additional restrictions on many financial entities, aiming to avoid the unhedged and highly leveraged risk-taking that characterized the financial crisis. But it did not take long for adherents to The Myth to begin watering down some of those regulations.[20]

The crisis revealed how much we revere our financial institutions. The number and variety of programs that were put in place to support the financial system in the wake of the financial crisis was stunning. Within months, the financial sector was back on an even keel, its stock prices rising, its profits rebounding smartly.[21] The level of support reflects the perceived importance of the financial systems in the United States. To some extent, that perception is justified, as key financial institutions indeed provide funds essential to nonfinancial firms, allowing them to keep the lights on and their workers paid. However, it is far from clear that all the activities of the largest financial entities are necessary to the success of nonfinancial business.[22] Much of those financial entities' resources were, and remain, devoted to improving the yields on high-wealth individuals' portfolios, adding minimal social value. The point is that we often overstate the fundamental importance of our largest financial institutions, and we overestimate the sagacity and prescience of their leaders. In failing to manage the risk inherent in large portfolios of mortgage-related securities, key financial institutions amassed losses that nearly toppled the financial system. In the process, they dragged down many nonfinancial businesses with them, contributing directly to the economic woes suffered by households.

The contrast between the outcomes for financial firms and the average worker is striking. The Obama administration and Congress were not able to put together aid sufficient to keep millions of families from losing their homes, a goal that may well have been feasible. Many millions more suffered protracted spells of unemployment.[23] One can reasonably argue that financial markets required a quicker policy response, and that, once repaired, financial markets could be expected to rebound more quickly than, say, unemployment. But that does not explain the seven-year period required to normalize unemployment and return the economy to its full potential. As former Treasury Secretary Timothy Geithner put it in a 2018 presentation on the response to the financial crisis:

> I think that in general the country would have been better served if we'd had a stronger program of, you might call them, fiscal stimulus: tax cuts, support for state and local governments, a whole range of things like that, larger, sustained longer. . . . I think that would have made a big difference. And we were successful in relaxing some of the political constraints on that, but not successful enough. Housing is, you know, tragically complicated; the broad thrust of the programs we did were not large enough to offset a substantial part of the damage from a recession in which millions and millions of people lost their jobs. . . . The programs we did to directly limit the risk people would lose their home unnecessarily, they helped 9 million people benefit from lower payments on their mortgages and millions of people refinanced who were underwater, but [the programs] were not large enough and they came late in the process. They came too late."[24]

Bernanke agrees. "More should have been done to help homeowners," he said, "although devising effective policies to do that was more difficult than many appreciate."[25] Difficult, but not impossible.

Finally, this episode reveals our national priorities. Our policymakers were willing to put vast sums of money at stake to rescue large and powerful financial institutions. Many of the benefits of those rescues accrued to high-income and high–net worth individuals—they are clearly the deserving in our economy—not to the average person. Evidently, ordinary people deserved something less. Nor did Americans collectively see the struggles of average people as unacceptable, and thus they bore the brunt of the crisis, a crisis in which almost all of them were innocent bystanders turned victims.[26]

In contrast, the response to the economic decline resulting from the COVID-19 pandemic provided much-needed help to households and workers. One might more easily be able to classify most people as the "deserving poor" in these circumstances: those struggling financially in the face of COVID were clearly harmed by forces beyond their control. In addition, during most recessions, the goal is to get people back to work, and thus some fear that unemployment compensation that is too generous will deter return to work. In this case, the point was to *keep people afloat while they could not work* for public health reasons, so there may have been less concern about employment disincentives. It may be risky to overgeneralize from this episode, but it does raise interesting questions about The Myth's assumptions regarding how households and small businesses use or misuse government aid, and about how much we can trust the recipients of such aid.

In spring 2010, I spoke with senior Boston Fed staff about lessons from the financial crisis and Great Recession. One lesson I highlighted was Secretary Geithner's: we saved Wall Street but left Main Street to languish. At the time, this was not a popular stance to take, and I received some flak for it. But I contend that it was a reasonable critique and one that holds up well today. The Federal Reserve as an institution appears to have learned that lesson, having taken policy steps consistent with it in the past decade.

In sum, financial markets don't always work well, and when they fail the repercussions are felt widely in the economy. Financial markets therefore require regulation and supervision. The debate over the appropriate degree of regulation is ongoing, and there are risks on both sides: too much regulation can restrict the flow of capital to businesses, and too little can lead to excessive risk-taking and macroeconomic disaster. Judging by the profitability of financial firms to date, it seems unlikely that we have over-regulated them on the whole.

Most Americans venerate capitalism and the financial markets that have grown up with it. The Myth imputes to their leaders the same qualities it does other high-earning individuals: brilliance and extraordinary vision. In *The Theory of Moral Sentiments* Adam Smith, a founding capitalist thinker but also much more, laments this "disposition to admire, and almost to worship, the rich and powerful, and to despise, or, at least, to neglect persons of poor and mean condition." He deems this attitude "the most universal cause of the corruption of our moral sentiments." He despairs "that wealth and greatness are often regarded with the respect and admiration which are due only to wisdom and virtue" and that "the contempt, of which vice and folly are the only proper objects, is often most unjustly bestowed upon poverty and weakness"[27]

As a consequence of this adulation, those in power are reluctant to regulate, interfere with, or question the decisions of financial firms, even as they lead us to the precipice of depression. The financial crisis and Great Recession showed that the costs of Americans' reverence for capitalism fell almost entirely on the average worker and disproportionately on families of color. Our very recent history makes such adulation of our economic system and its leaders appear rather misplaced.

Evidence on the "Trickle Down" Theory

An argument often used in defense of low tax rates and tax breaks for the rich is that when high-income families and businesses thrive, their prosperity will make its way down to lower-income families. High-income people are "job creators:" they own businesses that employ lower-income workers, and their spending circulates throughout the economy, generating demand for goods and services that are produced by low- and moderate-income workers. Allowing the rich to retain profits means more money can be plowed into investment capital, which in turn will also produce more jobs. The more the well-off have, the better off everyone will be.

In this way, the "trickle-down" element of The Myth defines a key part of our society's relationship with the poor: the best way to get money to the distrusted poor is to instead give it to the rich, proclaiming against all odds that it will make its way down to the needy. This theory has been widely discredited by economists, although its popularity remains. John Kenneth Galbraith described the trickle-down theory as the notion that "if you feed the horse enough oats, some will pass through to the road for the sparrows."[28] Joseph Stiglitz finds trickle-down's continued esteem puzzling, noting that "rising inequality has not led to more growth, and most Americans have actually seen their incomes sink or stagnate . . . the opposite of trickle-down economics."[29] Generally, studies that attempt to find a link between tax cuts for the well-off and increased investment spending or employment come up empty.

It was hard to find anything good trickling down during the most recent attempt at an application of the theory, the Tax Cuts and Jobs Act of 2017. The law reduced the corporate income tax rate from 35 to 21 percent and allowed companies to fully deduct certain types of capital spending from their earnings. The hope, as articulated by its proponents, was that lower tax rates would spur investment, employment, and economic growth and that the resulting increase in tax revenues would more than pay for the tax cuts.

Instead, an independent study by economists at the International Monetary Fund found that the reduction in the cost of investment capital played at best a "minor role" in explaining investment spending in the wake of the law's passage.[30] Meanwhile tax revenues, adjusted for inflation, were *lower* in 2018. As a share of GDP, tax revenues fell even more. And revenues were well below Congressional Budget Office projections made before the tax cuts were signed into law.[31] The law was billed as providing a significant tax cut for the middle and working classes, but research casts doubt on this proposition. Economist Joel Slemrod finds that "overall, more than half of the benefits go to the top 10 percent of earners."[32]

Despite trickle-down's repeated failures, it has proven a go-to justification for efforts to cut taxes on the wealthy and on large corporations and occasionally the middle class—actions that have over time exacerbated inequality and rarely if ever delivered the promised benefits for the majority. The evidence to date suggests that the top earners have indeed gained from tax cuts, but the effects never trickled down, and they probably never will. Nonetheless, trickle-down theory remains a popular element of The Myth.

9 This Is Not the Only Way: International Comparisons

Adherents of The Myth believe that US outcomes are best, reflecting our success in leaving capitalism to its own efficient devices. Doing so allows our system to provide the most benefit to the economy. In short, this is the way capitalism *should* work.

There is no reason why a free-market capitalist system must unavoidably lead to the undesirable outcomes documented above. For proof, we need only turn to comparison with other democratic, free-market capitalist countries. Among developed capitalist nations, the United States is an obvious outlier in key respects—with regard to our tax system; inequality of income and wealth; and access to health care, childcare, education, and economic mobility. This strongly suggests that Americans could make other choices and that capitalism can work without producing the thundering inequities that we observe in the United States.

While a common battle in Congress centers on lowering taxes, in fact US taxes are quite low by international standards. Judged by total taxes paid—the sum of income, payroll, sales, Social Security, property, and other taxes as a share of GDP—Americans pay little compared to residents of most developed countries, as figure 9.1 shows.

The appropriate level of taxation is a political decision that involves weighing costs and benefits. The cost of higher taxes arises from reducing net wages and capital income, which could in theory reduce the incentive to work or invest. The benefit of higher taxes lies in the social gains delivered by the government programs and services that the taxes pay for. It is clear from figure 9.1 that Americans have chosen a balance that errs well on the side of avoiding much-feared—but, in practical terms, usually insignificant—disincentives, at the expense of providing services.

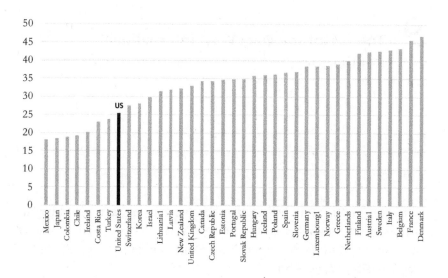

Figure 9.1
Total taxes paid as percentage of GDP, 2020. Source: OECD, "Tax Levels and Structures, 1965–2020."

Not only do Americans pay low taxes, but the US tax code is also not unusually progressive—that is, the IRS does not collect a highly disproportionate share of tax revenue from the highest earners. In thinking about the overall progressiveness of the US tax system, we need to consider a range of taxes. The rates for the *individual income tax* are indeed progressive, ranging from 10 percent for the lowest-income filers to 37 percent for the highest. But Americans also pay largely flat taxes for social security and Medicare. State income and sales taxes are also typically flat.

One way to gauge whether a tax system is more or less progressive is to compare the share of total taxes collected from taxpayers in a particular income range to the share of total income they earn. A common trope is that the top 1 percent of income earners pays 40 percent of the taxes.[1] This is quite misleading, as it covers only the individual income tax and ignores the fact that the top 1 percent of earners take home nearly 20 percent of total income, as highlighted by many researchers and as summarized earlier.

A better measure is provided by the Institute on Taxation and Economic Policy. Their 2019 report shows that the US tax system *overall* is very mildly progressive, with lower income deciles paying a bit less than the share of

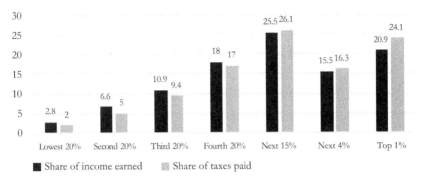

Figure 9.2
Shares of total taxes paid by each US income group, compared to shares of total income in 2019.

income they earn, while higher income deciles pay about 3 percentage points more than their share of income, not the 39 suggested by the trope described above. Figure 9.2 makes the point clearly.[2] In a completely neutral tax system, the shares of income would equal the shares of taxes paid. We're not too far from that.

It should be clear from this chart that we have not tipped the scales into absurd progressivity. Roughly speaking, taxpayers pay their share of income in taxes.

Between this observation and the statistics on the massive amount of income concentrated in upper income deciles, it would appear that Americans have chosen *not* to overburden upper-income earners. On the bright side, this relatively even burden of taxation suggests that the United States has significant capacity to reapportion income without doing great damage to any one group.

Like individual tax rates, US corporate tax rates are low by international standards. In fact, judged by tax revenues collected as a share of GDP, the United States has the lowest corporate tax rate among members of the G7 developed economies, as shown in figure 9.3.[3] The effective tax rate has fallen by a factor of more than five over the past seventy years.[4] These low rates suggest significant lost revenue that could be put to good use. We would need to weigh this benefit against the damage higher taxes could do to corporations' profitability, but this seems a small concern of late, as profits have been quite healthy in recent decades, as discussed earlier.

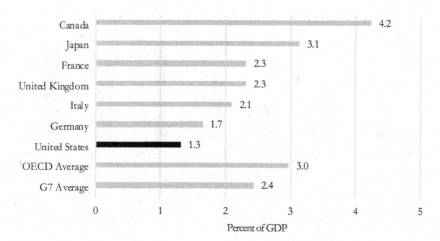

Figure 9.3
Corporate tax revenues as a share of GDP, 2020, among G7 countries.

Income and wealth inequality stand out in the United States compared to other developed economies—the United States has the sixth-highest income inequality among OECD members. As of 2020, it was in the top three for the share of residents below the poverty threshold and in the top three for the "poverty gap" (the ratio of average income among the poor to one-half of median household income for the entire population).[5]

The United States stands out just as much for wealth inequality. According to Credit Suisse's *Global Wealth Databook 2021*, wealth inequality in the US ranks behind only that of Sweden among developed Western nations. Among all countries, those that exceed the United States in wealth inequality are either very poor—Botswana, Namibia, Nigeria, Lesoto—or small countries with lopsided oil-based wealth—Saudi Arabia, Bahrain, and the United Arab Emirates (UAE).[6]

Data from the World Inequality Database show that the United States is not at the very top of the wealth inequality distribution—that distinction is earned by resource-dependent countries like Saudi Arabia, the UAE, and Russia. Among OECD countries, the United States stands fifth behind Chile, Mexico, Turkey, and Costa Rica. But the United States has the highest wealth concentration among Western developed economies.[7]

US health care choices similarly stand out. Despite being leaders in health care *spending*, Americans experience some of the worst health outcomes in the developed world. An analysis of OECD health care data highlights the gap between US health care spending and the health outcomes our system produces. Among OECD countries, the United States spends the most on health care as a share of GDP. US public spending is similar to that of other countries; the difference lies in private spending on insurance premiums and out-of-pocket costs. This likely reflects the extra spending by higher-income and better-insured families.

Despite high spending, Americans trail in many health outcomes. Among OECD countries, the United States has the lowest life expectancy, highest suicide rates, greatest chronic disease burden, highest rate of obesity, and second highest rate of hospitalizations due to preventable causes, including diabetes and hypertension.[8] Many of these outcomes are well known to be associated with lower income and wealth.[9] In these dimensions, too, we fail to provide basic needs to our poor. There is some evidence that high US spending is associated with higher-end health care services—the US is in the top three OECD countries for MRI scans. But overall, our high spending is fairly categorized as mis-spending, as it has not prevented relatively poor health outcomes.[10]

The United States is also an outlier when it comes to the care we devote to children in their earliest years. Despite overwhelming evidence demonstrating the importance of early childhood care and education, the United States is on the low end of developed countries in terms of public spending for child care and early childhood education. The United States spends approximately $700 on childcare per child age two and younger, versus an OECD average of $4,605.[11] Spain, Israel, and Mexico are the only OECD countries that spend less in this category. What spending there is in the US tilts towards lower-income families, but at about $1,000 per child per year, this support still lags other countries' provisions by a large margin.[12] Investment in elementary and secondary education, by comparison, is among the highest worldwide. In 2018 US public spending amounted to $28,000 per student over the course of primary and secondary school, placing the country fifth behind Luxembourg, Norway, Austria, and Iceland.[13]

The pattern continues when it comes to economic mobility: the United States does poorly. People born in poverty tend to stay there; people born in the proverbial lap tend to remain there. This is not the case around the globe. Other capitalist states do better. According to a study released by the Economic Mobility Project, "There is a stronger link between parental education and children's economic, educational and socio-emotional outcomes" in the United States than in its developed-economy peers. The study compared the United States to the United Kingdom, France, Germany, Sweden, Italy, Australia, Finland, Denmark, and Canada across five key indicators, examining the strength of the relationship between parents' outcomes and their children's. The United States ranked highest in the likelihood of a child inheriting her parent's cognitive (IQ and other test scores), economic (income and labor-market position), educational (grades and final attainment), physical (health and birthweight) and socio-emotional (mental health and childhood behavior) outcomes.[14]

This is not the only evidence of the weak US position in the economic-mobility rankings. Julia Isaacs of the Brookings Institution has found that the United States lags behind its developed-economy peers across a wide array of studies. A number of the studies she discusses find a closer tie between US fathers' and sons' earnings than is the case in other developed economies, and in some underdeveloped economies. For instance, Isaacs cites a study that finds that United States men born in 1958 in the poorest one-fifth of families were more likely to remain there than were their counterparts in Denmark, Norway, Sweden, Finland, and the United Kingdom.[15]

*   *   *

The evidence from other free-market capitalist economies is clear. It implies that Americans have made unusual choices about how to structure our economy. It is true that populations, geographies, and industrial landscapes are not identical across the globe. But on too many key measures—income, wealth, health outcomes, education, economic mobility—America's failure to bring prosperity broadly to our citizens does not jibe with our country's world-leading income and wealth. We have chosen to be broken in these ways.

If we keep saying The Myth is true, we abdicate responsibility for changing the worst outcomes in our country, blaming them on individuals rather than systems. Global evidence suggests that it simply doesn't have to be that way. We can do better without sacrificing overall prosperity. The alternative is to continue to pledge allegiance to The Myth, ensuring that our systems keep funneling income and wealth to the already insanely affluent.

IV Broken by Design: How We Have Chosen to Create and Sustain Our Broken System

The stunningly poor outcomes that characterize our broken economy reflect *choices* that Americans have made consistently over generations. We have again and again provided resources and opportunities to the white, the affluent, and big business. Our economy does not have to work as it does. We have chosen to ensure that it does. The history of choices in key areas—systemic racial and ethnic discrimination, the careful design of our free markets, tax policy, the safety net, working conditions for low-wage jobs, and macroeconomic policy—demonstrates the consistent desire of the powerful to perpetuate an economy that leaves millions behind, with little chance of success.[1]

Central to the critique of The Myth is that this narrative, while flawed and inaccurate, is not only used passively—to justify or interpret outcomes, or as an input to voting choices. *It has also played an active role in creating the reality it interprets.* Those with wealth and power use The Myth to manipulate tax policy, public programs, the safety net, and workplace norms to maintain or strengthen their dominant position. When convenient, wielders of The Myth defer to the wisdom of markets rather than promote policies that might lead to more equitable distribution of income, wealth, health, education, and opportunity. In ways subtle and not so subtle, the powerful use their political connections to shape tax and spending systems for their own benefit.

The Dance of Narrative and Policy

Prophets decrying the use of wealth and power to perpetuate a slanted economic system run a diverse gamut. Nobel laureate Joseph Stiglitz's *The Price of Inequality* details many of the ways in which private companies have shaped the rules of the game to their benefit. For example, Stiglitz notes that despite the well-known need for government intervention to correct key market failures in the financial sector—the cost that financial market meltdowns impose on the rest of the economy, for example—the financial sector successfully lobbied for less regulation in the years leading up to the financial crisis. As Stiglitz puts it:

> Deregulation in the 1980s led to scores of financial crises in the succeeding three decades, of which America's crisis in 2008–09 was only the worst. But those government failures were no accident: the financial sector used its political muscle to make sure that the market failures were *not* corrected, and that the sector's private rewards remained well in excess of their social contributions.[2]

Another Nobel laureate, Paul Krugman, avers, "In the past many influential people seized on economic arguments that could be used to justify high inequality. We can't raise the minimum wage, because that would kill jobs; we can't help the unemployed, because that would hurt their incentives to work; and so on."[3] Krugman goes on to report the evidence that has accumulated to refute many of these arguments—minimum wages do not lead to loss of employment; unemployment insurance does not stop workers from taking employment opportunities. Adherence to these elements of The Myth despite the evidence testifies to the hold they have over us but also to their usefulness in maintaining unequal power and wealth.

Miles Corak, an economist who focuses on the link between inequality and low economic mobility, similarly finds that the wealthy exercise their power and position to shape societies and policies. For example, with ready access to elite private high schools and colleges, "wealthy parents have little incentive to back spending on public education."[4] Corak finds that life outcomes for children are determined by "the care, nurturing, and direction they receive from their families, the structure and nature of inequalities in the labor market with which they must engage, and the degree to which public policy can level the playing field with human capital investments that are relatively more advantageous to the relatively disadvantaged." In the United States,

> all three of these forces are aligned in a way that reinforces rather than weakens the tie between socioeconomic status and adult outcomes. . . . And in spite of these greater challenges, public policy does less to level the playing field. Indeed, in some important ways, policies do just the opposite, tilting the playing field to help the more advantaged.[5]

It isn't just economists and policy wonks who have decried The Myth and the inequities it builds into our economy. In a 2013 exhortation, Pope Francis contends

The gap separating the majority from the prosperity enjoyed by those happy few . . . is the result of ideologies which defend the absolute autonomy of the marketplace and financial speculation. Consequently, they reject the right of states, charged with vigilance for the common good, to exercise any form of control. A new tyranny is thus born, invisible and often virtual, which unilaterally and relentlessly imposes its own laws and rules.[6]

The dance of narrative and policy continues.

10 The History of Systems That Have Been Shaped by The Myth

The dance between narrative and policy plays out in the interaction between The Myth and the decisions that sizable private actors—primarily larger businesses—and government make. This is a key difference between the realms of human behavior and the physical sciences. It doesn't really matter what I believe about the orbits of planets around the sun, but when it comes to human behavior, what we believe—the narratives we hold—shapes our actions, our decisions, and the economic structure within which we live.

The History of Institutional Racism, and Its Persistent Effects Today

In recent years, many Americans, both left- and right-leaning, have become more aware of our country's history of institutional racism. An important contributor to my (partial) knowledge dates back less than a decade. Following the Boston Fed's 2015 publication of "The Color of Wealth in Boston," members of our staff and more than twenty regional partners formed a working group with two purposes. First, to build a common understanding of the sources of racial and ethnic inequities through reading historical, legal, and economic research. Second, to agree on a shared agenda for actions that each of our institutions could take to reduce racial wealth gaps.[1] Participating in that working group and engaging in conversations with the "Color of Wealth" authors and other colleagues opened my eyes and changed my mind about the sources of wealth gaps.

At around this time, Richard Walker, a mentor of mine and former senior vice president and head of the Fed's community development efforts, came into my office holding a copy of Carol Anderson's *White Rage*. Having recently finished the book himself, he said simply, "You should read this." I did. I found it difficult reading because the history is uniformly depressing. In a very matter-of-fact manner, Anderson provides a harrowing account of the unrelenting record of our government's intentional institutional abuses of Black people. Anderson's book further propelled my own journey of learning about these painful truths about our national history.

The process of learning continues today—for me, for the Federal Reserve, and no doubt for many others. I believe that one cannot fully understand how America's economic system works without understanding the effects that racial and ethnic history continues to have on outcomes today.

It is imperative that Americans learn our nation's history of choosing to deny access to opportunity for people of color. Our centuries-long legacy of discriminatory policies and government actions, beginning with our interactions with Indigenous people, is well documented, thanks to the meticulous scholarship of authors such as Anderson, Richard Rothstein, Melvin Oliver and Thomas Shapiro, Darrick Hamilton and William Darity Jr., and Michelle Alexander, among many others. That literature also makes clear the persistent effects of past policies on people of color today, as well as the racism that remains embedded in many of our institutions and systems. The results of America's centuries-long program of discrimination are evident in the data presented throughout this book. The wealth gap is particularly informative, because it reflects the cumulative effect of blocked opportunities across generations. This research makes it painfully clear that the wealthy, white, and powerful *designed* our systems to exclude many.

The End of the Civil War, Reconstruction, and Jim Crow

While the story begins far earlier, this section will not touch on the country's origins, harrowing as they were for Blacks and Indigenous people but instead will begin with the post–Civil War period.

President Abraham Lincoln's initial plan, early in the war, was to ask African Americans to leave the country and take up residence in Chiriquí, now a province in Panama, as their removal from the country would eliminate what he saw as the source of the Civil War. "But for your race among us there could not be war," Lincoln lectured a small gathering of Black leaders he summoned to the White House in 1862.[2]

That plan was abandoned, and after the war responsibility for rebuilding the union fell to Lincoln's successor Andrew Johnson, who was hardly a civil rights activist. Johnson consistently opposed efforts to improve the lot of formerly enslaved people. For instance, one of the first acts of the Freedman's Bureau, created by an act of Congress in March 1865, was to provide newly freed families forty-acre parcels of land from abandoned plantations along the Georgia and South Carolina coasts. President Johnson rescinded that order, initiating a series of broken promises. Former Confederate states, one after another, passed laws denying African Americans the forty acres, along with many of the rights of citizenship, including the right to vote. Anderson argues that Mississippi's Black Codes, which reinstituted practices common among slaveholders before Emancipation, effectively reinstated slavery: "In this reconstruction of the Reconstruction, . . . African Americans now had neither citizenship, the vote, nor land."[3] Infractions of rules established by the codes were punishable by whipping and were so successful in restoring the status quo ante that they were soon copied by nine other former Confederate states.[4]

These initial betrayals met with backlash from Congress, which passed the Reconstruction Acts of 1867—deploying US troops to intervene between white Southerners and freed Blacks—and the Enforcement Acts of 1870 and 1871, which allowed the use of military force to protect African Americans' rights to vote, hold office, serve on juries, and receive equal protection under the law.[5] Countering Congress's intent and supporting Johnson, the Supreme Court ruled that Congress had overstepped its authority—that it was usurping state's rights. Subsequent rulings eroded the protections of the Thirteenth, Fourteenth, and Fifteenth Amendments to the Constitution, concerning citizenship, due process, voting rights, discrimination in hotels, restaurants and other public accommodations, segregation, and discrimination in school funding.[6] By the late 1870s, the promise of providing freed people a path toward economic and social opportunity had been largely discarded. As an illustration of the North's complicity in this cavalcade of horrors, the Compromise of 1877 settled the disputed presidential election of 1876 by withdrawing federal troops from the South, ending any hopes of ensuring civil rights for Blacks there.[7]

The history of the Jim Crow era—the period from 1877 until the Civil Rights Act of 1964—has been well-chronicled by many. It is sadly replete with documented lynchings; more Supreme Court decisions that allowed discrimination to persist, notably the 1896 *Plessy v. Ferguson* decision that established the doctrine of Separate But Equal; institutionalized segregation in the civil service (including segregation of occupations, lavatories, and lunch rooms) under Woodrow Wilson's presidency; and the resurgence of the Ku Klux Klan.[8] This era marks the postslavery period in which the white majority used all means at its disposal to continue to promote state-sponsored injustice, violence, and denial of opportunity to people of color.

The New Deal and the GI Bill

In 1933, as President Franklin Roosevelt assumed the presidency, the nation was reeling from the Great Depression. Nearly a quarter of the labor force was unemployed, food shortages were widespread, and one in six homes were in the process of foreclosure.[9] In response, FDR's administration constructed the New Deal for the American public, a suite of programs and institutions designed to mitigate the ravages of the Depression—for white families.

Passage of New Deal legislation required the buy-in of Southern Democrats, who remained fiercely committed to a white-dominated world. In order to appease this faction, Social Security, unemployment insurance (a provision of the Social Security Act), minimum wage protection, and recognition of labor unions "excluded from coverage occupations in which African Americans predominated: agriculture and domestic service."[10] Partially in response to a housing shortage in the 1930s, the New Deal also created the first public housing for civilian nondefense workers. The legislation featured separate programs for African Americans, or segregated housing by race, or excluded African Americans altogether. The Civilian Conservation Corps (CCC) echoed this preference for residential segregation, both in the South and the North. Governor Harold Hoffman of New Jersey refused CCC residences for African American corps members because of "local resentment."[11]

Similarly, the Fair Labor Standards Act (FLSA) of 1938 provided a host of work-related protections, including the forty-hour work week, a ban on child labor, and establishment of a federal minimum wage and overtime pay requirements.[12] Once again, by excluding domestic, agricultural, and service occupations from its coverage, it largely excluded African American, Hispanic, and Asian-American workers from benefits. Today agricultural workers are still excluded from overtime and minimum wage restrictions, and domestic workers and at-home aids—disproportionately people of color—are still excluded from many FLSA protections.[13]

The same discriminatory practices played out in the economic boom years after World War II. In theory, the Servicemen's Readjustment Act of 1944, best-known as the GI Bill, was colorblind, offering education and housing benefits to all veterans regardless of race. But in the case of housing, because the program was administered by states rather than the federal government, the GI Bill fell far short of its race-blind goals. While the Veterans Administration could cosign low-interest loans, mortgages were frequently originated by white-owned financial institutions that refused mortgages to Black borrowers.

One of the most powerful institutional mechanisms for denying wealth accumulation for people of color was initiated by the Home Owner's Loan Corporation, an entity formed as part of the New Deal to rescue households near default. This agency invented the policy of "redlining"—defining residents of Black and other minority neighborhoods as high-risk and not suitable for lending. Later adopted by the Federal Housing Administration, this practice systematically denied Black access to homeownership for decades.[14] In 1947, only 2 of Mississippi's 3,229 VA-guaranteed home, business, or farm loans went to Black borrowers. In New York and northern New Jersey suburbs, fewer than 100 of the 67,000 mortgages insured by the GI Bill went to people of color.[15]

Hilary Herbold suggests that "the segregationist principals of almost every institution of higher learning effectively disbarred a huge proportion of Black veterans from earning a college degree."[16] Sarah Turner and John Bound find a positive impact of the GI Bill on educational attainment for some Black men, although that benefit decreases significantly for Black veterans whose educational opportunities were limited to the South.[17]

The experience of Hispanics who served in the war appears somewhat more nuanced. To be sure, many experienced discrimination in finding housing and obtaining medical services after the war. However, a good number obtained life-changing educational benefits. And in a survey of over one thousand Hispanic war veterans, more than 80 percent of respondents reported that VA doctors and staff treated Hispanic veterans "with respect" or "the same as all veterans."[18] But the research on discrimination against Hispanics in the wake of WWII is not nearly as extensive as the research on discrimination against Blacks, a gap that needs to be filled.

*   *   *

For the first century after the Civil War, Blacks, Hispanics, many Asians, and Indigenous people were systematically denied the means to accumulate wealth—as Blacks and Indigenous people had been for many decades before that. In contrast, white families were supported in their efforts to build family wealth through savings, homeownership, profits from entrepreneurship, and government benefits that funded education and housing. Between 1940 and 1970, more than 4 million Blacks migrated from the South to the North, Midwest, and West, at which point some were able to begin investing in housing—where they weren't blocked by redlining and race-restricted covenants. The mass migration of Blacks coincided with migration of Puerto Ricans to the Mainland and northward migration of Mexican-American agricultural workers.[19] These nonwhite families have had much less time than their white counterparts in which to build housing equity.[20] More broadly, had racism ceased with the passage of the Civil Rights Act of 1964, it would still have been nearly impossible for the median Black or Hispanic family, over the ensuing sixty years, to build wealth rivaling that of their white counterparts. Those white families didn't face the racial barriers Black and Hispanic families did and in many cases had had centuries of opportunity to build wealth. The point is that these disparities in wealth accumulation have been centuries in the making. The effects of institutional racism over these many decades reverberate strongly today. They are not behind us, they are with us still.

The Civil Rights Era

The passage of the Civil Rights Act of 1964 explicitly forbade discrimination in hiring, promotions, and firing on the basis of sex and race and created the Equal Employment Opportunity Commission (EEOC) to implement some of its provisions. The EEOC was authorized to make rules to help end discrimination, which were later interpreted to include affirmative action on behalf of minorities. The law was subsequently amended, expanding protected classes to include not only race and sex but also color, religion, national origin, age, disability, and genetic information. The law now applies to other work-related situations as well, including harassment, training, wages, and benefits.[21]

Yet, in many respects, practice has not followed the spirit of law. The evidence on wage inequality certainly implies that discrimination in the workplace has been far from eradicated. Proving discrimination in wage-setting or advancement is difficult, as a pattern must be established, and doing so requires controlling for a host of other factors that could (justifiably) influence an employee's appropriate pay and advancement in an organization.

Careful and clever research documents racial, ethnic, and gender discrimination in hiring decisions. Early research in this vein distributed identical resumes to employers with job openings, differing only by the name on the résumé—one would have a "Black-sounding" name, the other a "white-sounding" name. Applicants with white-sounding names enjoyed significantly higher chances of being contacted by potential employers.[22] A recent meta-analysis of twenty-eight field experiments on hiring discrimination finds that white job applicants receive an average of 36 percent more callbacks than African Americans and 24 percent more callbacks than Hispanics. The analysis controls for applicant education, gender, occupational groups, local labor-market conditions, and the methodologies of the original studies. None of these alter the results.[23]

One reason that discrimination continues is that the EEOC does not adequately enforce its rulings and regulations, not least because it lacks the resources to do so. The EEOC's inflation-adjusted budget per resident has declined since 1980, with a commensurate decline in its employee base. Expressed in 2018 dollars, spending per resident fell from $1.67 per person in 1980 to $1.15 in 2018. The EEOC's workforce fell from 3,390 employees to 1,968 over the same period. By 2018, the agency had accumulated a backlog of nearly 50,000 unaddressed cases.[24]

Not only is discrimination alive and well, but our institutions have also scaled back their capacity to redress it.

*   *   *

This history speaks mightily to the litany of systemically discriminatory policies our government has put in place, aided and abetted by the private sector. As Martin Luther King Jr. put it, just weeks before his assassination:

> At the very same time that the government refused to give the Negro any land, through an act of Congress our government was giving away millions of acres of land in the west and the Midwest, which meant it was willing to undergird its white peasants from Europe with an economic floor. But not only did they give the land, they built land grant colleges with government money to teach

them how to farm; not only that, they provided county agents to further their expertise in farming; not only that, they provided low interest rates in order that they could mechanize their farms; not only that, today, many of these people are receiving millions of dollars in federal subsidies not to farm, and they are the very people telling the Black man that he ought to lift himself by his own bootstraps. And this is what we are faced with, and this is the reality. Now, when we come to Washington in this campaign, we are coming to get our check.[25]

Free Designed Markets

Free markets go hand-in-hand with capitalism. How could one wish for something other than free markets? Freedom is good! Freedom is American!

The term "free markets" is perhaps used too freely, often as an incantation to ward off the evil spirits of market-obstructing government interference. Rarely is it well defined. The aim of this section is to remind readers that *all* markets are designed, created, supported, and curated by a partnership of government and private actors.[26] The infrastructure that supports markets did not arise organically but is instead the product of a host of narrative-rich choices. Markets are no more "natural" than are industrial chemicals. Markets that spring fully formed from the womb do not exist, and probably could not function if they did. As Dean Baker puts it in *Rigged*, "Markets are never just given. Neither God nor nature hands us a worked-out set of rules determining the way property relations are defined, contracts are enforced, or macroeconomic policy is implemented. These matters are determined by policy choices."[27] Thus an appeal to leaving markets free as a justification for policy inaction is misguided. Instead, the question is how we choose to design and support markets to achieve both efficiency and reasonable social outcomes. So far, we've achieved only efficiency.

Work in economic development emphasizes the host of infrastructures (broadly construed) that are required for economies to thrive. Many of these are government supports for market functioning. They include the establishment and maintenance of the rule of law, including of property rights and contract enforceability, which are essential to ensuring that investors can reliably collect the returns to their investments. These basic elements of the political and economic infrastructure allow markets to function, however they are designed. Empirical studies confirm the importance of such government supports in driving economic growth.[28] Consider a recent example that highlights what can go wrong in the absence of government-provided legal infrastructure: private investors in China's economy are facing a number of infrastructure challenges, not the least of which is widespread intellectual property infringement.[29]

Interestingly, even the conservative-leaning Heritage Foundation recognizes that countries with substantial government intervention still have markets that are at least as free as the United States. Its Index of Economic Freedom tracks property rights, judicial effectiveness, government integrity, business freedom, labor freedom, investment freedom, and tax burden. In 2021, the United States scored 72.1 on this index (higher is better), ahead of Japan (69.9) and France (65.9) but behind the United Kingdom (72.7), Germany (76.1), Canada (76.6), Sweden (77.9), Ireland (82.0), and Singapore, the top-rated country at 84.4. Countries that fall below the United States are largely developing or autocratic countries such as the Slovak Republic, Croatia, Romania, Indonesia, Kazakhstan, and Guatemala.[30] Despite the rhetoric about the merits of the US brand of free-market capitalism, this (more-or-less) objective measure concludes that European countries with higher taxes and more generous social services have *not* limited the free exercise of economic activity.

A relatively young field in economics, the study of market design, focuses on all the ways in which supposedly free markets are bound by rules. Alvin Roth, who won the 2012 Nobel Prize in Economics, for his work in market design, explains:

> A new field of economics, known as "market design," recognizes that well-functioning markets depend on detailed rules. For example, supply and demand drive both stock markets and labor markets, but someone who wants to buy or sell shares in a company goes through very different procedures from those followed by a job seeker or an employer. Moreover, labor markets work differently from one another: Doctors aren't hired the way lawyers, professional baseball players, or new MBAs are. Market designers try to understand these differences and the rules and procedures that make various kinds of markets work well or badly.[31]

Roth focuses primarily on market design features that bring together a large enough number of buyers and sellers so that it is safe for them to reveal or act on information that only they may hold. In addition, a large scale of participation enables the means—time and technology—to "make satisfactory choices when faced with a variety of alternatives."[32] These aspects of market design are much more narrowly focused than the government-provided infrastructure discussed above. But they often inform the ways in which government will interact with markets—for example, by auctioning licenses to operate in the radio spectrum. The markets for radio broadcasts, wireless internet, and cell phones would not operate well, or perhaps at all, without a government-run system for allocating bandwidth rights. Again, this highlights the fact that markets are *designed* to do specific things, with all kinds of support from government. They can't work any other way.

Tax Policy

The US tax code has been a constant focus of Myth-fueled manipulation, maneuvering, and deception. A recent investigative report documents the revolving door through which senior private-sector accountants pass temporarily into top Washington positions that shape tax policies. This pipeline has fueled policies that work in the interest of accounting firms' clients, many of which are the largest and most well-positioned companies in the United States.[33] For instance, proponents of the "stepped-up basis" for capital gains have mounted a strong defense of this loophole.[34] An arcane provision, stepped-up basis raises the tax valuation from which capital gains are calculated, so as to avoid paying capital gains taxes at inheritance. This loophole allows wealthy families to pass more of their money down to the next generation, perpetuating wealth concentration in already-rich families—probably not the first group that could use some relief via our tax system.

Popular press articles and academic research have shown how powerful businesses and wealthy individuals influence the tax code to their own advantage, through campaign contributions and lobbying at the state and federal levels. The benefits to using both levers are sizable. Estimates suggest that one dollar of campaign contributions at the state level yields more than six dollars in reduced corporate taxes. And research shows that a 1 percent increase in lobbying expenditures yields a decline of 0.5 to 1.5 percentage points in tax rates the year following. The incentive for businesses to exert influence on tax rates is significant.[35]

Private equity firms have spent years pursuing legal changes and allegedly skirting existing laws to minimize their tax burdens. One estimate holds that private equity investors who fail to report their income accurately cost the United States $75 billion in taxes annually.[36] The overall lost revenue from all unpaid taxes is estimated at approximately $600 billion annually, an amount that would go a long way toward fully paying for early childhood education and building affordable housing.[37] The odds of being audited are *three times higher* for someone with income of less than $25,000 than for the richest 1 percent of Americans.[38] Yet the Treasury Department's estimates find that the top 1 percent of wage earners account for more than one-quarter of lost tax revenues due to nonpayment and underpayment. In contrast, low- and middle-income workers whose taxes are deducted automatically from their paychecks are highly likely to pay what's due.[39] This last point speaks powerfully to the political use of the dominant narrative, specifically the mistrust of the poor: the gatekeepers of our tax system believe it is more important to audit the lowest wage earners than those who earn incredibly high incomes, and who with the aid of lobbyists and accountants shield themselves from their appropriate tax liability.[40]

The 2017 Tax Cut and Jobs Act provided opportunities for the highly compensated to pay even less in taxes. While the law famously reduced the corporate profit tax from 35 percent to 21 percent, it made only a small change to the rate affecting salaries. This of course opened the opportunity for top executives—at least those who shared in the companies' profits—to take more compensation in the form of a profits distribution rather than salary, significantly reducing their tax burden. IRS data show that salaries paid to top executives dropped after the law went into effect. The data cannot prove that the drop in salaries is entirely due to this reclassification of income, but the timing is highly suggestive.[41]

These are just a few examples of how accounting and other tax-avoidance tactics have been used mostly, but not entirely, legally by corporations to shift tax burdens to others. These behaviors also fit very tidily into the "maximize shareholder value" narrative. It is completely understandable that corporations will seek to lower their tax burden, given the tax structure and their desire to raise profits by reducing tax payments. But these behaviors effectively shift the burden of paying for necessary government services from the well-heeled to the less fortunate who do not have the means to so directly affect tax policy. And to the extent that these maneuvers reduce tax revenues, they rob us of the ability to make long-term investments in human potential. Tax avoidance, much of it legal, undercuts high-return investments in America's future.

Unweaving the Safety Net

We have already summarized the current state of the safety net, the programs and policies that limit how far residents can fall economically. The
tortuous path from the safety net's inception to today's incarnation reveals
both longstanding and evolving national views on the objectives of the
system as well as the share of national resources that can appropriately
be devoted to it. Recent research highlights the link from The Myth to
the design of the safety net. It suggests that the public's changing views
of who is deserving are in part responsible for many changes in safety net
programs.[42]

A few key programs and their acronyms are noted below.

Acronym	Program
AFDC/TANF	Aid to Families with Dependent Children/Temporary Assistance to Needy Families
SS	Social Security
UI	Unemployment Insurance
SSDI	Social Security Disability Insurance
EITC	Earned Income Tax Credit
SNAP	Supplemental Nutritional Assistance Program (food stamps)
SSI	Supplemental Security Income

From the Reagan era through the mid-2000s, benefits were systematically shifted toward the elderly and the disabled—through SS, SSI, and
SSDI—and toward married-parent families, largely through changes in the
AFDC/TANF program. The losers were the very poor and single mothers
with children. The redistribution away from the poorest families, defined
here as earning less than 50 percent of the poverty level, is striking. Among
the poorest nondisabled, nonelderly, single-parent families, the decline in
benefits amounted to 35 percent. Among the poorest nondisabled, nonelderly, married-parent families, the decline in benefits was 31 percent.
Benefits to nondisabled, nonelderly childless individuals and families also
declined, although in general these individuals receive much smaller benefit amounts.[43]

If the redistribution of safety net benefits arises in part from the public's
determination of who are the deserving poor, then Americans today view

the deserving as those who work, those who are married with children, the elderly, and the disabled. Others—single parents, those out of work, adults without children—are undeserving. Of course, many of the poorest families in the United States are single-parent families—the poverty rate for single-mother families in 2020 was 23.4 percent, compared to 4.7 percent for married couples.[44] These characteristics of deservingness fit well into The Myth: those who work, who remain married, who have children within wedlock have been industrious and made good choices. The Myth argues that those who are not working are lazy or have made bad decisions. They don't deserve public assistance.

In an August 2021 survey commissioned by the *Washington Post*, 59 percent of respondents said that recipients of government benefits should be required to work at least some of the time, while 31 percent said they should *always* be required to work. Respondents were similarly much more supportive of social programs that help the elderly and disabled (81 and 85 percent respectively) than of programs for families with dependent children (63 percent) or low incomes (65 percent). As the Post suggests, "Americans are fairly united in seeing older and disabled people as 'deserving'—but are more divided about whether poor people or people with children universally deserve support."[45]

Interestingly, for all the damage Milton Friedman may have done through his shareholder-value maxim, he advocated a welfare system that provided assistance based on income and family size. He saw no reason for using other characteristics, such as age or occupation, to determine eligibility or benefit levels. He called his favored approach a "negative income tax"—a policy whereby people who fall below a certain income threshold receive an income subsidy in proportion to their shortfall relative to the threshold.[46] Households above the threshold pay taxes in proportion to their income.

The earned income tax credit is just such a policy. The EITC is a key component of the safety net, as it efficiently augments the incomes of low-earning families. While it does not lift families out of poverty, it clearly makes a difference and along with SNAP may be the most effective strand in the safety net. Its history clearly reflects the dance between our narratives about the poor and the policies our nation has chosen to mitigate poverty.

In the Johnson administration's 1964 declaration of the War on Poverty, we hear once again the old "deserving poor" narrative that has shaped US welfare policy for many decades. As Johnson's Council of Economic Advisors wrote:

> Conquest of poverty is well within our power. About $11 billion a year would bring all poor families up to the $3,000 income level we have taken to be the minimum for a decent life. The majority of the Nation could simply tax themselves enough to provide the necessary income supplements to their less fortunate citizens. . . . But this "solution" would leave untouched most of the roots of poverty. Americans want to earn the American standard of living by their own efforts and contributions. It will be far better, even if more difficult, to equip and to permit the poor of the Nation to produce and to earn the additional $11 billion, and more. . . . The major thrust of our campaign must be against causes rather than symptoms.[47]

Dennis Ventry suggests that this approach to poverty reduction derives from the characterization of poverty as "a temporary condition of the working poor and a permanent condition of the disabled and aged." In contrast, welfare dependency is adduced as a "pathological and voluntary condition of the indolent." Ventry observes that this position "conflated social policy with morality."[48]

Policymakers recognized the limited impact that modest reductions to tax rates would have on the poor: the lowest-income households don't pay taxes, so they of course would not benefit from tax cuts. Through this logical open door walked the negative income tax that Friedman had espoused. An important advantage of a negative income tax is that it's always better to earn more income than not—as your income rises, your subsidy declines, but your income even after taxes is always rising. Some earlier welfare programs completely dropped benefits once income rose above preset limits, which discouraged individuals from earning more than that limit. They would suddenly lose all of their benefits as income rose just a dollar above the limit. As a consequence, their after-tax income would *fall* as income rose just above the limit. Why work and earn more if you make *less* money after taxes?

There was confusion within the Johnson administration on these points: the president viewed the negative income tax as a cash benefit, and thus a *disincentive* to work, despite the arguments just made.[49] Johnson decided not to put forward a negative income tax and instead went with a variety of self-help programs meant to give a "hand up, rather than a handout." President Nixon tried again with a welfare-reform package, the warmly named Family Assistance Plan. This included a negative income tax alongside changes to the AFDC program to limit work disincentives. The policy failed to pass Congress.[50]

Throughout the 1970s, the meaning of the "poverty problem" changed. Instead of motivating the War on Poverty, the poverty problem came to be understood as a Welfare Problem: a deep concern that too many were or would become dependent on the welfare system, and that proposals to address poverty needed to keep costs down and motivate beneficiaries to work. A wide array of proposals was considered, including replacing the entire welfare system with tax credits for low-income families or with a comprehensive negative income tax. A 1974 report from the Joint Economic Committee noted that "since any aid given to the poor reduces the need for work, a benefit program must be carefully constructed if it is not to crush efforts at self-help and independence."[51]

Under the Ford administration, the Earned Income Credit, a version of Friedman's negative income tax, was passed *for one year*. This system paid low-income taxpayers 10 percent of the first $4,000 they earned. The percentage paid decreased to zero as income rose to $8,000. Households with incomes above $8,000 paid taxes in proportion to their income above $8,000. The Senate Finance Committee favored the proposal because it would "assist in encouraging people to obtain employment, reducing the unemployment rate and reducing the welfare rolls." Over the next three years, the income credit was extended and modified slightly, always adhering to its "pro-work, anti-welfare charter."[52]

Efforts to further modify the program under President Carter were unsuccessful, and changes over the half-dozen years following Carter's presidency were minor, although the income-cutoff levels were raised in recognition of the erosion in the purchasing power of the credit due to high inflation. Despite those adjustments, the value of the maximum credit fell by 35 percent between 1975 and 1984 after adjusting for inflation.[53]

In pushing his anti-welfare campaign, President Reagan slashed welfare expenditures. But the EITC remained intact, seen as a viable replacement for other social programs. The Tax Reform Act of 1986 expanded the EITC, significantly reducing the tax burden on low-income families. Expansion enjoyed bipartisan support from liberals like New Jersey Democratic Senator Bill Bradley and fiscal conservatives like New York Republican Jack Kemp. The law appealed to liberals' desire to lower the tax burdens faced by low-income people and to conservatives' interest in pushing taxpayers off the welfare rolls and into the workforce.[54]

In the end, the EITC was successful in lowering the tax burden for low-income families. Throughout its evolution, the narrative struggle between providing aid to the poor and avoiding disincentives to work pushed the program back and forth between greater and lesser generosity. Research has shown that the disincentive effects of the EITC have been smaller than expected, while the incentive to work in order to gain eligibility for the tax incentive has been substantial, solidifying its status in the safety net. The EITC succeeded because it appealed to a bipartisan desire to reduce welfare roles and avoid work disincentives. The debates about the EITC highlight the nation's ambivalence about providing aid to the poor, including who the "deserving" poor are—those who work, those who have children in wedlock. That debate continued through welfare reform under the Clinton administration.

*   *   *

Officially the Personal Responsibility and Work Opportunity Reconciliation Act of 1996, the Clinton-era welfare law reveals in its title plenty about how the country thought about aid to the poor. Despite all the evidence to the contrary, personal responsibility apparently needed to be restored in our welfare system—a bow to the welfare-queen tales that President Reagan spun in the 1980s. The bill passed with significant bipartisan support.

The law dramatically reshaped the welfare program, with the largest changes altering the contours of AFDC, which became TANF. The opening text of the bill is interesting and revealing, as its high-level goals make no mention of poverty reduction. The first paragraphs of the bill read as follows:

The Congress makes the following findings:

(1) Marriage is the foundation of a successful society.

(2) Marriage is an essential institution of a successful society which promotes the interests of children.

(3) Promotion of responsible fatherhood and motherhood is integral to successful child rearing and the well-being of children.

(4) In 1992, only 54 percent of single-parent families with children had a child support order established and, of that 54 percent, . . . only about one-half received the full amount due. . . .

(5) The number of individuals receiving aid to families with dependent children . . . has more than tripled since 1965. More than two-thirds of these
recipients are children. Eighty-nine percent of children receiving AFDC benefits now live in homes in which no father is present.[55]

The focus is completely on family structure, including marriage and the
presence of a father. The implication is that poverty is due to irresponsible
or nontraditional parenting. The bill goes on to document the disadvan-
tages faced by children reared outside traditional family circumstances. The
purposes of the bill, outlined in the text, are as follows:

To devolve welfare responsibility to the states to operate a program that will . . .

- end the dependence of needy parents on government benefits by promoting job preparation, work, and marriage;
- prevent and reduce the incidence of out-of-wedlock pregnancies and establish annual numerical goals for preventing and reducing the incidence of
  such pregnancies; and
- encourage the formation and maintenance of two-parent families.[56]

By blaming poverty on poor people's choices—in this case, with respect to
family life—the legislation harkens back to Josiah Quincy's 1821 report on
the deserving and undeserving poor. To couch the argument in terms of
The Myth: if only the poor would get married, get to work as they should,
and stop exploiting government programs, all would be right and as a primary benefit, our welfare rolls would be reduced.

TANF, the centerpiece of this legislation, imposes work requirements,
devolves many program implementation decisions to the states, funds the
state programs via block grants, and sets a lifetime sixty-month participation limit that can be reduced by the states if they choose. As safety net
expert Rebecca Blank suggests, as cash assistance "became far less available, welfare recipients were pushed much harder to find employment and
leave the rolls."[57] Importantly, state leeway to choose benefit levels and the
rate at which benefits tail off as income rises led to wide variation in the
benefits available across states. In 2000, cash welfare available during the
first 24 months of work for a welfare recipient with two children varied
from nothing (Arizona, Indiana, Maryland, and others) to $13,478 (Alaska).
The mapping does not correlate well to high and low-income areas—high-
income New Jersey offered $1,551, middle-income Virginia offered $6,984,
and very-high income Washington, DC, offered $1,296 for those work-
ing a thirty-hour work week.[58] State-level choices about how generously

to implement the program were arguably more important than Congress's intent in designing it.

Why did the bipartisan attitude toward welfare culminate in this dramatic change in 1996? The macroeconomic background no doubt had an effect. With unemployment at 5 percent or lower, it was a good time to push former ADFC recipients into the workforce. But as the discussion of the EITC highlights, the nation had always held ambivalent feelings about who were the deserving poor, about how much cash assistance should be provided, and about how to reduce the welfare rolls and minimize work disincentives. In some ways, this reform was a long time in the making.

Robert Moffitt provides evidence that the rise in the number of single mothers with out-of-wedlock children in the 1980s was a development that voters "disliked," according to attitudinal data from the General Social Survey. Voters' distaste for this family configuration may in turn have partly explained the popularity of changes in welfare that provided fewer benefits to single mothers with out-of-wedlock children.[59]

Kent Weaver provides a thorough summary of the political tensions and compromises that led to the 1996 reform. Public opinion, shaped by political message, played a key role. As a presidential candidate, Clinton vowed to "end welfare as we know it," and his persistent capitulation to conservative demands likely led some moderate voters to support reform. National Opinion Research Center polling in the 1990s showed declining support for welfare spending and "spending on the poor" more generally.[60] Research from institutes across the political spectrum drew attention to rising out-of-wedlock birthrates, even as birthrates for teen mothers generally were on the decline. As Weaver emphasizes, the interpretation of this research varied by party, but on balance it helped move politicians and the public toward the view that AFDC had to be replaced by a new program that included work requirements and other incentives to reduce birthrates and welfare tenure.[61]

These policy changes led to a marked decline in caseloads. By 2000, 57 percent fewer people were receiving TANF benefits than the number that had received AFDC benefits in 1996, with sizable declines experienced uniformly across states. Perhaps more importantly, the program changes led to a 10 percentage point increase in workforce participation by single mothers with young children. Families with other characteristics experienced smaller increases in workforce participation. In the short run, poverty rates for families with children declined, no doubt aided by what was at the time the longest postwar expansion of the economy.[62]

However, these effects were not felt equally across race and ethnicity. To begin with, recipients of AFDC prior to the reform were disproportionately people of color. Marianne Bitler, Jonah Gelbach, and Hilary Hoynes find a 17 percent decline in household income for children of Black families in 1997, compared to insignificant changes in income for white and Hispanic families in the same year. As our survey of the data on income, employment, and benefits showed, over time members of these poor families disproportionately ended up in low-wage jobs with inadequate health and retirement benefits, uneven provision of paid leave, and unpredictable schedules.[63]

Welfare reform provides a clear example of US policy choices made on the basis of stories the well-off believe about the poor. Lack of trust in poor people is central to our design of public policy. Although the evidence suggests that low-income families use money for the same things everyone else does—food, shelter, clothing, utilities—Americans are enduringly suspicious of entrusting money to them.[64] The Myth is powerful and guides the design of our economy in a host of ways.

A central irony in the current structure of our welfare system is that it was designed to induce families to work their way out of poverty, yet even working welfare recipients struggle to survive. As Janet from Boston, a Hispanic woman who has lived in subsidized public housing for the past twenty-two years, puts it, government aid "helps, but it doesn't make the difference—it doesn't get you out of the hole you're in." Like many of the interviewees, despite working a solid job and receiving a housing subsidy, she still has to "juggle a little bit" to pay bills. She makes ends meet with a number of "side hustles."[65] We have crafted a system that provides scant aid to the nonworking poor and meager aid to the working poor.

The welfare system leaves millions below the poverty line, and millions more below reasonable living standards. Not exactly a success story, but our narratives imply that most poor people deserve nothing more.

Workplace Norms: The Role of Unions and the Shareholder-Value Maxim

Dalida R., a Black Cape Verdean immigrant in Worcester, Massachusetts, worked for some years for small nonprofit organizations, which "aren't able to pay a livable wage," she says. Among employees, "there's always a fear" of not quite making it. Dalida's life changed when she went to work for a large service workers' union. "The union is when I felt like there was a shift in my life—you know, great benefits, 401k, and all that, that allowed me to set myself up to be able to purchase a home and felt some type of security." The union—which provided its employees the kind of benefits it provided its members—put her life on a new trajectory. She is now the executive director of a nonprofit. We'll hear more about Dalida later in the discussion of ways to change our prevailing narratives.[66]

Unions have played a critical role in addressing problems associated with low-wage work. In their heyday in the 1950s, they motivated the expansion of company-provided employee benefits—which were designed to slow the spread of unions. But corporate strategies and government action—with public opinion on their side—gradually ejected unions from most sectors of the economy. The dramatic decline in the share of workers represented by unions aided in the cost-cutting, streamlining, labor-busting strategy of Friedman acolytes. It also tilted the balance of power back toward ownership and away from workers. As we have seen, the results of that tilt are particularly bad for low-wage workers.[67] Rick Wartzman characterizes this shift in the employer-employee relationship in this way: "The American corporation used to act as a shock absorber. Now, it's a roller coaster."[68]

Here I trace the saga of unions' rise and fall—and the resulting rise and fall of workers' conditions—beginning at the end of World War II. As the war drew to a close, a group of industry leaders, the Committee for Economic Development, banded together to plan for postwar production. They focused on the role private industry could play in promoting economic stability for its workers. Alfred Sloan, chairman of General Motors, suggested industry should "lend a helping hand to its workers . . . against the vicissitudes of life."[69] This largesse reflected not simply a benevolent disposition toward employees but also a response to the rising power of labor unions in the first half of the twentieth century. As Lemuel Ricketts Boulware, vice president of employee and public relations for General Electric, put it in the early 1950s, "It must now be obvious to our employees that membership in a union will not get them anything they would not be able to get without a union."[70]

The 1940s and 1950s yielded a string of wins for workers at large corporations, encouraging a management culture that competed for workers and staved off unionization by offering increasingly generous compensation and benefits. The addition of automatic cost-of-living adjustments to wages, health care, and pension benefits; extensive training and specialized training facilities; and on-site recreational facilities prompted a leader of the Conference of Industrial Organizations to observe in 1950, "Ten or fifteen years ago . . . there were so many things I was mad about. But what can I agitate for now? We don't have any really big issues left."[71]

Some of these corporate benefits offered support that is today covered by government programs. An example is the supplemental unemployment benefits fund at Ford and General Motors, which in 1955 set aside five cents per employee per hour worked for a fund that could be used in the event of layoffs. Combined with state-funded unemployment insurance, workers could receive 60 to 65 percent of regular pay for up to twenty-six weeks. Other automakers soon followed, as did firms in the shipping and steel industries. General Electric extended a form of unemployment benefits to its employees in 1931, before the New Deal implemented unemployment insurance nationwide.[72] On-the-job training, a benefit less and less common among current employers, became an important element of the overall compensation and benefits package at large companies such as General Electric and General Motors.[73]

The National Alliance of Businessmen (NAB), a privately funded and federally subsidized training program, was founded in 1968. Initiated in part in recognition of the lopsidedly white male workforces that large corporations had hired historically, the alliance counted Ford, Coca-Cola, McDonnell-Douglas, and Mobil among its members.[74] In remarks to the Alliance in May 1968, Vice President Hubert Humphrey noted that the rationale for the Alliance was of course economic. However,

> as persuasive as economic justification is—and its logic is unassailable—we fundamentally support the NAB effort for another more important reason: It is an attempt to save lives . . . to rescue persons who have been denied a full and equal chance in our industrialized economy . . . to reach those who have been left out with the message that America needs everybody.[75]

While likely an exercise in political rhetoric to some extent, the message recognizes that there are many who "have been denied a full and equal chance" in the economy, and that it is the joint responsibility of private industry and the government to do something about it. It would be refreshing to hear more today about the merits of such a private-public partnership with those same goals.

In short, during the fifty-year span from the pre-Depression 1920s through the 1960s the United States developed a relatively benevolent social norm that guided employer-employee relationships. This compact was formed as the result of a variety of complex economic and social pressures, including the rising power of labor unions, the threat of "socialist" reforms that would reduce large private corporations' power to determine how work was conducted, and the recognition that many citizens—largely people of color—lacked access to the kind of stable employment that these companies offered. The compact brought a sizable measure of economic security and stability to workers.

That security dissolved in the ensuing decades. Union membership declined and support for free-market capitalism rose at the expense of workers' wages, benefits, and voice—in essence, the power shifted from workers back to employers. That power imbalance remains today and lies at the heart of the poor working conditions documented earlier.

*   *   *

How did this transformation occur? Something catalyzed change in the early 1980s, and history suggests that something was the Professional Air Traffic Controllers Organization (PATCO) strike in 1981.[76] PATCO endorsed Reagan in his 1980 presidential bid, and Reagan in turn promised a "spirit of cooperation," acknowledging the difficulty of controllers' jobs as well as the outdated equipment they had to work with. Emboldened by what seemed to PATCO a favorable audience in the White House, the union began bargaining in February 1981, pushing ambitious demands including a sequence of pay increases with cost-of-living adjustments and a four-day work week. But several rounds of negotiations went nowhere, and 13,000 air traffic controllers walked off the job on August 3.[77] President Reagan quickly laid down the law. Within hours of the onset of the strike, he delivered a speech and an ultimatum: "I must tell those who fail to report for duty this morning they are in violation of the law, and if they do not report for work within forty-eight hours, they have forfeited their jobs and will be terminated."[78]

Reagan's action reverberated throughout organized labor. Within a week of the episode, the president of the United Auto Workers, Douglas Fraser, worried the strike could cause "massive damage to the labor movement."[79] It did. The administration quickly hired permanent replacements for the striking controllers, a response that was to be used repeatedly in subsequent labor actions by many unions. Corporate leaders felt increasingly empowered to hire temporary and even *permanent* replacements for striking workers. If workers could be replaced without public pushback, the power of the strike was gone. The ability to hire replacement workers depends, of course, on the availability of additional workers to hire. Thus the early 1980s, when unemployment was quite high and many were looking for work, proved an ideal time to push this part of the antilabor agenda forward. The president appeared to have turned public sentiment against labor, in part because PATCO's action was illegal—unlike many unionized workers, air-traffic controllers are barred from striking—and in part because the demands of PATCO just seemed excessive. The narrative about unions was changing.[80]

The Reagan administration likely had larger goals in mind when it put an end to the PATCO strike. As one expert put it, "The administration . . . wanted to send a strong unambiguous message to organized labor . . . that organized labor—unionism—was essentially incompatible with the emerging free-market philosophy of the administration."[81]

This is precisely where the free-market, shareholder-value narrative collides with public policy, private business philosophy, and the fate of workers. To keep profits high and thereby satisfy shareholders, labor costs had to be minimized, or so the narrative goes. The first step in managing the cost of labor is to slash the power of unions. The Reagan administration led the way in this, but dozens of companies followed in the decades to come. Employers flouted labor laws, discriminating against, coercing, and firing workers who supported unionization.

But employers didn't have to break the law in order to bust unions. They could legally mandate that employees attend antiunion meetings, drag out negotiation of labor contracts, and distribute antiunion literature. Unions responded, but "every major effort to change the labor laws since the 1960s has failed."[82] Under President Reagan, the National Labor Relations Board, charged with ensuring the right to unionize and maintaining a balance of power between labor and corporations, was understaffed, leading to large and growing backlogs of antiunion grievance cases.[83] Long delays in handling cases worked to the companies' advantage: they could fire union organizers and replace them. But the fired worker could ill afford to lose months or years of earnings while awaiting a decision in the reinstatement case. In this way, employers further eroded the power of unions.

The political battle to reduce unions' prevalence and influence was highly successful. Union membership rates peaked at over 30 percent in 1960 and have fallen to one-third that rate since.[84] Despite their decline, unions retain considerable public support, as indicated by a 2021 Gallup poll that shows approval outnumbering disapproval by a two-to-one margin.[85]

*   *   *

One cannot impute all of workers' losses to declining unions. Instead, union decline and the shift in the employer-employee bargain reflect a common underlying cause. That cause is intimately tied to the Friedman maxim. And in the 1980s, no one individual used that maxim more powerfully to change the employment compact than Jack Welch, CEO of General Electric.[86] In his own words, Welch pooh-poohed job security and "contracts" between employers and workers at large firms:

> Any organization that thinks it can guarantee job security is going down a dead end. Only satisfied customers can give people job security. Not companies. That reality puts an end to the implicit contracts that corporations once had with their employees. Those "contracts" were based on perceived lifetime employment and produced a paternal, feudal, fuzzy kind of loyalty. . . . I wanted to create a new contract, making GE jobs the best in the world for people willing to compete. If they signed up . . . we'd do everything to give them the skills to have "lifetime employability," even if we couldn't guarantee them "lifetime employment."[87]

Clearly not a fan of the "paternal, feudal, fuzzy" working arrangements that prevailed at larger corporations in the 1950s and 1960s, Welch worked to streamline GE, eliminate what he considered unnecessary bureaucracy, and ensure that the company was a leader in any markets in which it operated. He presided over a massive reduction in GE's workforce, just in time for the 1981–1982 recession. Tens of thousands of workers were fired from plants in Louisville, Kentucky; Pittsfield, Massachusetts; Erie, Pennsylvania; and elsewhere, leaving former industrial cities in depressions that would last for decades.[88] To be sure, Welch was not to blame for the rising global competition GE faced or for national economic decline. But he played a critical role in shifting the company's attitude of responsibility for its workers in the face of those challenges, and his example proved influential.[89]

Today foreign competition, rising health care costs, and lagging worker skills all challenge the profitability of companies. A key question is *how the private sector and the government should respond in the face of these pressures.* The simple approach is to leave government out of it, pursue cost-cutting measures, and not worry about the fate of workers. That is not the only choice, although it is a choice that employers have made consistently over the past four decades.

Whether or not you are a fan of unions, you have to be a fan of the objectives that unions were created to achieve: ensuring livable wages; reasonable working conditions; benefits that improve family economic stability; and, as important as all of these, worker voice. The last serves as a counterbalance to the incredible financial and political power of large corporations and as an offset to the still-prevalent shareholder-value dictum. At the risk of getting all Marxist, without this balance of power, workers—especially lower-wage workers—will continue to sit at the bottom of the economic pyramid, falling short in wages, benefits, working conditions, and power. Most people, upon viewing the current slate of working conditions among the low-wage, nonunionized workforce, would not be delighted. They might, however, believe that free markets will solve that problem. It's been over forty years, and throughout that period, when it came to looking after low-wage workers or providing racial justice, the invisible hand of the free market was nowhere to be seen.[90]

Macroeconomic Policy: Excess Unemployment by Design

In September 2011, in the aftermath of the financial crisis and Great Recession, hundreds of protesters representing the "99 percent"—those not among the 1 percent who garner so much of the income and hold so much of the wealth in the United States—gathered at an encampment across the street from the Boston Fed. Inspired by their peers in New York City, Occupy Boston settled in Dewey Square and demonstrated for three months, bringing attention to a number of issues around economic inequality.[91]

At a senior management meeting in early October, the Boston Fed considered whether to engage the protesters. I argued that we could do much good simply by listening to the protesters, but the prevailing view among my colleagues was that their demands were too diffuse (there was some truth to that) and that there was risk in talking with protesters in a format the Fed could not control. We chose not to engage the protesters at that time. Some months later, key members of management reconsidered that decision, but by that time the protesters had disbanded. In my view, we missed an opportunity.

While just a dozen years ago, the Fed, surely aware at that time of many of the economic disparities, was concerned about becoming directly involved in the national discussion. But that episode marked the beginning of a transition from a central bank that studied, convened, and wrote about economic conditions to one that began to take action to make a difference. Just a year after Occupy, we began to discuss in earnest a new partnership for the benefit of lower-income communities in New England.[92] Dubbed the Working Cities program, its goal was to bring change to low-income cities outside of Boston, fostering a collaboration of local nonprofits, government, philanthropy, and the private sector that works toward common development goals and guided by the voices of residents and community representatives.[93] Critically, the program emphasized a strong focus on racial equity.[94]

*   *   *

Many people find macroeconomic policy rather abstract and difficult to warm to, and for good reason: the macroeconomy is a fiction, a story that economists tell about the sum of all the behaviors of individual businesses and households. Yet, abstract as its target is, macroeconomic policy has been pivotal in creating many of the unsatisfying outcomes we have discussed. It has played a central role in perpetuating unequal outcomes.

The two pillars of macroeconomic policy are monetary policy—the setting of interest rates by the Federal Reserve to achieve low and stable inflation and maximum sustainable employment—and fiscal policy, which refers to taxing and spending policies that provide vital services, redistribute income, and promote long-run economic growth.[95]

Figure 10.1 provides a simple demonstration of the net effect of these policies on the economy. It compares the unemployment rate—the share of workers who would like to be employed but are not (the solid black line)—to our best estimate of the unemployment rate that corresponds to a healthy economy in which everyone who wants to be is employed (the dashed black line). Economists call this the "natural rate," although the data suggest it is not quite so natural as we might like. The figure shows

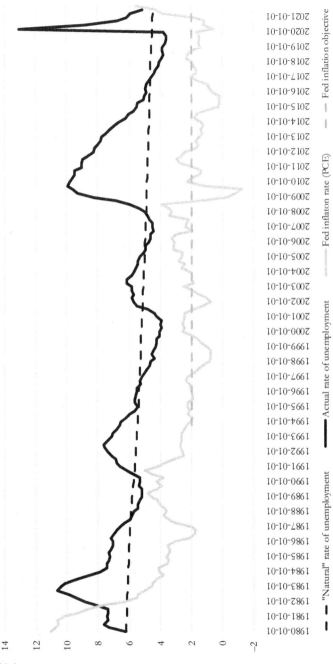

Figure 10.1
Falling short for decades.

these two measures over the past forty years, roughly the span of my career with the Federal Reserve System.[96]

The simple story this figure tells is that the proportion of the workforce that is unemployed has been chronically high for decades. The argument is not that we should always be at the dashed black line. The economy suffers real disruptions for a variety of reasons that make it impossible to remain always at full employment. The point is that the combination of fiscal and monetary policy has to some degree accepted chronically high unemployment.

Is high unemployment necessary in order to contain inflation? Many economists believe so. In theory, that might explain this persistent policy bias. But in fact the opposite has been the case. For most of the twenty-five years leading up to the pandemic, actual inflation (the solid gray line) has been quite low, averaging a bit *below* 2 percent, which is the Federal Reserve's official inflation goal (indicated by the dashed gray line).[97] The growing recognition that inflation appeared to be persistently low guided monetary policy under Fed Chairs Janet Yellen and Jerome Powell in the late 2010s, as they kept interest rates low, spurring the economy even as the unemployment rate dipped to 3.5 percent, because the long and vigorous expansion posed no obvious tradeoff in terms of undesirably high inflation.

Interestingly, we achieved the opposite of these outcomes in the three decades between World War II and 1980. As shown in figure 10.2, on average, unemployment was below its natural rate for the majority of this period.[98] Of course, this was also the period in which inflation rose above 10 percent, as shown in the right panel, which prompted a vigorous Federal Reserve response that sent the economy into its deepest recession in decades.

One way of interpreting these two episodes is that the Fed learned its lesson from the 1970s a bit too well: it is wise not to allow high inflation to become embedded in wage- and price-setting behavior, as it is notoriously difficult to reduce inflation when that happens. But in response, the Fed, and arguably the European Central Bank and others, have erred too far on the side of restraining the economy, fearing an inflation outbreak that did not occur—at least not because of an overheated economy—at the expense of chronically elevated unemployment.

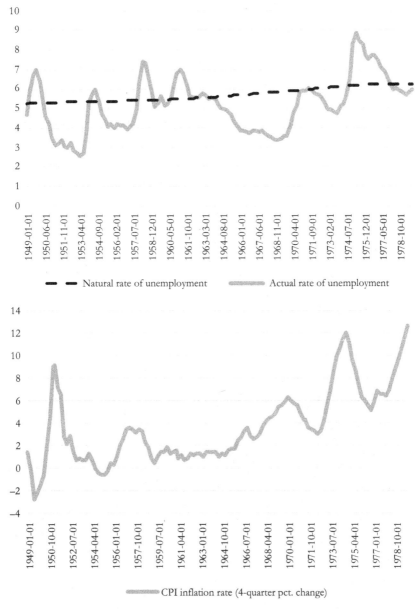

Figure 10.2
Learning the lesson of the past too well?

Apart from overlearning the lessons of history, it is not by accident that inflation received disproportionate attention during the period following the 1980s. The difference between a 1.5 percent and a 2.5 percent steady rate of inflation is, for most households, negligible. So whom is the low-inflation outcome meant to benefit? Financial markets, particularly those that trade in government and other bonds. A rise in inflation means that lenders are repaid in less-valuable dollars as prices rise faster, which is not something lenders are hoping for.

Unemployment, on the other hand, is bad for working families, and worst for the least advantaged in the economy. Today, an unemployment rate that is 1 percentage point above the best we can do means an additional 1.6 million people out of work.[99] But the distributional consequences are at least as important.

Figure 10.3 shows the difference between Black and Hispanic unemployment rates and the white unemployment rate.[100] Black and Hispanic unemployment rates are consistently higher than those of whites. In addition, during recessions—periods of economic contraction indicated by the gray

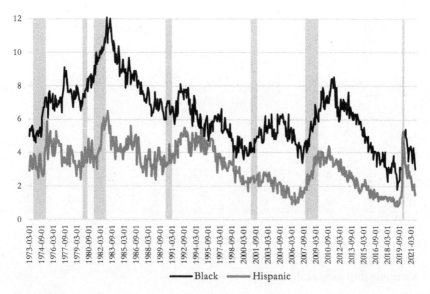

Figure 10.3
Black and Hispanic unemployment relative to white unemployment, with periods of recession indicated by the vertical bands.

vertical shaded areas—Black and Hispanic unemployment rates rise *much more* than white rates, by 4 to 12 percentage points.

The implication is that the most recent forty-year period of excess unemployment was suffered disproportionately by people of color. Recessions are bad for almost everyone. For Blacks and Hispanics, they're awful. Over this forty-year period, who has won? The financial sector. At whose expense? Workers, most especially Black and Hispanic workers. This of course oversimplifies the outcomes, but the big picture is clear.

In 2019–2020, the Federal Reserve conducted the first comprehensive review of its monetary policy framework—the strategy, tools, and communications practices it employs to meet its congressionally mandated goals of maximizing employment and stabilizing prices.[101] As part of that process, the central bank embarked on a Fed Listens tour, in which it convened retirees, low-income people, and community representatives with whom it does not routinely discuss the effects of its monetary policy actions. I was involved in this process, primarily in Boston, but also systemwide.[102] The Fed regularly talks to financial market and business leaders on matters of monetary policy. It also routinely works with community development groups but does not usually engage them on monetary policy matters. From my perspective, Fed Listens was a welcome development, an important component of the opening-up process. In my view, the Fed really did listen, and it learned.

One key takeaway of the tour that a community participant suggested: for some neighborhoods with persistently high unemployment, "it's always a recession." The recessions indicated in figure 10.3 exacerbate chronically poor conditions.[103] During the prolonged expansion preceding the pandemic, unemployment rates in some Chicago neighborhoods exceeded 15 percent. High as they were, Fed Listens panelists noted that these rates were among the lowest unemployment rates these communities had seen, although they would be considered "catastrophic for the country as a whole."

A second takeaway from Fed Listens was validation of the Fed's policy in the late 2010s of keeping interest rates low to run the economy "hot"—supporting robust growth accompanied by very low unemployment. While some economists worried about the inflationary repercussions of the hot economy, feedback from these communities made it clear that the prolonged and robust economic expansion had provided work opportunities that they would never have seen otherwise.[104] While still doing much worse than the nation overall, these communities benefitted significantly from a hot economy, especially when such conditions did not cause inflation troubles, as was the case pre-pandemic. It's not that the Fed hadn't had access to the data on Black and Hispanic unemployment; it's that hearing the stories of people living those numbers appears to have reached Fed policymakers far more effectively than any statistical analysis could.

*   *   *

A discussion of inflation during the pandemic may seem somewhat far afield, but it matters in the context of this book. Prior to 2020, the Fed was able to keep interest rates low for quite some time, even as unemployment dipped into historically low territory, reflecting a very vibrant economy. This was possible because *inflation remained quite low, below its 2 percent goal.* There was no apparent tradeoff to negotiate between lower unemployment and higher inflation. But recent history suggests a risk that we can no longer rely on inflation to cooperate in that way. If so, the Fed may have to keep interest rates higher, slow the economy more, causing a loss of employment that is clearly most damaging for people of color. We may thus lose some of the gains made in the late 2010s.

Of course, apart from its implications for interest rates and employment, high inflation directly harms low-income families. The prices of necessities—rent, gasoline, food, heating fuel—have risen dramatically, making already-precarious economic existence even more perilous. When inflation is this high, the Fed's desire to lower it is not (just) about aiding financial markets, it's about helping ordinary households.

As of this writing, it is unclear whether the pandemic-era inflation surge will prove persistent—lasting more than a couple of years—or transitory. Even a transitory burst of inflation *could* turn into a sustained rise in inflation, if workers and businesses come to expect higher inflation on average for the foreseeable future. For example, if most people believe that inflation will be 4 or 5 percent for the next five to ten 10 years, they will likely not be happy with wage increases of just 2 or 3 percent. If they are successful in pushing for higher wages based on this expectation, then the resulting increased cost of labor will pass through to consumers in the prices of everything that is produced using labor—which is just about everything. In this way inflation could persist. To date, we don't see significant rises in expected inflation beyond the coming year. A variety of inflation expectations measures for long-term inflation have remained relatively stable.[105]

Importantly for lower-income families, wages rose faster in 2021 than they had in the preceding decade, and they rose fastest among the lowest 25 percent of wage earners.[106] However, very few workers' wages rose as fast as inflation, so workers still lost ground after adjusting for the increased cost of living. In the wake of the pandemic, prices rose more than enough to cover rising labor costs, yielding record-breaking corporate profits.[107] A suspicious interpreter might suggest that companies took advantage of shortages in labor and other supplies to boost prices beyond cost increases, raising profits and, don't forget, maximizing shareholder value![108]

The key takeaway is this: it is vital that we to return to the prepandemic goal of supporting low unemployment and long spans of strong growth. The Federal Reserve needs to reduce inflation to stop the direct harm caused by rapidly rising prices for basic necessities. But the Fed also needs to restore an economy in which low inflation allows policymakers to support prolonged economic expansion that will mightily benefit the poor people and families of color whom our economy has historically left behind.

Update: The Impact of COVID-19

This book was largely written during the second and third years of the COVID-19 pandemic. The pandemic threw the economy into an upheaval unlike any it had experienced since the Great Depression, when the structure of the economy was dramatically different than it is today.[109] What happened during the pandemic that might alter the pattern formed by the data that we have seen throughout this book?

Certainly a lot happened! The government engineered massive aid to businesses (two rounds of the Paycheck Protection Program, or PPP), individuals (extended unemployment insurance benefits, direct stimulus checks, and an expanded child tax credit), and financial institutions (similar to the suite of programs put in place during the financial crisis of 2007–2009). Some of these programs clearly had an effect: the increase in the child tax credit, some of it paid in advance, gave families an additional $1,600 per year for each child under age six and $1,000 per year for children ages six to sixteen.[110] The child poverty rate fell from over 18 percent before the pandemic to 11.9 percent in July 2021, the first month that advance child tax credit payments were made. After the expiration of the policy in December 2021, the child poverty rate jumped from 12.1 percent to an estimated 17 percent in January 2022.[111]

Not all policies enacted in response to the pandemic were successful. The PPP, designed to avoid some of the employment loss that pandemic-induced shutdowns could have caused, achieved its goals in part. According to economist David Autor, the program likely saved 2 to 3 million job-years of employment over fourteen months. But the cost per job saved was somewhere between $170,000 and $260,000, far above the full cost of compensation for these workers. That implies that the balance of the funds distributed—roughly 70 percent of the $800 billion total—went not to workers but to business owners and shareholders. Another victory for the wealthy and white. This contrasts markedly with the two other programs aimed at helping workers—the stimulus checks and expanded unemployment insurance benefits—which distributed $800 billion and $680 billion respectively, directly to households and to the unemployed specifically.[112]

Despite an improved labor market and public commitments by some firms, there has been no improvement in scheduling practices for low-income service-sector workers in the wake of the pandemic.[113] Disparities in educational attainment likely widened during the pandemic, due to the differential effects of remote and hybrid instruction on lower- and higher-income students.[114]

Awareness of racial economic justice has heightened—there is now greater attention to racial injustice among (some of) the media and many media consumers. But outcomes have yet to change. The disparities in income, wealth, health care, and education have not budged over the past two years. For example, the Census Bureau's Pulse Surveys suggest no discernible improvement in the gaps between Black, Hispanic, and white outcomes for health insurance coverage or food insecurity since before the pandemic. Blacks and Hispanics remain two to three times as likely as whites to be uninsured or suffer food insecurity.[115]

A more persistent, concerted effort to address racial inequities will require a more widespread and persistent change in narrative. Results from the Pew Trust's ongoing survey on support for the Black Lives Matter (BLM) movement highlight the challenge in moving this narrative. In 2017, 55 percent of respondents registered support for BLM. In the weeks immediately following the murder of George Floyd, support rose to 67 percent, and opposition fell from 34 to 31 percent. However, by September 2020, support had fallen back to its previous level of 55 percent, while opposition *rose* to 44 percent. These levels were essentially unchanged through September 2021.[116]

Let us hope that the pandemic, which exposed persistent weaknesses in our economy across racial and ethnic lines, and the racial upheaval provoked by growing awareness of racially motivated violence, have taught us something. Perhaps attention has now been focused, the Pew results notwithstanding. Action that leads to enduring change is yet to come.

*   *   *

It is clear from the evidence above that our systems have been consistently subject to the influence of those who have power and resources. Our lopsided distribution of economic rewards is the result of design, not accident. In many cases, powerful institutions, lobbying groups, and voting blocs have employed key elements of The Myth as justification: the poor are different from us, not to be trusted with aid. They need to be encouraged to work harder (and to build traditional families). The power of labor, largely expressed through unions, grew too strong and needed to be shut down if corporations were to succeed in pleasing shareholders.

And yet our current safety net largely *requires* recipients to work. The tragedy is that despite working, many remain desperately poor and dependent on relatively meager government aid to survive. The decline in worker voice has indeed led to robust profitability among most corporations—at the expense of a large cohort of workers who are properly characterized as the working poor. The voice they exercised through unions has been silenced, to their detriment. Meanwhile, the burden of paying for our nation's public goods and services—including the frayed safety net—has been sloughed off by the most affluent, through the exercise of their economic and political power.

The system is broken, working just as it was designed to.

V The Wreckage

What hath The Myth wrought? The principal loss is that of human potential. Countless millions never get the chance to build their knowledge, skills, and experience so that they can put their innate and acquired skills to best use. That loss reduces the size of the economy, stunts the personal and financial development of many, and denies us the benefits we would all accrue if there were millions more productive and innovative workers in our economy.

On the face of it, the human loss entailed is simply staggering. Why this is an acceptable outcome for our country is bewildering, although it is clear that our national mythology has deafened us to the constant cries of genuine anguish.

I will consider two ways of thinking about the size of the losses incurred. In terms of more hard-headed calculus, one method for estimating losses is to look backward, assessing the loss of wages, accumulated wealth, health, or lifespan for various populations over US history. Because it is probably impossible to account for losses due to all injustices across all peoples across all of US history, the estimates I develop should be considered distinctly a lower-bound approximation to the true costs of The Myth.

With this in mind, I will estimate the magnitude of key losses that loom large in America's history: the loss due to the displacement, mistreatment, deprivation and murder of the Indigenous people who lived here well before white people landed on this soil; the losses due to Black enslavement, derived from the estimated costs for reparations; and losses due to systemic discrimination, reflected in wealth differentials.[1] I will also compute losses that will accrue going forward as large segments of the population—including Indigenous, Black, Hispanic, and Asian people—participate partially or not at all in the labor force, lose earning potential, suffer from poor access to health care, and miss the opportunity to accumulate wealth. All of these estimates involve debatable assumptions and approximations. But to be clear, the goal is not to obtain the precise value of the losses, but to develop a rough estimate of their overall magnitude. As we will see, the degree of precision will be a secondary concern, given the size of the losses.

11 The Loss Looking Backward

Original Sin: Losses Due to Land Theft from Indigenous People

The history of governmental abuses of Indigenous people is long and sordid and includes land theft, displacement, and genocide, among other abuses. The difference in net worth of Indigenous white Americans serves as one estimate of the cumulative losses suffered. Today, Native Americans possess only about 9 percent of white people's wealth, per household, implying a loss of about $900 billion.[1]

But that reckoning ignores one of the largest losses suffered by Indigenous people: the theft of their land. Essentially all of the land that now forms the literal foundation of the United States belonged to—or perhaps more accurately, was inhabited and stewarded by—Indigenous people when Europeans first landed here.[2] Now a small fraction of that land is set aside in reservations, totaling about 2.3 percent of the area of the United States.[3] The Bureau of Economic Analysis periodically estimates the value of the land in the contiguous forty-eight states.[4] As of 2009, their estimate came to $23 trillion. However, 2009 immediately followed the housing and financial crisis, a time when land values remained severely depressed. Since then, taking account of the rise in real estate values, a conservative estimate of the value of stolen land is closer to $40 trillion.[5]

Losses from Systemic Racism

In promoting a case for reparations, William Darity Jr. and Kirsten Mullen survey several ways of estimating the losses suffered by Black people due to slavery. Some use the current value of land promised but not delivered to slaves in the wake of the Civil War. Some use the value of wealth gained by slaveowners from their slave holdings. Some compute the value of what was produced by slave labor, deducting the costs of production—the profits from slavery. The value today implied by these estimates ranges from $5 to $42 trillion, depending on the loss computed and the interest rate employed in inflating 1860s losses to the present.[6] Most of these estimates do not include an accounting of the impact of injustices heaped on Black Americans in the twentieth century.

Darity and Mullen ultimately prefer estimates derived from net worth, which they view as "a more powerful measure of economic well-being than income." They write, *"We view the racial wealth gap as the best single indicator of the cumulative economic effects of white supremacy in the United States."*[7] Updating their calculations using the latest available data, one can take the 2019 Black-white average household wealth gap of $838,000 and multiply by the number of Black households in the latest US Census (about 17.4 million) to yield the amount needed to close the gap: $14.5 trillion.[8] Alternatively, one can apportion the total value of US household net worth—$114 trillion as of 2019—to Blacks according to their share in the population (about 14 percent) to arrive at $16 trillion. Subtracting 2019 holdings of net worth among Black families yields a net worth gap of $13.5 trillion.[9]

The wealth gap of course grows even larger and would require trillions more to close if we include the wealth shortfall among Hispanics. For Hispanics, the gap relative to whites is about $815,000 per family. With approximately 18.3 million Hispanic households in the United States, this represents a total wealth gap of $15 trillion. Alternatively, allocating a share of total US wealth to Hispanics in proportion to their share of the population (about 18 percent in 2019), we arrive at a wealth gap of over $17 trillion.

These estimates are necessarily crude, but they capture the approximate magnitude of the losses inflicted by systemic racism over the decades and centuries.

Points of Comparison: Reparations for Japanese Internment and the Holocaust

In the twentieth century, the United States attempted to address historic losses arising from systemic injustices, paying reparations to specific populations. Beginning in 1942, the US Government forced more than 120,000

Japanese Americans from their residences and into internment camps, following President Roosevelt's Executive Order 9066. The camps were located in California and Oregon. Living conditions were abysmal, security was tightly enforced using barbed wire and armed guards, and prisoners lost their homes and businesses. The rationale for relocation and imprisonment was that Japanese Americans might be spies, a fear heightened by reports that the Pearl Harbor attack was enabled by Japanese American spies. No investigation has ever uncovered incidents of espionage or treason committed by a Japanese American.[10]

Internment ended in December 1944 by presidential proclamation, but Japanese Americans found it difficult to return to their previous lives. Little action was taken to address the wrongful incarceration until the 1970s, when the Japanese American Citizens League issued a resolution seeking reparations. Legislation sponsored by Senator Daniel Inouye, a Hawai'i Democrat, called for the formation of a commission to study wartime incarceration. The commission's 1983 study recommended monetary reparations.[11]

After several years of deliberation, the Civil Liberties Act of 1987 was passed, providing a modest payment of $20,000 for each individual affected by evacuation, relocation, and internment during World War II. Eligibility was to be determined by the US attorney general. The restitution paid was not to be "included in determining eligibility to receive certain income-based Federal benefits," thus it did not inadvertently push low-income Japanese Americans off the rolls of public programs. Importantly, the legislation also provided restitution for Aleutian and Pribilof Islands residents, who also were relocated during the war, in the amount of $12,000. The bill further provided appropriations to establish the Civil Liberties Public Education Fund (CLPEF) and includes a formal apology from the nation for its actions during the war. Today the CLPEF continues to inform the US public about the internment program. Nearly half of the residents affected by internment had died by the time reparations became available.[12]

The roughly $1.6 billion in payments authorized by the law cannot be considered fair compensation for the individuals and families who were imprisoned for one to three years from 1942 to 1945. Taking as a baseline the average hourly earnings for manufacturing workers at the end of the War (about 90 cents per hour), three years in an incarceration facility implies a loss of about $6,300 in 1942 dollars. That would correspond to about $65,000-$75,000 in income in 1988.[13] Thus the $20,000 payment does not even compensate the interned for their lost wages. And, as suggested above, the loss of houses and businesses represents a considerable additional loss of net worth that would likely double or triple properly estimated lost income.

Reparations were made, and the apology was an important admission of responsibility. But the amounts involved only went a small way toward true repair. That said, this remains an important US precedent for recognizing and paying losses caused by systemic racism.

*   *   *

German payments to victims of the Holocaust provide another point of comparison. Jews in the wake of the Holocaust were successful in obtaining reparations, some of which continue to be paid today. I should note that I am in no way equating the historical episodes of the Holocaust and Black enslavement. I am, however, using the German reparations response to the Holocaust as an example of a country that took seriously its obligation to survivors and descendants of a population that it had systematically murdered and abused.

Reparations occurred in two waves, the first immediately following the end of the War and the second in the 1990s. The first wave paid both Jewish victims and first-generation heirs for suffering in concentration camps and for loss of property. Between war's end and 2000, West Germany and then Germany paid approximately $53 billion in compensation. This first wave may have been easier to realize, as many victims were still alive, and international sentiment was clearly aligned behind the need for reparations. Konrad Adenauer, who was chancellor of West Germany from 1949 to 1963, acknowledged the wrong done to Jews.[14] Payments were made to Israel for costs associated with the influx of survivors, to the Conference on Jewish Material Claims Against Germany on behalf of survivors, and directly to survivors who could reasonably establish specific harms or losses.[15]

There are important parallels between the Holocaust and Black slavery in assessing the magnitude of reparations required to compensate the victims. As Leslie Sebba points out, there was significant debate in 1952 about "the morality of accepting monetary payment as reparation for the atrocities inflicted in the course of the Holocaust."[16] That is to say, putting a price on the suffering endured by Holocaust victims or enslaved Blacks is a fraught enterprise, mixing cold-hearted economics with the moral reckoning of human atrocities. Did Germans hope that, by paying reparations, they would elicit international forgiveness for war crimes?

The initial 1953 Holocaust Indemnification statute provided for compensation for a broad range of damages that included wrongful death, disability, injury, incarceration, professional and economic losses, and property loss. Over time, the program was clarified and broadened, raising maximum benefits for property and earnings damages. Importantly, amendments to the statute set an objective standard for the extent of reparations, tying them to payments the deceased would have earned from a German civil service pension corresponding to their economic status prior to their deaths. In the first ten years following the implementation of reforms in 1958, more than 1.7 million applicants were registered for compensation.[17]

The lessons to draw from this ongoing program of reparations are that West Germany rather quickly came to a reckoning of the vast scope of damage inflicted by the Nazi regime during the Holocaust, ultimately using a fairly broad definition of damages to determine the scale of reparations. Its program likely benefited from the relative proximity to the time of the Holocaust. The program also benefited from West Germany's strong desire to reintegrate into the economies of Western Europe, including its desire to receive Marshall Plan funds (which may not have been forthcoming if West Germany had not moved forward on reparations). And the program remains open-ended to this day, providing payments to survivors and increasingly next-of-kin. In reckoning the actual cost of these injustices, the wide lens employed by postwar Germany serves as a significant benchmark.

To date the United States has clearly not been so generous in recognizing the breadth of damage that slavery did to the descendants of enslaved people, that institutional racism has caused for people of color, or that our current system does to millions of working poor people. We have allowed decades to pass since the abolition of slavery. We will need a national change of heart to pay what is due.

12 The Loss Looking Forward

The preceding discussions assess the losses for specific racial and ethnic groups in the context of slavery, Japanese internment, and the genocide of Indigenous people. For the United States, reparations should be an important part of the calculus in considering the economic potential lost due to centuries of suffering.

But the losses that our system will continue to cause going forward could easily be as great as those already incurred. And as we have seen, those losses will span multiple demographic groups, including poor white families left behind by our particular brand of capitalism. Can we compute the loss of what could be? Though inevitably any determination is debatable, we can use data and historical experience to arrive at an estimate that captures the order of magnitude of the losses likely to accumulate in the future.

The Cost of Childhood Poverty

A number of authors have produced estimates of the losses entailed in childhood poverty in the United States. These estimates attempt to capture losses broadly, including not just lost income but also the costs of conditions associated with poverty, such as the increased incidence of crime and ill health among adults who grow up poor. Economists Harry Holzer, Diane Schanzenbach, Greg Duncan, and Jens Ludwig properly describe the losses inherent in childhood poverty as an opportunity cost—the harm that arises "because the opportunity to be productive and generate earnings is lost."[1] The losses so calculated include not only those suffered by individuals born in poverty but also the costs borne by society due to increases in crime and health care expenditures after these individuals reach adulthood.

These authors note that assessing the loss from childhood poverty quite likely understates the overall cost of poverty, as many people experience poverty for the first time in adulthood. Of course, some who grow up poor are fortunate enough to exit poverty, but the estimates reproduced here represent the *average* costs to those who grow up poor, which comprises both those who escape poverty and those who slip even deeper into poverty as adults. However, the estimates do not reflect the costs of those who do not start out poor but end up poor in adulthood. While experiencing poverty in the earliest years of childhood is likely most damaging to adult outcomes, not all studies can control for the timing of poverty in a child's life, so the estimates may understate the actual costs.

Using similar approaches and surveying a number of studies of childhood poverty's statistical association with subsequent income, crime, and health care outcomes, Holzer et al. estimated the annual cost of childhood poverty at $900 billion. Another group of researchers arrived at a figure of $1.2 trillion.[2] Given how difficult it is to measure costs of childhood poverty, the results are reassuringly similar. They are also huge. Costing between 4 and 5 percent of annual GDP, the burden of childhood poverty represents a staggering loss of human potential. Over just one generation, childhood poverty likely costs the country $25 trillion, an amount in the same ballpark as the accumulated losses due to Black enslavement. And the authors of these two studies, and of many studies that they cite, suggest that these figures likely *underestimate* the true cost of childhood poverty.

The Cost of Lost Earnings: Compared to What?

The losses of earnings in the childhood-poverty studies cited above use the official poverty level as a benchmark against which to measure earnings. But as we've seen, a family at the poverty line—about $27,000 for a family of four in 2021—is nowhere near able to meet even its basic needs. An alternative measure of loss calculates the gap between actual household earnings and the level required to meet basic household expenses.

Recall that by several different income measures, between one-fifth and one-quarter of all households earn total income of less than $30,000. Median family income by the standard US Census measure was about $70,000 in 2021.[3] As outlined earlier, the budget for necessities—housing, food, childcare, transportation, health care, taxes (if applicable), and so on—ranges from $65,000 in low-income US counties to more than $90,000 in moderate-income counties.

To arrive at a conservative benchmark for lost earnings, I start with the three family budgets presented earlier, paring back the amounts of some spending components.[4] I use the midpoint of these adjusted budgets, which is a bit below median family income for 2021, as the earnings benchmark. The estimates of loss due to childhood poverty are derived from what it would cost to move those families up to the poverty level. Here I add to this by calculating what it would cost to move those families from the poverty level all the way up to the midpoint of the adjusted family budgets. I then add the cost of moving those already *above* the poverty level up to this income level. The sum of these two amounts to an annual loss of about $1.9 trillion—*in addition to the losses due to childhood poverty calculated above.*[5] Reducing the income benchmark to $50,000 cuts the annual loss to $1.5 trillion. Alternatively, we might consider moving the lowest income families *part way* toward the benchmark, closing more of the gap for them and less of the gap for higher-income families that still fall short of the benchmark. This method implies a loss of $1.3 trillion annually. These estimated losses are larger than those for childhood poverty—almost twice as large—because I am comparing the lost income to a higher (and I believe more reasonable) benchmark, and because more families fall short of that higher benchmark. Over a working lifetime, these *annual* costs add up to staggering amounts.

Losses are borne disproportionately among racial and ethnic minorities. I compute the loss in earnings relative to the household-income benchmark by race and ethnicity and assess the share of the total loss borne by any demographic category relative to its share in US population. Households headed by a Black individual bear a share of the loss that is 38 percent higher than their representation in the population. Native American, Aleutian, and Alaskan families bear a share 22 percent higher than their population share. Hispanic-headed households bear a share of the losses that is 16 percent higher than their representation. Asian/Pacific Islander households bear a roughly proportional share of the loss. To be sure, white families bear some of the loss. But they are alone in bearing about 11 percent *less* than their representation in the population.[6]

Losses Due to Unequal Education Outcomes

We have learned much about the effects of educational attainment on later earnings, among other life outcomes. To be sure, isolating the causal effect of secondary school education on adults' earnings is difficult, as many other factors influence earnings. David Card examines a number of studies that attempt to unravel causal links between education and earnings and finds that an additional year of schooling adds between 7 and 13 percent to lifetime earnings.[7] The significant gaps in educational attainment by family income, race, and ethnicity thus imply a tremendous gap in earnings over the lifetimes of workers. A 2019 Census Bureau study shows white adults are much more likely to attain bachelor's, master's, and doctoral degrees than are Black and Hispanic adults, whose highest degree is more likely to be something shy of an associate's degree or high school diploma.[8]

Using these data, one can compute the aggregate loss of lifetime earnings relative to two modest educational benchmarks—if one hadn't attained a high school degree, how much would one have lost in potential earnings, and similarly for an associate's degree.

I add up the number of years by which one fell short of a high school diploma for all those adults in 2019 who were not high school graduates. I then apply the midpoint of Card's estimates of the increase in income associated with another year's education—about 10 percent per year—to the average weekly earnings of those who had not completed high school, to approximate the lost earnings per year of lost education for this group. Combining lost years of education with earnings lost per year produces the estimated loss: obtaining a high school degree would have added $290 billion in earnings per working year for these people, or about $11.5 trillion over a forty-year working life. Using the same method, I estimate that going even further—completing an associate's degree—would have added another $1 trillion per year, or another $40 trillion in aggregate lifetime earnings.[9] To put it colloquially, the lifetime losses to lower educational attainment are massive.

Not surprisingly, the losses fall disproportionately on people of color. Of the total losses incurred due to reduced earnings, non-Hispanic whites bear a much smaller share relative to their proportion in the population. Conversely, Hispanics bear losses that are two to three times their representation in the population. Blacks and Asians bear losses that are closer to proportional to their share of the population, according to this measure.

Are these estimates reasonable? In a 2015 study of OECD countries, Eric A. Hanushek and Ludger Woessmann estimate the effect on countries' GDP from raising the average achievement of their student body to mastery of basic skills, as defined by a learning assessment for fifteen-year-olds from the Program for International Student Assessment. In the United States, only three-quarters of fifteen-year-olds attain this achievement level. Hanushek and Woessmann estimate that, if the United States were to raise achievement levels so that all students master basic skills, total economic gains would be approximately $27 trillion over the working lives of these students.[10]

Another interesting point of reference is Hanushek and Woessmann's 2020 study of the loss in GDP from pandemic-induced remote and hybrid schooling. These authors estimate that for the United States, the long-run impact of one-third year of lost schooling in terms of educational attainment and a reduced skills is $20.6 trillion.[11]

The earnings losses attributed to education in this section likely account for a good portion of the overall income gaps that we considered in the preceding section. These estimates are imperfect, but they do suggest the massive cost of unequal access to educational attainment.

Deaths Due to Poverty, Inequality, Racial Segregation, and Poor Education

So far we have not considered the reality that inequality, poverty, and racial inequality cause deaths, which of course adds greatly to the tally of losses.

A team of public health professionals has estimated the number of deaths attributed to low education, household poverty, low "social support," area-level poverty, area-level income inequality, and area-level racial segregation.[12] Drawing on forty-five studies, Sandro Galea and colleagues find that, in 2000, about 875,000 deaths could be attributed to these causes. Scaled to today's population, that implies about 1,029,000 deaths in 2021. It seems a bit heartless to put a dollar value on lives lost, but in fact the US government does so all the time. The value of a life used by the EPA in 2016 was $10 million, and the Department of Transportation uses a higher number at $11.8 million.[13] Using a round number of $10 million, the roughly one million lives lost annually can be given a statistical value of $10 trillion.[14]

Losses That Are Harder to Quantify

As detailed above, the wealth gap across racial and ethnic categories is enormous. Wealth can facilitate a number of economic opportunities—the down payment on a home, the capital needed to start a business, the funds to pay for or defray the cost of education—as well as serving as a source of financial stability in the event of loss of employment or hours worked, or in the event of a large and unexpected expense such as a medical bill. Even so, the lifetime loss suffered from homes unpurchased, businesses not started, and education not pursued is not directly captured by wealth-gap calculations, although these are indeed consequences of having little or no wealth.

Liquid assets—assets readily converted to cash—serve the important role of a buffer in case of economic hardship. For example, if a family loses income, balances in its checking and savings accounts might be used to make up the difference for some time. Many families have small to nonexistent holdings of these buffer assets. Ten percent of families with a white head of household hold liquid assets of $400 or less, and 17 percent report cash-like assets of less than $1,000. And the picture worsens for families of color. Between 25 and 44 percent of Black- and Hispanic-headed households have less than $400 or $1,000 on hand to meet financial emergencies. Almost half of Black and Hispanic households would find it nearly impossible to come up with a $50,000 down payment for a home—even if they had $50,000 in total assets, they would have to liquidate *all* of their holdings, both financial and nonfinancial. The share of white-headed households that are similarly constrained is less than half that of Black and Hispanic households.[15]

It is difficult to put a dollar value on the number of homes not bought, the businesses not started, the retirement lives plagued by insufficient savings, or the turmoil experienced when a spell of unemployment forces increased debt or loss of a home. What is clear from these data is that due to the lack of wealth accumulation, such opportunities are missed by an alarmingly high fraction of the population.

Equally difficult to quantify are the losses due to unequal leadership representation. Despite much discussion of the importance of diversity, equity, and inclusion (DEI) as societal goals and drivers of business performance, progress in changing the representation of women and minorities among company's boards and executive teams over the past several years has been remarkably slow. A recent study by McKinsey shows that among firms first surveyed in 2017, gender representation on boards and executive teams was roughly unchanged as of 2019, with women accounting for only 15 percent of executive teams (up one percentage point) and 24 percent of boards (unchanged). Though they account for more than one-third of the US population, ethnic minorities accounted for only 14 and 16 percent of executive teams and boards as of 2019 (versus 12 and 14 percent in 2017).[16] The same report notes a positive correlation between diverse leadership and boards and company performance, although it is difficult to know which way the causation runs in such data. It may be that high-performing firms with healthy profit margins are more likely to put in place robust DEI programs, or it may be that DEI programs have contributed to these firms' profitability. I personally believe that more diverse leadership is essential for progress among the racially and ethnically diverse populations in the United States, but I am disappointed by the lack of serious research that might provide even more compelling support for that belief.

So it is difficult to put a number on the cost of unequal representation in our country's leadership. However, it seems a priori reasonable to assume that drawing from only a subset of eligible leaders cannot be the best way for Americans to manage our country's private and public enterprises, to say nothing of our political bodies. How many trillions of dollars have been lost in this way I can't say, but we have almost surely set aside an enormous amount of potential.

Final Tally of the Losses

No matter how one accounts for the loss—as a historical reckoning of accumulated losses from slavery and institutional racism or as a forward-looking reckoning of the cost of leaving the system as it is—the United States has suffered enormously from leaving so many behind. Given the losses quantified in this chapter, it is reasonable to arrive at a conservative annual number of at least $14.3 trillion, and perhaps as high as $17 trillion, both of which are well over one-half of annual GDP. Note that this annual total expresses accumulated losses due to slavery and systemic discrimination—$30 to $40 trillion—as the equivalent indefinite annual flow of income that these stocks of (missing) wealth would produce—$0.9 to $2 trillion annually, if they earned three to five percent per year. The total similarly expresses the accumulated value of land theft from Indigenous Peoples as an annual income flow.[17]

This estimate of the overall loss very likely understates the true loss. It excludes a number of harder-to-measure losses: it does not directly include losses inflicted by a broken prison system, or the loss due to unequal representation among business leaders. Losses due to wealth disparities are captured crudely by the investment income such assets might have produced. Those losses do not include the value of lost housing, education, or entrepreneurial opportunities that wealth provides. Estimates of childhood poverty are likely underestimates, according to the studies' authors.

In the end, there is no completely satisfying way to calculate such losses. What is clear is that they are suffered, year in and out, by millions of citizens who are working hard and persevering, but not making it.

Unless something changes, we will continue to add to this toll for generations to come. Lives will be lost, families will struggle, children will receive poor educations, wealth will go to the already wealthy.

I offer two positive spins on these observations. First, because we constructed our economy, we can change it. Second, one can think of most of these forward-looking losses as potential future gains. This suggests that we could gain about $15 trillion annually if we successfully integrate millions more of our residents into the economy, avoiding unnecessary deaths, lifting children out of poverty, and improving education and earnings.

VI   What Are You Prepared to Do? The Way Forward

We have a choice.[1] We can leave our less-fortunate fellow citizens to their own devices, pitching them into an economic tournament where the luckiest win. Good luck to them!

Or we can build a system that provides real pathways to success—the opportunity to build human and financial capital. This system would recognize that few of our poorest outcomes reflect the inevitable result of well-functioning free-market economic processes. Instead, they flow from a system that has been designed to yield poor outcomes for many and to concentrate wealth and power among the few. The challenge is to use the power that has been wielded throughout our history to instead craft a very different, inclusive economy.

In that economy, luck will play a smaller role in determining success, opportunity to build human capital will be widely available, the benefits of a healthy and necessary symbiosis between government and private enterprise embraced, and the continuing effects of our history of racial injustice acknowledged and addressed.

What specifically needs to be done to get there? Both narratives and policies need to change. If we undertake the program outlined below, we will go a long way toward repairing the wreckage that has just been tallied.

13 Change the Narrative

Dalida R., whom we met before, has achieved a measure of economic stability, after coming from financially strapped beginnings. Adopted at age four by a big-hearted family in Cape Verde when her own family did not have the financial means to support her, she immigrated to the US at the age of fifteen to live with her adoptive sister in Boston. Dalida has enough income to meet basic needs, with a small amount set aside for emergencies. (How much? "It depends on what goes wrong. If it's the roof, I don't have that.") She rejects the meritocratic/individual effort narrative. She exhorts her three children, "Don't believe the whole 'work hard and pull yourselves by your bootstraps.' I don't think anyone worked harder than slaves. And all of us who are slave descendants are poor, and still trying to make something for ourselves."[1]

Unprompted, she articulated for me an alternative narrative:

> I wouldn't be here without the support of teachers, without the support of my community—[it] goes to show that we don't do it on our own, it's not all about hard work—it's about a community caring for each other. . . . That's why I am able to break the cycle of poverty that has been in my family for so long. And hopefully I'm able to help my children go even further than what I've been able to accomplish.

In this narrative, community support—in Dalida's case from an early age—is essential to success. Hard work still matters. Dalida's high GPA in high school earned her a spot in the school's academic honor society. But without the support of her communities—in Cape Verde, in Boston, and in Worcester where she now lives—she believes she would not be where she is today: the executive director of a nonprofit, a first-time homebuyer raising three children, active in giving back to those who have less. Individual effort is simply *not* sufficient.

As long as the majority of the population—and their elected representatives—believes in The Myth, it will be difficult to make the changes necessary to more equitably build human capital. As Natasha Hicks and colleagues put it,

> We cannot build power to change the rules that have resulted in low wealth levels among Black people without shifting narratives about Black people, neighborhoods and institutions that are steeped in deficits, falsehoods, and stereotypes. We must shift mental models that lead people to believe that wealth accumulation is predicated on hard work and making the right economic decisions.[2]

A prerequisite to systemic change is narrative change.[3] Consistent and widespread dissemination of the facts about brokenness, along with consistent efforts to expose and dispel the false narratives of The Myth, may help to move the center of opinion closer to reality, laying the groundwork for change.

Holding On to Our Narratives and Misperceptions

Why is it that we hold so tightly to manifestly false narratives? For the wealthy and powerful it is easy to see why The Myth is so popular. That narrative has for decades supported them in building and sustaining a system that maintains their economic and political status. Simple self-interest, coupled with willful ignorance of unpleasant facts, explains the enduring popularity of The Myth among this cohort.

But as the popular-media references and the polling data cited earlier demonstrate, The Myth remains remarkably popular not just among the affluent but also among ordinary citizens. Why is that? A wealth of psychological research has examined this issue, but it boils down to a few simple factors. First, we want to believe that the world is set up to do good and fair things. Second, we trust our beliefs more than we trust evidence. And third, we find it psychologically easier to discard evidence that challenges our beliefs rather than change those beliefs.

On the first of these points, a strong desire to believe in societal fairness appears to bias perceptions towards the ideal of equality and away from the reality of disparity. This resilient belief in fairness may "stem from motivations to protect the self from the uncomfortable realization that societal outcomes . . . are unfair." Furthermore, economic and geographic segregation makes it easier for those who live in less diverse networks to place more faith in the ideal than in the reality. Segregation implies little regular contact across racial, ethnic, and economic groups. Without regular exposure to populations who experience outcomes different from our own, it can be difficult to form an accurate picture of how those differences arise.[4]

It is understandable that we wish deeply to believe in the virtues to which our country has always aspired—equality of opportunity, reward according to merit—as well as ideals of newer vintage, such as nondiscrimination on the basis of race and gender. That such beliefs can profoundly and persistently shape perceptions and decisions despite evidence to the contrary has been studied by psychologists for decades and falls under the category of "motivated reasoning"—the triumph of belief over incongruent evidence. In discussing reluctance to accept scientific guidance, Joshua Blank and Daron Shaw find that "deference to scientific evidence . . . depends on the availability of such alternative points of view as religious faith and political ideology. When scientific results conflict with a readily available alternative view, individuals are less likely to defer to the research."[5] Michael Kraus and colleagues point to

> one fundamental aspect of the psychology underlying these misperceptions of equality; namely, the desire to see society as fair, just, and merit-based. These underlying motivations are strong enough, we argue, to lead individuals to pay greater attention to confirming information and considerably less attention to information that suggests society continues to be both unequal and unjust, especially on the basis of race.[6]

Because narratives about societal fairness are deeply embedded in Americans' psyches, these narratives are readily available to us and likely account for some of the resistance to accept counternarratives that are evidence-based. An important insight in this research is that people choose the *easiest* way to resolve conflict between their narrative and the facts. It's much harder to change your view of the world than it is to downgrade some evidence that challenges it.[7]

A related literature points to the tendency toward "system justification," the "general ideological motive to justify the existing social order."[8] According to this theory, individuals want to hold favorable views about themselves and the groups they identify with, but also about *social and political systems that affect them.* A key finding is the strong tendency to believe in "fair market ideology," which presumes that "procedures and outcomes generated by market-based systems are not only efficient but fair and just."[9] This belief sits at the center of a key tension: while most Americans believe in fair market ideology, thus perceiving our economic system to be fair and legitimate, many simultaneously recognize that substantial inequality exists.[10] System justification allows Americans to accept as fair and just the inequality inherent in our system, believing it must have been the appropriate product of markets that they believe generally deliver fair and just results.

The Political Uses of False Narratives

Our history is replete with examples of using false narratives ("the deserving poor," the primacy of free markets, the preeminence of maximizing shareholder value in guiding business decisions) to win political gains that have profoundly shaped our safety net, welfare system, and tax code. Overtly racist political decisions reflected the nation's inability to move decisively away from slavery in the post–Civil War period. In the twentieth century, our system overwhelmingly slanted wealth supports toward white families. It should be clear at this point that false narratives—all the components of The Myth, including the notion of a post-racist country—have driven momentous political and policy decisions.

More recently, as overt racism has become widely unacceptable across political parties, politicians have resorted to coded language—"dog whistles"—to unite white voters behind policies that feed into their unfounded fears, fears that are in turn fed by The Myth. Few are willing to say that Black voters are lazier and routinely abuse government programs, but many politicians eagerly appeal to white voters by suggesting that abusers of government programs—once again, the undeserving poor—are essentially siphoning hard-earned money from the pockets of middle-class whites. What's in it for the white voters moved by these appeals? In the end, not much. But for politicians aligned with the rich and the powerful, there is plenty to gain: these strategies exploit underlying racial fears and misperceptions to help the rich and powerful stay that way. In office, they reduce the size of government programs and keep taxes low and profits high, all to the benefit of those at the top tier of the economic pyramid.[11]

As we have seen, false narratives about race and ethnicity have been used to deflect attention away from institutional and systemic causes of inequities and toward the memes of personal responsibility for choices that lead to success. As Hicks and colleagues point out, an emphasis on personal responsibility "blames Black people for their depressed financial position and the inequities they experience," while the "bootstraps" narrative ostensibly provides the way out of that position: "Anyone can achieve economic prosperity through sheer determination, hard work and playing by the rules." Your failure is your fault, your success is up to you. Pay no attention to the man behind the curtain who is pulling the economic levers and making up the rules.[12]

How to Change Deeply Embedded Narratives

It is one thing to note the centrality of narrative change in moving forward. It is quite another to make that happen. While narratives are clearly powerful, they are at the same time a bit slippery, remarkably persistent, and likely difficult to change because they are held somewhat unconsciously in the population at large. Is it simply too much to ask to change the narratives that spring from our nation's founding and speak to our deepest aspirations?

I don't think so. Some influential narratives have indeed changed over time. Witness the change in narrative around LGBTQIA+ rights from the 1960s to the present. One critical impetus for this change has been the recognition that those asking for basic rights are family members, friends, colleagues. It is painful and embarrassing to recall the kind of homophobic rhetoric and slurs my friends and I used growing up in the 1960s and 1970s. But as coming out became more common, more became aware of relatives, friends, neighbors and colleagues who belonged to the LGBTQIA+ community. Thinking about LGBTQIA+ rights in the context of relationships changes the dynamic from "the mainstream versus the other" to "one of us." It is far more difficult to deny rights to people we know and love than it is to an abstract, distant population with whom we believe we have little connection. There may be a lesson here for dispelling The Myth. Helping adherents to The Myth to see lower-income families and families of color as "us" rather than "them" would very likely change the narrative that many carry about low-income families.

Throughout this book, I have interwoven the stories of low-income people, most often people of color. My hope is that their stories of struggle and survival, told in their own words, may help close the distance between poor people and those who would blame them for their poverty. I have chosen the interviewees to *reflect* the disparities we see in the data. They are not a random sampling of the population and should not be thought of as a source of objective data. Rather, they put flesh on the skeletal representation of reality that the data afford. I hope that these stories might connect the reader more closely to the people our economy leaves behind. Their stories in their own words may be more powerful than the reams of data presented in this book. This book is not about data. It's about people who have been denied the opportunity to succeed.

While reducing prejudice at scale is a tall order, some approaches may hold promise.[13] Research by Salma Mousa confirms that racial and ethnic groups that have consistent contact can change their behaviors toward one another, although there are some limits. In one experiment, Christian members of a soccer team in northern Iraq improved their behavior toward Muslim team members; however, that change in behavior didn't necessarily translate to the Muslim population in general.[14] It may be easier to think of one's few Muslim teammates as exceptions to a broad anti-Muslim narrative rather than as evidence suggesting that one ought to revise one's antipathy toward Muslims generally.

While some narratives emerge and collapse with historical episodes ("house prices never fall nationwide"), many of our deepest-held narratives are entrenched over decades and will likely be very difficult to change. Psychologists recognize that "entrenched norms are an obstacle to social change." One promising method for altering persistent norms employs key influencers to spread messages about norms in social groups. For example, providing information about drinking norms to the most influential students in a high school can change their behavior, with effects on perceptions of drinking across the entire high school class. This strategy of encouraging behavior change among "social referents" can be used to modify social norms generally.[15]

Research also suggests that false perceptions can be changed by engaging "those who have the experience of being disempowered and marginalized . . . to partner with policymakers to make more evidence-based decisions." We have a strong tendency to rely on our own experience and our own powers of imagination, even when others are the experts on the matter at hand. Gaining perspective from others has been shown to be a "powerful tool for changing judgments and opinions about marginalized groups." Researchers note a number of hurdles to clear in bringing these experts into the decision-making fold. Decisionmakers, like the rest of us, tend to overweight the opinions of those with whom they have frequent interactions. They might thus discount the perspectives of those who have actually experienced disadvantage. Determining who are the appropriate experts in the experience of inequality is contentious, as decisionmakers disagree on which experts are "legitimate, persuasive, credible and constructive" and which should be dismissed as "rude complainers."[16]

Echoing the widespread misperceptions of racial inequity discussed earlier, Michael Norton and Dan Ariely find that Americans dramatically underestimate the actual level of wealth inequality in the United States.[17] Respondents to a nationally representative 2005 survey were given the choice between a very unequal distribution like that of the United States, a more equitable distribution like that of Sweden (where the top quintile owns 36 percent of wealth), and a hypothetical equal distribution. On a hopeful note, and especially germane to the issue of changing the narrative, 47 percent preferred Sweden's wealth distribution, 43 percent preferred the equal distribution, and 10 percent preferred to leave the US distribution as it was. Those notions of the ideal distribution were shared across all demographic groups, political affiliations, genders, and income classes, with only modest variations. (Results by race and ethnicity were not tabulated.) Overall, people claim they wish for a distribution more equitable than even their mistakenly optimistic estimate of the current distribution.[18]

14 How to Get There: A Program to Build Human and Financial Capital

The wreckage that our system leaves behind is real, tangible, and personal. Millions suffer a loss of human capital—the accumulated education, training, skills and work experience that can allow each of us to contribute to the economy in the way that best suits our native abilities and interests—and financial capital. Thus we need to focus on building an economy that equitably provides access to education, employment, and wealth.[1]

The rough tallying we've done of the immense losses inherent in the current systems—which should be viewed as potential gains if they are eradicated—suggests that the proposed investments in building human and financial capital will pay back handsomely. But it seems prudent to explicitly tally the costs entailed in making the proposed changes, rough though the reckoning may be.

Early Childhood Education

I focus first on the very beginning of lives. Economic, medical, neurological, and sociological research all confirm the centrality of supporting early childhood development—particularly important from birth but extending at least to kindergarten—in setting children up for lifetime success.[2] As many have noted, the gap between resources available for education and enrichment from years zero to five and years five and older is tremendous. Estimates vary, but the United States spends on average between $500 and $1,500 per child annually in the first five years of life versus $13,000 per child annually for the next thirteen years. And yet these early years appear most important for development and success in adulthood. They are also the years in which most parents earn the smallest portion of their lifetime income and are least able to borrow and could thus benefit most from assistance. In these important senses, we are notably lopsided in our programmatic and financial focus on secondary versus preschool education.[3]

As we've seen, the United States has fallen well behind other countries in its attention to early childhood education, highlighting the critical *choices* we have made as a country in designing a system that makes it difficult for many to succeed, starting from birth. One might wish for a free market solution to the problem of early childhood education, but that's not likely to occur, for at least three reasons. First, decisions about early childhood education by parents bear consequences not only for themselves but also for their children, the future communities in which their children live, and the public generally. The first of these is critical for many elements of economic brokenness—children do not get to choose their families' income, wealth, place of residence, or access to health care. And yet these starting conditions make a huge difference to economic success later in life. These "externalities" or "spillovers" are problems that most economists and policymakers agree cannot be solved by markets.

Second, the quality of early childhood programs is difficult to observe. In the absence of the information needed to make decisions about childcare, free markets cannot guarantee good outcomes for parents or children. Third, as just mentioned, decisions about early childcare most often occur during families' most-stressed financial circumstances. The inability to borrow against future earnings—a well-documented credit-market failure—implies that many parents with low income during early adult years will underinvest in early childhood education.[4]

The racial and economic inequities in early childhood outcomes are dramatic. From birth weight to overall health and cognition measures at age five to degree of food insecurity, children in low-income families fare significantly worse than their luckier counterparts.[5] Black and Hispanic children are respectively 17 and 15 percentage points less likely to be ready for school than their white counterparts; a good portion of this gap is related to the disparities across racial and ethnic populations in parental income, maternal education, and employment.[6] Resources for early childhood are not only inadequate, they are also quite unequally distributed.

Successful early childhood education programs have focused not only on providing childcare for disadvantaged families, but on supporting language skills, cognitive development, socioemotional skills that facilitate task orientation, independence and communication, supports for parental involvement, and routine medical checkups.[7]

Ultimately, the promise of early childhood education lies in the sustained boost it provides for participants. Sneha Elango, Jorge Luis García, James Heckman, and Andrés Hojman provide a thorough review of four demonstration programs that began in the early 1960s, the 1970s, and the mid-1980s. These pilots provided invaluable data and experience that was used subsequently to design the Head Start and Early Head Start programs. Participants in each of these programs were selected randomly, avoiding the problem of self-selection that plagues many social interventions. (Self-selection means that participants may *choose* to participate, perhaps because they possess characteristics that would have made them more successful even without the benefits of the program, thus clouding inferences about the effects of the program.)[8]

The authors conclude that all of the programs provided important early-stage effects, such as improvements in IQ and school readiness. For those studies that allowed for follow-up measurements in adulthood, significant improvements were reported in high school graduation rates, employment, income, health, probability of participation in welfare, and propensity toward criminal activity. Where they can be measured, the programs' effects are more significant for children that begin in more disadvantaged circumstances.[9] A study focusing on two of these programs found the overall benefit-to-cost ratios to be 6.6:1 and 3.2:1, respectively. The authors suggest that these estimates likely understate the benefits that one can expect from more recent and better-designed programs.[10] This is powerful evidence of the efficacy of early childhood support. These investments pay back their costs many times over.

A more recent study revisits the now-grown participants in two early childhood programs and finds significant improvements in lifetime income, health outcomes, incidence of crime, and parental income. The returns to these programs are sizable, even as the costs are substantial. Recently available data for adults from the Perry Preschool Project who are now age fifty-four show sustained and substantial benefits—even at this age, participants have higher average earnings, are 26 percent more likely to be employed, and are 11 percent more likely to be in good health.[11] Thus despite the costs, the researchers find an overall benefit-cost ratio of 7.3:1 for the two programs across males and females.[12]

In view of these results and the observation that benefits appear to accrue disproportionately to the disadvantaged, Heckman, a Nobel-winning economist, favors a targeted or means-tested approach. "Every child needs quality early childhood education," he notes. "Those most in need should receive the most help from policy makers. Those with means do best on their own—and that is best for everyone."[13]

Careful evaluative work by many economists and practitioners over decades demonstrates the remarkable potential of a well-targeted and systematic approach to early childhood education. The key features of the most effective programs include starting at birth, providing continuous center-based care (full-day, all week, all year), providing transportation to these centers, focusing on building cognitive and social-emotional skills, enabling consistent parental engagement in providing a supportive family life, recognizing the importance of health and nutrition, employing highly trained educators and staff—in general, a "whole child" approach to early education.[14] Such programs are expensive. But if offered consistently to children from disadvantaged backgrounds, whose other options for early childhood education are of poor quality, the payoffs are likely very high—many multiples of the cost. And those payoffs benefit not only the children and their parents but also the community more broadly, as more adults thrive, supported by the building block arguably most essential to the formation of human capital: a stable, safe, enriching childhood.[15]

Cost estimate High-quality early childhood education is expensive. Drawing on work by Heckman and colleagues, such programs would cost about $21,200 per student annually.[16] About twenty million children aged five and under currently reside in the United States.[17] If we assume for the sake of argument that one-half of those do not have the family resources to pay for early education, the total annual cost of providing early childhood education for these children would be $212 billion per year, assuming the annual per-child figure noted above.[18] Full support for half of all children this age may be too generous. If we scale back the level of public support as families approach median income, then the cost could be lowered to below $200 billion. Apart from reparations, this constitutes one of the largest costs of the programs I recommend, but it is also likely the one with the greatest long-term benefits and the best research-tested results.

As Art Rolnick, a former director of research at the Minneapolis Federal Reserve Bank and long-time advocate of early childhood education says,

"It might be expensive, but it's actually more expensive not to do it."[19] Lower rates of employment, lower earnings for those employed, worse health outcomes—all of these losses and more will continue to occur in the absence of robust early childhood programs.

Using Our Community College System More Effectively: School-to-Work Education Programs

Many hold up the four-year liberal arts degree as the gold standard of post–high school academic achievement. While I am a product of such an education and feel privileged to have had exposure to a broad array of disciplines, I recognize that the four-year liberal arts degree may not be ideal for all students. Indeed, the nation's community colleges provide vital educational services to a very large proportion of our undergraduates—about 41 percent of all undergraduates in 2019 attended one of the country's roughly 1,200 community colleges. And community colleges disproportionately serve students of color; more than half of Native American and Hispanic college students are in community colleges, along with about two in five African Americans and Asian/Pacific Islanders. While preparation for transfer to a four-year institution is the goal for some community college attendees, community colleges do much more than prepare students to transfer elsewhere.[20]

In particular, community colleges have for decades served as key sources of technical training, offering degrees and certificate programs for careers in medicine, information technology, manufacturing, engineering, and hospitality, to name a few.[21] Despite the efforts of community colleges to date, employers in medicine, IT, engineering, manufacturing, and other sectors chronically complain about a shortage of skilled workers. Indeed, citing a shortage of skilled workers is so common at business gatherings that it became a running joke among economists who speak to business gatherings—"I'll bet they mentioned a shortage of skilled workers. Did they talk about raising wages?" That's the glib Econ 101 response to the observation of a shortage of any kind: pay more for the stuff you need more of.[22]

It is fair to say that despite their well-intended efforts to train the skilled workforce that employers need, many community colleges are struggling. Enrollments are declining and have been since well before the pandemic. For those students who enroll, rates of degree and certificate attainment are chronically low.[23] And in part due to perceptions that community college students are less academically able and less skilled than peers at four-year institutions, employers may be hesitant to rely on community colleges as key sources of talent.[24]

A solution both to these woes—and, more importantly, to the problem of providing educational opportunity more equally—may lie in a more uniform use of pipeline programs.[25] These well-articulated pathways from schooling to employment incorporate deep partnerships with businesses, curricula that propagate backward into high schools, training that aligns neatly with employers' desired job skills, and job exposure through internships, apprenticeships, cooperatives, and ultimately placement in well-paying and stable positions. This kind of program has the potential to aid significantly in building human capital for those who otherwise would be left behind.[26]

Internships and cooperatives have long been a feature of the community college landscape, apprenticeships less so. Less than one-tenth of 1 percent of the US workforce is engaged in apprenticeships today, despite their widespread adoption in developed Western European economies.[27]

Pipeline programs are quite a bit newer, and much less widespread, than traditional internship and coop programs. A typical pipeline program involves a partnership with an employer who works with the community college and a regional high school system to design courses that include hands-on training to prepare students for work in the partner company (or companies), or in their industry more generally. Such programs typically include the following elements:

- Identifying local and regional employer and labor market needs
- Modifying existing courses or developing "new courses with direct employer input to reflect the skills required for positions they need to or anticipate to fill"
- Sharing start-up and other costs across partners
- Adapting programs to suit nontraditional students with limited time and financial resources[28]

A leading example of such a program is the Pathways in Technology Early College High School (P-TECH) program pioneered in Brooklyn in 2011. Today, P-TECH covers 127 schools in ten US states with more than 600 industry partners. Programs vary to some extent, but they typically include one or more employer partners, focus on developing skills valuable for STEM careers, and provide significant job exposure with partner employers via mentoring and paid internships or apprenticeships. Most P-TECH programs have not been around long enough to produce a crop of seasoned graduates, so evaluation of the programs' success in realizing pathways to employment is not yet available. Because many students in the earliest New York P-TECH programs were selected by lottery, an evaluation study that takes advantage of this random assignment is underway. The results, according to interim measures, appear promising. The New York program, at least, has been successful in serving otherwise-underserved minority populations: 85 percent of students entering the New York City P-TECH programs self-reported as Hispanic or Black.[29]

Research indicates that this may be a successful model for community colleges seeking to build human capital, especially among disadvantaged populations.[30] Improved earnings associated with similar career-oriented technical education programs at community colleges range in one careful study from 14 to 45 percent, with the increases varying by field and length of study. Health-related certificates produce the greatest increase in earnings, followed by certifications in agricultural and natural resource–related careers.[31] Taking into account the cost of attaining certifications and degrees, the returns to higher education—the net of increased earnings less the cost of education—are quite high and have risen in recent decades.[32] This rise in returns, coupled with increased Pell grant funding, motivated increases in college enrollments. But the returns only benefit those who *complete* their degree and certification programs, and completion rates at community colleges have been perennially low. This has been especially troublesome for poorer students, who may run out of funding or need to leave school to take jobs or both, prior to obtaining their degree.[33]

An issue to consider in such programs is who controls the design of curricula. Some schools are reluctant to turn over too much curriculum design to a partner business or group of businesses, fearing that their school will devolve into a specialized training site. This might be attractive to businesses, whose training costs will be at least partly borne by the community college and in turn by whatever entities fund them. The community college, however, needs to maintain academic integrity while balancing that goal with the need to provide predictable pathways to employment, especially for disadvantaged students.

While promising and beginning to spread, pipeline programs that truly integrate private-sector participation are not nearly so widespread as they could be. A pipeline program that was initiated by Toyota was adopted by the National Association of Manufacturers with the goal of scaling nationwide, but as of 2021 it had been adopted by only 38 of the 1,200 or so community colleges.[34] Despite support from the federal and state governments, "employers still largely play a limited role in informing community college career and technical education programs."[35]

More widespread use of such programs, and more careful research assessing impact, would almost surely lead to significant improvements in acquiring the human capital needed for economic stability and success. A 2019 report from the Aspen Institute's bipartisan Economic Strategy Group agrees, proposing significant investment in community colleges. In their view, the investment, which would take the form of a federal grant program with performance incentives, would achieve the key goals of "(1) increasing the supply of college-educated workers; (2) responding to unmet demand for midcareer skill development and training; and (3) providing better pathways into the workforce for non-college-educated workers through the expansion of high-quality, short-term certificate programs."[36]

Such a push might reap the benefits that the United States enjoyed from the earlier high school movement in this country, a period during which the country made substantial investments in secondary education. As we saw, from 1910 to 1935, the high school graduation rate increased from below 15 percent to 40 percent. This increased the productivity of the US workforce relative to that of the rest of the world and contributed to growth in per capita income.[37] A more intelligent use of our community college system might achieve similar gains.

Cost estimate   A high-quality community college program costs $6,000 to $10,000 per student per year, with costs varying depending on the field of training or study.[38] The costs of pipeline programs might well be greater, although those costs could be shared by the public and the private sector. Assuming that per-student costs are $12,000 per year, 1 million additional pipeline slots would cost $12 billion per year. A ballpark estimate for a program that would build human capital by significantly improving the flow through community college programs to employment would be about $25 billion or more annually for overlapping two-year cohorts. Adding funds for work stipends and competitive grants as recommended in Holzer could bring the total to a generous $50 billion.[39]

Restructuring the Workplace

Earlier we discussed the prevalence of low-quality jobs in our economy, a shift from the 1950s and 1960s when employers of many stripes provided high wages, excellent benefits, and job security. Today's workers would drool at what their predecessors got. But the loss of worker power amid the dissolution of unions has led us to a new kind of employer-employee relationship that features low wages, poor benefits, little job security, and otherwise-poor working conditions.

One can hope that well-intentioned companies will right this ship, and a few have indeed adopted better working conditions. Companies that implement such changes enjoy improved productivity, higher worker engagement, and greater profitability, so self-interest could prove a significant motivator.[40]

But relying on firms to "do the right thing" is unlikely to be a systemic solution. In any given industry, the first firms to try high-road measures put themselves at a competitive disadvantage, as raising wages and adding benefits and scheduling stability increase their costs. If these first-mover firms are lucky, improvements in productivity and worker retention will eventually offset these costs. But making the leap without the certainty of a positive payoff within a reasonable time horizon is a difficult ask for the many companies that operate in highly competitive environments with tight profit margins. Even benevolent companies are self-interested, and relying exclusively on their good will would almost surely leave the bulk of the low-wage workforce behind. A more coordinated solution is likely required.

One approach to fixing the suite of problems associated with lousy jobs is to address each of the attributes one by one. Here I consider reforms of wages, health benefits, childcare, work schedules, and paid family medical leave.

Wages

States and municipalities have enacted new minimum wage laws in the past decade, in many cases establishing or moving toward a $15-per-hour floor.

Individual corporations have taken similar actions. As of January 1, 2023, only California, Massachusetts, Washington, and the District of Columbia have at least a $15 minimum wage. Eight states—Maryland, Florida, Delaware, Connecticut, New Jersey, Rhode Island, Virginia, and Illinois—plan to raise their minimum wages to $15 no later than 2025. A number of other states will increase their minimum wage annually to keep up with increases in consumer prices.[41] The federal minimum wage of $7.25 is the official or de facto minimum wage in twenty states.

Whether raising minimum wages helps or hurts workers remains a subject of debate, and much of the debate splits across partisan lines. Increased wages are obviously a good thing for those who remain employed, but a high minimum wage can also cause unemployment or reduced work hours: if employers must pay workers more, they might hire fewer of them and might lay off existing staff or reduce their hours. Thus the crux of the issue is whether the wage gains of those who remain employed—net of any reduction in hours—outweigh the earnings losses of those who are laid off. The jury is still out to some extent, but many more economists are now willing to entertain minimum wage increases as part of a suite of solutions for low-income workers, and I am among those favorably inclined.[42] The most recent evidence, from a careful evaluation of Seattle's city-wide minimum wage increase, suggests that a higher minimum wage yields a net *benefit* in earnings.[43]

Ellora Derenoncourt and Claire Montialoux have undertaken a powerful study of the benefits of expanded minimum wages. Their analysis looks at the results of Congress's decision, in 1966, to extend the federal minimum wage to cover workers in previously excluded fields, such as agriculture, restaurants, nursing homes, and other sectors in which black workers were disproportionately employed. The study finds a 20 percent reduction in the black-white wage gap in those industries, with no discernible negative effect on employment.[44] This extraordinary result should lend courage to those like me who want to see minimum wages increased.

Smaller businesses with lower profit margins and less ability to raise prices are more likely to be harmed by a minimum wage increase than are major employers, as small companies may find it harder to absorb what is effectively a transfer of profits to workers. As an offset, the federal government could offer a tax credit to smaller employers who augment wages for low-wage workers. David Neumark suggests that such a mechanism, if properly designed, could be more effective than a minimum wage, raising wages without unduly harming small businesses or employment. Depending on specifics, such a program would cost $10–15 billion per year, according to Neumark's estimates.[45] Such a policy could also be combined with a rise in the minimum wage, excluding larger and more profitable firms from the tax credit while providing the credit to smaller firms less able to bear the cost of a wage hike.

What would be the direct impact on incomes of a $15 wage, assuming that adverse employment effects are not significant?[46] For a full-time worker, a $15 wage amounts to about $30,000 of annual income—above the current poverty level for a family of four, but not by much, and not enough to cover a real household budget even in a low-cost US city. Still, raising minimum wages would increase incomes for a large proportion of families. We've seen that, under a variety of income measures, roughly one-fifth to one-quarter of all families earn less than $30,000 annually after taxes and government transfers. A recent study found more than 50 million US workers earning less than $15 per hour. Nearly two-thirds of working women of color fall short of the $15-per-hour benchmark.[47]

Turning to the effects of a minimum wage increase on the economy overall, simply put, some would win and some would lose. That is, the increase in earnings to low-wage workers would come at the expense of net income earned by business owners. On average, a rise in labor cost can be expected in part to reduce profits, as many firms will not be able to fully pass on this cost increase, due to competitive pressures. The part of the labor cost that is absorbed by firms reduces income to business owners.[48] The fraction of the cost that's not absorbed in profits is passed on in higher prices and acts as a tax on consumers. If a one-time increase in wages leads to a one-time increase in prices, this would partially reduce the gain in purchasing power of incomes (reducing their "real" or inflation-adjusted value), effectively taxing away some of the income gains induced by the rise in wages.

Conventional economic models suggest that, while a higher minimum wage would increase prices somewhat, the inflation-adjusted earnings of low-income workers would still rise significantly—that is, their wages would rise faster than prices. Any loss of employment that results from businesses cutting back hiring due to higher wages would further reduce the income gain. But it is quite likely that the net effect on earned income for low-wage workers would be positive, as the income increases for those who remain employed would be quite a bit greater than losses for the much smaller number who would lose their jobs. According to the Congressional Budget Office, raising the minimum wage is an almost purely redistributive action: the net effect on total income after adjusting for inflation—net gains for low-wage workers minus losses of business income to higher-income owners—is nearly zero.[49]

Cost estimate   Because the loss of profits to businesses is largely offset by the gains to low-wage workers, the overall cost of a minimum wage increase is very small. This same logic applies to more widespread increase in wages that address chronically low pay. This is a tradeoff that we should be willing to undertake, given the high-value benefits to low-wage workers and the relatively low-value uses to which businesses these days direct profits—stock repurchases, for example.[50] The costs of a tax incentive to smaller businesses that raise wages would be moderate, on the order of $10–40 billion depending on the scale of the incentive.

All things considered, I suggest that *wage increases* in general should be firmly on the table. Many of the other improvements in human and financial capital-building that I recommend, such as improved early childhood education, improved access to health benefits, assistance with childcare expenses, and community college pipelines, should also improve wages over time. But in the meantime, we need to ensure that families take home earnings sufficient to cover basic expenses.

Health Benefits

It is a consequence of historical accident that health benefits are largely obtained through employment. A shortage of workers during World War II, coupled with a federal freeze on wages, made the provision of health insurance the way for employers to compete for employees.[51] Labor markets have certainly changed since that era, but the coupling of health insurance to employment status remains. Fortunately, there are new options for obtaining health benefits outside of employment. The Affordable Care Act (ACA) has increased the fraction of Americans insured in part by augmenting the available choices for direct purchase of insurance outside of employment, through federal and state marketplaces. As of 2020, 54 percent of the population was insured through an employment-based plan,

10.5 percent were covered via direct purchase of insurance outside of employment (3.3 percent through marketplace coverage), and a bit more than a third were covered by public insurance—Medicare, Medicaid, and veterans' benefits. The remaining 9 percent of the population, 28 million people, were uninsured.[52]

It is unfortunate that health benefits are so tightly linked to employment, as losing work often means losing health insurance. But even among those with jobs, access to health benefits is far from even. While access to health benefits is nearly universal among high-wage earners, only about 40 percent of those in the bottom 25 percent of the wage distribution receive health benefits. The share receiving coverage drops to about one-fourth for the lowest 10 percent of wage earners.[53]

The uninsured generally receive worse health care. They often enter the health system through the emergency room, when their needs are most acute, rather than obtaining preventive care or care that can manage ongoing conditions.[54] Still, the cost of health care for the uninsured is substantial. Prior to the ACA, these costs averaged $63 billion per year from 2011–2013. From 2015–17, after ACA implementation, they dropped to a still-hefty $42 billion per year—a price tag that has likely increased since then, in part due to the economic downturn induced by the COVID-19 pandemic. These costs are largely borne by federal, state, and local governments through reimbursements to providers.[55]

The federal government could increase the penalties levied on smaller employers for not offering insurance coverage. The court challenges to such an action would likely be formidable. In addition, small businesses might genuinely find it difficult to cover the costs of either insurance coverage or a hefty fine. That could necessitate some aid in terms of tax relief or direct subsidies to these businesses or to the uninsured, the cost of which could exceed the current federal expenditures on the uninsured.

Cost estimate   Whatever the mechanism for providing better health care for the uninsured, the cost would be substantial. We can develop an estimate starting with the observation that the uninsured incur a bit less than one-half the health costs of the insured.[56] I believe the goal should be to provide the 28 million uninsured with national-average health care coverage, which would roughly double annual health spending for this group from $42 billion to $84 billion.

Childcare

As we have seen, low-income people face a sizable mismatch between household incomes and the cost of childcare. Far too many lower-income households spend high fractions of their income on the childcare that enables them to go to work. For a family at twice the poverty level or lower, childcare costs 35 percent of income, an unsustainable burden.[57] The US government recommends that families spend no more than 7 percent on childcare. It is time to subsidize the cost of childcare, ensuring that low-income households spend a reasonable amount on childcare expenses.

Cost estimate   The federal government already subsidizes childcare, but it could do more. Increasing subsidies so that low-income families would not have to spend more than 7 percent of their income on childcare would add about $8.5 billion to the annual federal budget.[58]

Work Schedules

Congress has recognized the cost to working families of unpredictable work schedules—hours that vary from week to week, often with little notice, complicating workers' busy lives and making their earnings unpredictable. Correspondingly, the Schedules That Work Act was introduced in the Senate in 2015 by Massachusetts Democrat Elizabeth Warren and in the House in 2019 by Connecticut Democrat Rosa DeLauro. The bill has been referred to relevant subcommittees, but no action has been taken. The bill provides for a request to change work schedule, requirements to provide baseline schedules, advance notice of at least fourteen days for changes in schedules, a $75-per-day fine for employers that fail to provide adequate notice of schedule changes, mandatory rest time between work shifts, and time-and-a-half compensation for shifts that don't allow for the required rest time between shifts.[59] If passed, this bill would appear to address many of the relevant concerns surrounding scheduling for low-wage workers.

Cost estimate   I assume that this is approximately a wash in terms of cost to the employer, as the cost of reduced flexibility would likely be offset by the increase in employee productivity and engagement. A separate but related change—workers moving from part-time to full-time employment and thus qualifying for benefits—would impose costs on the businesses affected. As with wage increases, this would entail a transfer from owners (read: profits) to workers. There may be room in profits, especially among larger corporations, to absorb such a cost increase.[60]

Paid Family Medical Leave

Paid family medical leave (PFML) would require employers to provide paid leave for specific medical needs, including birth, adoption, or foster-care placement of a child; care of a spouse, child, or parent with a serious health condition; or a serious personal health condition that leaves the employee unable to perform their job. Current federal law requires employers with more than fifty employees to provide *unpaid* time off under these circumstances. As of mid-2021, eight states and the District of Columbia had enacted paid family medical leave laws, with four more moving to implement new laws in 2022.[61] As of 2021, the provisions in the eight states plus DC that required PFML at that time covered about a quarter of US workers.[62] The state measures vary in terms of the types of leave that are paid, the amount of time during which employees can take paid leave, which employees qualify, who pays for the cost of their absence and how much they pay, and what fraction of salary the leave benefit must cover.

Cost estimate Existing state programs tax earnings at a rate of 0.3–1.2 percent to fund PFML. Expanding PFML to the states that do not already provide it could be funded by taxing about 0.75 percent of salary for residents in those states, with the levy paid by some combination of employers and employees. That would amount to about $50 billion per year, shared by workers and employers.[63]

Changing Work Norms

The alternative to this piecemeal approach to altering working conditions among low-wage workers is to more generally change the norms surrounding work—the set of prevailing expectations for the explicit and implicit agreements between workers and their employers concerning wages, benefits, and work conditions. It is too simplistic to appeal to an earlier era in which employers "took care" of their employees, as companies during that period provided benefits and compensation in response to the influence of labor unions that no longer hold much sway. But from this era we can infer that the coincident rise of labor unions and better working conditions in both union and nonunion jobs reflects more than chance. Labor unions

organized workers to exert collective power over working conditions, coun-
terbalancing the power of large corporations and achieving improvements
in compensation, benefits, and conditions for their own members as well
as nonunion workers.

What this implies is that finding our way back to better working conditions for low-wage workers entails *a fundamental shift in power toward
workers and away from corporations*. At the heart of such a change is the
recognition that economic stability for all workers contributes to overall
economic stability. If this shift in norms were only about taking from the
corporate rich and giving to the working poor, it might stand little chance
of success. But acknowledgement that such a shift need not be a zero-sum
game could make it more palatable to all sectors of the economy.

Housing

Housing is foundational for economic success and stability. As graphically
depicted in Matthew Desmond's *Evicted*, the upheaval entailed in repeatedly moving from one residence to another makes it impossible for children to benefit fully from schooling and for parents to be productive at
work. No one should be scrounging for decent and affordable living space.

But many millions do. Pam A. was evicted in August 2021 and had to
find new lodgings within weeks. Her meager income, coupled with the
requirements of her housing voucher—if she can't pay her utility bills and
electricity or her heat is shut off, she risks losing the voucher—makes housing stability a far-off dream.[64] Mariela, a recently arrived immigrant, shares
her five-room apartment with six family members across three generations.
She shares a bedroom with her partner and her daughter. From January
through March 2022, their rent was paid by a refugee agency. After that,
they had to figure out how to pay on their own.[65] Rosada has been in the
same apartment for five years, but it is "not high-quality—it has rats and
bug infestation."[66] Tasha moved from a home in a middle-class Boston
neighborhood to public housing at the age of eight. She said that while her
previous neighborhood was "quiet and nice," her new home was "noisy,
with lots of gun violence . . . I heard a lot of gun shots and thought oh, my
goodness, what is this?" People were "not as nice and used language I was
not used to hearing." Schooling was different, kids were more aggressive.
She called that move "definitely traumatizing."[67] Safe, affordable housing
makes a huge difference, and its absence can leave long-lasting scars.

The number of adequate affordable housing units falls well short of the need. Here "adequate" includes working plumbing, heating and electricity. Affordability is determined from income limits set by the Department of Housing and Urban Development for its rental programs, and varies by household size and location.[68] A 2017 Urban Institute study estimated that for every hundred affordable units needed by extremely low-income households, about forty-six were available. There are essentially no counties in the country that have an adequate stock of affordable housing, although the situation is worst in urban counties, where such housing is available for only forty-two of every hundred families that need it.[69] The shortage has been made worse by the demolition of many affordable units over the past two decades.[70]

In terms of raw numbers, roughly 6.8 million extremely low–income families do not have adequate, affordable rental housing. These families are largely concentrated (almost 90 percent) in metropolitan areas; two-thirds reside in counties with populations above 250,000. Roughly half of the available affordable units are "naturally affordable" without federal or other assistance.[71] Extremely low-income renters are disproportionately families of color: 20 percent of Black (non-Hispanic) households fall in this category, as do 18 percent of Native American and Alaska Native households, 14 percent of Hispanics, and 10 percent of Asians, compared to just 6 percent of White, non-Hispanic households.[72] We clearly have a long way to go before we meet the needs of affordable housing just for the very poorest of our residents.

Analyses of the sources of the housing shortage often point to local zoning restrictions as one of the leading culprits, although of course increased family income, aided by a robust safety net, would significantly improve housing affordability.[73] Rising materials and labor costs contribute as well, but a shortage of land appears to be the most significant contributor to underbuilding.[74] Given the plethora of local and regional zoning restrictions, some have appealed for a coordinated, top-down approach to offsetting zoning restrictions, perhaps by making certain federal funds contingent on relaxation of zoning restrictions for development of affordable housing.[75] Given the share of land cost in the cost of most metropolitan-areas housing, increasing the density of housing units is one of the most obvious ways to reduce their cost, and that requires a nationwide shift in zoning policies. But increased density might also require a shift in community norms.

Jim Parrott and Mark Zandi suggest using community development block grants (CDBG) and transportation aid—which in 2021 amounted to $9.2 billion and $74 billion, respectively—as leverage to effect zoning changes.[76] After all, affordable housing development is one of the explicit goals of the CDBG state program, so targeting funds to communities that make progress with affordable-housing goals is consistent with the intent of the program.[77] In total, the federal government grants over $1 trillion annually to state and local governments, so there is considerable potential in using these funds as a means to achieve affordable housing and other economic development goals.[78] Almost all zoning—single-family requirements, minimum lot sizes, and so on—is local, and local resistance to rezoning for affordable housing is considerable. The NIMBY (not in my backyard) movement resists many kinds of development, whether smaller, denser housing; public housing or other housing with affordability requirements; or housing for the homeless.[79] NIMBY residents may not employ the explicit language of The Myth—"We worked hard, we don't want poor people living near us, they're not like us, we can't trust them"—to maintain their geographic and economic segregation from poverty. But this is exactly what they achieve by supporting restrictive zoning.

Cost estimate   Using existing state and local transfer programs to encourage affordable-housing development is a promising idea. This will involve attaching to these programs incentives that strongly encourage reforms to zoning, transit, and other policy areas with the goal of promoting housing construction and density. Those additional incentives could entail costs in terms of additional transfers or lost tax revenue. A very healthy budget for this effort would target 10 percent of current transfers, or about $100 billion.

Given the current housing gap of about 6.8 million very low-income housing units, an ambitious goal might be to provide funding to close this gap over ten years. At a cost of roughly $200,000 per unit for higher-density units, this would add $136 billion annually for ten years.

Transit-Oriented Development

My reading of the research literature and history is that we are unlikely ever to be able to build sufficient affordable housing stock in the highest-cost urban areas. Even after the biggest housing crisis in modern history, the premiums paid for housing in vibrant cities remain enormous. In New York, Chicago, Boston, San Francisco, Los Angeles, Miami, and Washington, DC, prices have more than rebounded: at one-and-a-half to four times higher than the national average, housing in these cities is at least as expensive as it was prior to the 2007–2009 housing crisis.[80]

It is simply not realistic to consider construction or repurposing of millions of housing units in these high-cost areas. It should be more feasible to build affordable housing in satellite communities around these hubs. However, an affordable residence is of little value if employment and services (groceries, health care, childcare, and so on) are not easily accessible. As a result, this solution requires a critical complement to housing: affordable transportation that brings workers from satellite communities to their places of work.

"Transit-oriented development" (TOD) and "transit-adjacent development" have been on economic development practitioners' radar for some time. The idea is to build housing and complementary spaces in lower-cost areas alongside public transit, or to bring public transit to new housing in such areas. TOD projects can provide affordable housing, connect workers to other cities that have jobs, foster stable employment, and reduce space used for roads and parking. But often, the benefits of TOD accrue to those who least need economic help—the well-off and wealthy. As Tracy Corley and colleagues note, TOD projects too often develop property near a transit node "with little or no effort to improve the quality of life or advance the economic prospects of people and businesses in the district and surrounding neighborhoods."[81]

Establishing new transit and strengthening existing transit often raises property values, sometimes *in advance of* project completion, which risks driving out poorer residents, often residents of color, rather than bringing them more affordable housing. A number of studies, most of which are quite recent and focus largely on US experience, have found mixed evidence about the links between TOD and gentrification. While the evidence is not unequivocal, on balance, it appears that TOD risks some degree of gentrification, so this is a concern that needs to be addressed in designing transit-oriented policies aimed at reducing poverty.[82]

An important component of the TOD strategy is what kind of transportation to partner with affordable housing and community development. Much of the discussion around transit centers on light rail and commuter rail. Where rail lines already exist, that can be a reasonable component of the solution. But part of the problem is that rail lines do not serve many lower-income communities, especially those located in smaller cities, towns, and rural areas.[83] Just over 4 percent of all workers used public transportation of any kind in 2021.[84] In 2019, almost 90 percent of commuters outside metro areas who used public transportation rode buses.[85]

Building new rail is costly, perhaps prohibitively costly, at over $100 million per mile in the United States, and that does not factor in the costs of obtaining rights-of-way.[86] As a lower-cost alternative, bus and minibus systems may be a viable way to connect affordable suburbs to nearby high-cost cities, enabling people to get more easily from home to work without imposing the high ecological and economic costs of driving. Electric or hydrogen–fuel cell buses, which are now readily available, would help to mitigate the climate impacts of transportation.[87] Los Angeles, San Francisco, Chicago, New York, and Seattle have all committed to full electrification of their bus systems no later than 2040.[88]

The evidence to date suggests that while TOD is a promising mode of economic development, achieving success on all desired fronts is difficult. Furthermore, TOD relies on local, cross-agency collaboration that is in short supply. But those obstacles should not overshadow the critical importance of access to transit for lower-income workers. Well-located transit can enable workers to live in more affordable areas while providing ready access to the jobs that will help them succeed.[89]

Cost estimate   The transit infrastructure required to make affordable housing part of a "complete neighborhood"—a community that offers residents a full array of readily accessible services—represents an additional cost to the housing plan.[90] Replacing diesel and hybrid buses with electric buses would likely *save* on total lifetime operating costs, although initial purchase costs are typically high.[91] Communities that require additions to their bus fleets could face significant upfront cost, though of course much lower cost than that required for a rail system.[92] Consider here a crude estimate. Among the roughly 5,000 US cities with population greater than 5,000, if one-half need to implement new bus systems at a cost of $100 per resident, the annual cost of the new vehicles alone would be about $5 billion nationally.[93] Personnel and other costs are roughly 2–3 times capital costs, so a robust electric bus system would cost $15–20 billion nationally, each year.[94]

There is still one firm conclusion to draw with respect to affordable housing, and that is that restrictive zoning lies at the heart of the shortage of affordable housing. Reforming zoning to allow construction of multifamily dwellings in what are now lower-density areas—and especially in areas that feature, or could feature, easy access to public transit—will be essential to closing the affordable housing gap.

Baby Bonds and Reparations

Wealth provides access to educational opportunity, capital for the formation of small businesses, savings for retirement security, and financial stability in the wake of disruptions to employment, income and health. It plays a central role in building human capital and family economic stability.

Both baby bonds and reparations are meant to address inherited inequities in wealth.[95] Proposals for each recognize that our country *created the wealth inequities* in need of redress. While private markets were complicit in creating wealth inequality, policy lies at the heart of the problem. As a consequence, the government bears primary responsibility for fixing this.

Baby Bonds

Baby bonds provide an at-birth deposit of funds into an account whose use may be restricted.[96] As commonly proposed, baby bonds constitute a "big tent" investment, with deposits for children of any background, scaled by family income *and* wealth. Here, means testing is used to efficiently allocate funds where they are most needed, disproportionately benefiting families of color, as their wealth and income tend to be especially low. My affluent kids would have received nothing at birth, appropriately.[97]

Particulars of such a program matter quite a bit, both in terms of how the accounts are structured and how the deposits are paid for. Following the seminal work of William Darity and Darrick Hamilton, I recommend a potentially significant deposit, to be placed in trust until the child reaches age eighteen. Children of families with the least income and wealth could receive deposits of $50,000 or more, and families with above-median wealth would receive small deposits, or no deposits. The funds provided could be use-restricted to ensure they are reserved for asset-enhancing activities at adulthood, such as buying a home, starting a business, or paying for education. Key decisions center on how to invest the accounts in the first eighteen years: Should stocks be included, putting at risk some cohorts whose accounts may decline in value due to a string of bad years in the stock market? Or should the accounts be invested only in secure Treasury bonds and bills, held to maturity to avoid capital losses? If the goal is to provide a reliable source of wealth at adulthood, an argument could be made for focusing only on such safe investments.

Over the past fifteen years, a number of states and cities have implemented programs similar to baby bonds but on a much smaller scale—children's savings account or child development accounts. Save for College, a New York City pilot program, deposits a small amount ($100) into kindergartners' tax-preferred college savings accounts. Other programs provide initial deposits of up to $500 and, in some cases, matching funds if parents contribute to the account. Rather than explicitly trying to close the wealth gap, the aim of these plans has been to encourage families to prepare and save for college. Research suggests that, although the amounts deposited by the state or municipality are modest, students experience improvements in academic performance in grade school and are more focused on attending college following secondary school.[98]

Cost estimate   The approximate cost of baby bonds is relatively simple to estimate. As of 2020, about 3.6 million children are born annually in the United States.[99] If the average deposit is $25,000, and payments taper off for families with net worth above the most recently measured median of $122,000, the total cost would be between and $45 and $65 billion annually, depending on the rate of tapering above the median. A strict cutoff with no deposits above the median yields a cost of about $45 billion. This may sound like a lot, but, by way of comparison, the federal government currently spends more than twice that much annually on prisons, to say nothing of $700 billion on defense. A conservatively invested $25,000 baby bond could grow to $60,000 or more over the course of eighteen years. That amount would represent a sizable down payment toward closing the wealth gap *per child*.

Reparations

While baby bonds have gained increasing attention and support in recent years, reparations remain divisive. I have been counseled after public appearances to stop using the word "reparations," as it apparently offends some (white) audience members. I have chosen not to take this advice.

Despite the common intent of baby bonds and reparations to address generational wealth inequities, the programs differ in three respects. First, baby bonds are a universal program, providing deposits to all families in need, regardless of race. Reparations, in contrast, are designed to target people who can demonstrate a family relationship to an enslaved Black person. Second, because baby bonds provide a seed deposit at birth, the results of this investment accrue some years later, as the child reaches adulthood. Reparations, on the other hand, would provide payment to adults who can immediately benefit from the wealth infusion. Third, because baby bonds are paid only to newborns, no one alive before implementation of such a program receives payment. As a result, the wealth-equalization potential of baby bonds is to be realized entirely in the relatively distant future.

Specifics of reparations programs vary, but the program laid out by Darity and Mullen provides sensible guidelines. They suggest the following:

- The US government should foot the bill.
- Congress should establish a commission that would investigate the history of racial injustice.
- That report would be used to widen public support for a reparations project.
- Eligibility would be limited to US citizens who can prove that they had at least one ancestor who was enslaved in the US and who have self-identified as "Black" for at least twelve years before program enactment.
- The size of the payment should be based on the current differential in average wealth owned by Black versus white families.[100]

A host of important details should be the subject of debate: What are the most effective means for building political support for reparations? Should payment be made as a lump sum, or in installments over time? What information would the federal government use to verify slave ancestry?

I am uncertain at present about the political viability of a significant reparations program. The United States is beset by general political discord, and, more specifically, political coalitions are trying to attract voters by denying the existence and effects of institutional racism. As a pragmatic matter, reparations would also cost a lot. Still, the logic of reparations is compelling, and my heart says it is right. Our citizens created the racial wealth gap, starting with the institution and support of slavery and continuing through the Jim Crow era up until today, building wealth almost exclusively for white families. And Americans have previously recognized the moral responsibility to right a wrong; our nation has paid reparations to Japanese Americans and Alaskans, after all.

There is also good news in terms of changing the narrative on this issue. The trajectory of support among white Americans for reparations is quite distinctly upward. A 2000 survey found only *4 percent* of white Americans in favor of Black reparations. A 2016 survey showed significant progress, with 15 percent of white Americans onboard. Most recently, in 2021, the figure was up to 18 percent. Overall, almost 30 percent of a representative sample of the US public supported reparations in the most recent survey. What has seemed nearly impossible for decades is now closer to hand.[101]

Cost estimate   The cost of reparations would be huge—far greater than the other potential initiatives discussed. Using the aggregate wealth gap as the measure of accumulated disparity, the cost for reparations for Blacks is about $15 trillion. Including Hispanics more than doubles that. Reparations that address the systemic damage inflicted on Indigenous people, reflected in their wealth gap, adds at least another trillion dollars. I have estimated the value of land stolen from Indigenous people at $40 trillion. Even if spread out over thirty or more years, this amounts to more than a trillion dollars per year. Spreading reparations payments out over time may seem like a sensible alternative, but the more spread out the payments are, the smaller the advantages of reparations over baby bonds.[102]

A Non-institutional Reform: Mentors and Allies

In Horatio Alger's formulaic stories, the poor boys (they were always boys) who succeeded were taken under the wing of a benevolent adult man. That extraordinary lift—coupled with hard work and perseverance—propelled them far beyond what was expected of boys who began in their circumstances. As Alger emphasized, his stories were not a recipe for widespread exit from poverty but instead a means of calling attention to the plight of thousands who were unlikely to benefit from divine intervention.[103]

Similarly, in many workplaces, there are opportunities for white male leaders to help women and people of color reach their potential. The 100 Black Men of America mentoring organization says it well: "Mentoring begins with the trust and ability to see everyone's potential. Not every person begins at the same stage, but they all could create a positive impact on society, which begins with the guidance of mentors."[104] The Hispanic mentoring organization *Conexión* links their mission to the sociologist Robert Putnam's pathbreaking work on social capital:

> CONEXION's model is built on the concept of Social Capital ". . . social networks have value." What we saw missing for many people who are at the margins is a lack of access and Conexiónes, or reciprocal networks of value. We created a model that would be intentional about making bridging conexiónes (through the mentors) and bonding networks of value (through the other mentees in the cohort). [The] CONEXION model is Social Capital in action!"[105]

The research documenting objective benefits from mentoring relationships is not deep. Some of the best studies make use of the US Army's system for assigning junior officers to senior officer mentors. The details of this system make it plausible that mentor-mentee pairings are determined by factors other than the attributes of the mentor or mentee. One such study finds that those mentees who worked with a high-performing mentor were significantly more likely to be promoted ahead of schedule. The study's conclusion is that attention should be devoted to the quality of mentors: mentoring per se does not guarantee improved performance, as a low-quality mentor can have no effect or, worse, can lower the performance of the mentee.[106]

A second set of studies examines the outcomes for junior economics faculty randomly assigned to a mentoring program. The studies compare publication rates, outcomes of grant applications, tenure status, and academic employment between program participants and others and finds a significant increase in all measures for participants.[107] While it would be nice to have more research on mentorship, what we know so far suggests that mentoring can significantly improve career outcomes.

At a more personal level, I received the gift of being able to mentor dozens of colleagues and professional contacts over my career. Those relationships provided me a window into the experiences of men and women who often came from backgrounds very different from my white, middle-class roots. In addition, for about a decade, I oversaw the Office of Diversity, Equity, and Inclusion at the Boston Fed.[108] Along with my experiences in economic development and studying racial injustice, these relationships and responsibilities made it abundantly clear to me that my experience was not shared with all my colleagues and professional contacts. I had a wealth of opportunities that were simply not available to my friends of color. In other words, mentoring relationships are good for mentors as well as mentees, and can broaden the thinking of people in positions of influence.

Mentorship relationships will not close all the gaps highlighted in this book. But experience shows they can be powerful equalizers. There is no doubt some opportunity cost involved in devoting time to mentoring that could be spent in other work-related activities. But relative to the magnitudes of loss and opportunity discussed so far, these costs amount to rounding error.

Cost estimate   This initiative is relatively low cost; virtually all the costs are imputed, reflecting the opportunity cost to spending time on mentoring versus other work activities. If we assume for the sake of argument 5 million mentor/mentee pairs working together in a given year, and if we assume that each partnership absorbs an aggregate of one work week per year, and if we further assume an average wage of $100,000 per worker, we arrive at an imputed cost of $20 billion per year. This is a very generous estimate.

Table 14.1 sums the costs of my recommended human and financial capital-building programs.

How do these costs stack up against the losses (or potential gains) that we tallied in part V? As noted in the last line of the table, the total losses come to $14–17 trillion annually. Putting aside for the moment the transfer of wealth involved in reparations (including land theft from Indigenous people), would the expense of $727 billion yield $14 trillion in gains? Probably not. However, these investments in human capital building would almost surely provide benefits that greatly exceed the outlay. According to the research presented earlier, the annual investment in early childhood education would provide lifetime benefits valued at three to seven times the cost. Using the average of benefit-cost ratios estimated in the studies cited, one could reasonably expect lifetime benefits to each cohort of children of $1.2 trillion from the $212 billion outlay. Already, the returns from this one program would cover the cost of all the other investments. Enabling an additional one million people to graduate community college, as suggested in the discussion of community college pipeline programs, would yield $245 billion in increased wages for each cohort at an expense of $25 billion.[109]

Table 14.1

Program	Cost (billions, annually)	Duration	Comments
Early childhood education	$212	Until outcomes achieved—at least one generation	Means-tested, but generous to recipients
Community college programs	$50	Until outcomes achieved	
Workplace reforms	$140	Indefinite	Health care, PFML, childcare. Wage raises are partly paid out of profit losses, offset by tax credit for small businesses that pay higher wages (approx. $40 billion tax cost).*
Baby bonds	$55	Until wealth equalized	
Housing	$251	10 years	Very rough estimate of cost to incentivize zoning and transit changes and provide funding for 6.4 million affordable units over 10 years.
Mentorship and allies	$19	Until outcomes achieved	
Reparations	$1,000-$2,000	30 years?	
TOTAL	$1,727-$2,727		
MEMO: Losses under current system	$14,300–$17,100		

*This figure is roughly four times that in Neumark, "The Higher Wages Tax Credit," to reflect broader coverage at a significantly higher wage rate.

Raising wages by transferring profits to low-income workers would turn idle profits into real spending on housing, food, clothing and education, stimulating the economy much more powerfully than record profits have in recent years.[110] One can quickly envision trillions of dollars of gain for hundreds of billions spent, which is exactly why investment in human and financial capital opportunity is such a good idea.

Even if the costs in the table above are optimistically low, or the losses estimated pessimistically high by a factor of two or more, the cost of reforms would still be *substantially* less than the benefits obtained. Additional reforms might well be required to eliminate *all* the losses tallied here. But as a rule, the distinctly positive balance of benefits in excess of costs for human capital investments should tilt policymakers strongly in favor of taking action.

The recommended programs all aim to achieve permanent changes to a system that rations access to human and financial capital building, changes that would provide benefit indefinitely not only to those who accumulate human capital but to all in the economy. Over time, these structural improvements would accumulate to enormous aggregate economic gains. And this does not account for the human gains in terms of potential realized and misery avoided.

These are investments we can and should make. The payoffs are simply tremendous.

How Do We Pay for This?

Even though the social returns to these investments would be overwhelmingly positive, we still need to pay for them. If these programs are successful at building human capital, then over time many of the programs will pay for themselves. This is not magical thinking, it is sound economics: programs that improve the education and skill level of workers, bring more into the workforce, equalize wealth outcomes, and improve working conditions. As a consequence, workers' productivity increases, and so does the nation's. That increase will *over time* yield higher incomes, greater demand for goods and services, and greater accumulation of wealth, all without causing inflation, as the increase in demand is met—indeed, caused—by a commensurate increase in supply. As incomes rise, tax revenues will also rise.

In the short run, however—perhaps for the first generation of implementation—there will be a shortfall of resources, as it takes time to accumulate human and financial capital. This could entail deficit spending—paid for by issuing new government debt—and/or tax increases on the wealthiest and highest-earning, both households and corporations. As suggested in the discussion of income distribution, there is enormous opportunity to raise taxes on wealthy people and businesses without materially altering their lives and operations. The political will to grasp that opportunity is another matter.

Borrowing to pay for beneficial investments should be viewed as sound economic policy. If financed by long-term government debt, which currently commands relatively low rates of interest, these investments would earn returns that far exceed the cost of borrowing. Undertaking such debt-financed investments is almost always a good idea. It might also be viewed as a moral obligation for a country that aspires to be the land of opportunity. Turning that good idea into reality is a job for courageous political leaders.

15 The Other Half of the Battle: Implementation Matters

Passing legislation, realigning programs, and altering incentives to change key systems are critical first steps. But in addition, we need to do things *better* even after we have the courage to enact them. That is, we need to focus on an area we often ignore: implementation. Much of this section derives from my years of experience advising community-development efforts within the Federal Reserve. By observing low-income communities and their leaders on the ground, participating in a variety of projects aimed at improving outcomes in these communities, and talking to experts in the field about their accumulated wisdom, I have come to realize the importance of implementation.

So how do we implement well?

Community Engagement

"Engagement" sounds a bit like a community-development buzzword, but it matters. Community members and their representatives should be involved in interventions from inception through design, implementation, and evaluation. This seems a common-sense recommendation—if you want to make a difference in a community, shouldn't you talk to the people you're working with to get their perspective on the definition of the problem, the proposed solution, and how best to measure outcomes? Of course you should. And yet, in many, many such interventions, community engagement is an afterthought. To the extent that residents are involved, this comes too late to hear their perspectives on problem definition and solution design.[1]

Effective community engagement is not an amateur sport. At the Federal Reserve's Working Cities program, my team and I routinely engaged experts to guide us in our interactions with community stakeholders. These professionals had spent their careers figuring out how best to connect with representatives of the communities we were working with. Their depth of experience showed, and the program was much the better for their contributions.[2]

In Fitchburg, Massachusetts, for example, the Working Cities team's early assumption that residents in low-income neighborhoods were disengaged from community life was turned upside-down after employing more promising community-engagement approaches. Team members were pleasantly surprised to see "hundreds of people attending community design sessions and . . . contributing to productive dialogues about what change should look like in their city."[3] Well-designed community engagement really makes a difference.

Big Tent

Where possible, I would advocate implementing "big tent" policies. Some interventions, such as reparations, must be narrowly directed. But otherwise, policies that help people in proportion to their need should have no demographic boundaries. The big tent approach is not meant to downplay the role of systemic racism but instead to acknowledge that our broken economy has harmed white families as well as many families of color. The fact that harm is dramatically greater on average for families of color means that these families will benefit most from big tent policies, even as these policies can help any person who suffers for our economy's failures.

Means Testing

If big tent policy is meant to apply to everyone in need without demographic boundaries, then we need to determine who is in need. This points to another critical aspect of implementation: means testing. We will always be constrained by limited resources, so it makes sense to deploy them where the need is greatest. Means testing of income and wealth will focus policy on the poorest, which includes a disproportionate share of people of color.

But of course, means testing will also bring greater opportunity to some low-income, low-wealth white families. No mechanism for means testing will be perfect. As we've seen, income can be measured in a number of ways, and comprehensive wealth measures that capture financial wealth as well as property (homes, cars, household durable goods) could be difficult to implement.

Opponents of means-testing worry that the cost of proving eligibility falls disproportionately on those least able to afford it. As Representative Alexandria Ocasio-Cortez put it in an October 2021 tweet, "Means testing=more bureaucracy, red tape, & waste. That's why programs where means testing gets implemented are less popular, not more popular. It's also why many people who are eligible for means-tested programs still don't get healthcare or help at all—it's too hard."[4]

Some arguments against means testing are essentially political—the public will only accept so much in the way of programs that explicitly target the poor. During a 1973 debate with Milton Friedman, Wilbur Cohen, one of the architects of the Social Security system, argued against Friedman's criticism of the Social Security program as regressive—the poor worked longer and collected fewer benefits than the rich. "You are right," said Mr. Cohen. "However, a program for poor people will be a poor program."[5] Which is to say that programs designed to serve the poor would not garner the political support needed to pass and sustain them. Universal programs such as Medicare and Social Security are popular and have higher participation rates (rates of use among eligible people) than means-tested programs, such as the EITC and the child tax credit. This could be because universal programs suffer less from the stigma that often attaches to means-tested programs[6]

These concerns about the politics of universal programs and the burdens of means testing are legitimate, in my estimation. But my conclusion is that they argue not for scrapping means testing but for simplifying the process for determining eligibility—removing "sludge," as Cass Sunstein calls it. Doing so requires balancing the desire to reach as many eligible recipients as possible with the recognition that some number of ineligible recipients may also receive the benefit.[7] The IRS has much of the data on income and (to some extent) financial assets that might be required to establish eligibility, though there are of course confidentiality and trust hurdles to clear. Coordination with the IRS for key programs should make it feasible to means test without undue burden on poorer families. As Andrew Biggs puts it:

> The provision of relatively generous entitlement benefits to rich and poor alike must shift over time to a more targeted approach. But that targeting must bear in mind . . . that individuals and the economy as a whole . . . respond to incentives in ways that can stymie the seemingly simple answers suggested by static economic analysis. . . . The challenge for today's policymakers is to craft policies that make the most of the benefits of means-testing while avoiding its worst consequences.[8]

While we want program participation to be high and administrative burdens to be low, omitting means testing—say, by distributing baby bonds, tuition benefits, and housing to all comers—would be drastically inefficient, with less help going to those who need it most. Means testing will always be imperfect, but it is nonetheless essential to get the help to where it's most needed. However, I remain open-minded to well-reasoned arguments showing that even careful means testing will do more harm than good.

Learning Orientation

Humility is an underrated virtue. In this context, humility means simply recognizing how much we do not know. We do not yet know all that we need to know about how best to build and rebuild human capital among populations that have been left behind. This implies that a third vital aspect of implementation is the adoption of a *learning orientation*, or more prosaically, open-mindedness. There are many efforts already underway, and many have been for decades. Despite this, we have made insufficient progress in providing opportunity at scale—that's what the data show and what my interviews illustrate. We should be prepared to learn from our struggles. And we need to be patient: some of the current efforts may well end up being successful and scalable, which leads to the next principle.

Evaluation

While it may seem a bit academic, we need to maintain a strong focus on careful *impact evaluation*. Does the intervention really have the desired impact on the populations we are trying to reach? It's not just my background as a researcher that leads me to conclude that we devote far too small a share of our resources to evaluation. It's that decades of well-intentioned work to bridge opportunity gaps have not done nearly enough, as the disheartening aggregate statistics testify. So we clearly don't yet know enough about what is effective and what isn't.

During my years working on economic development with the Federal Reserve, we partnered with many high-quality not-for-profit institutions that have been building up lower-income communities, often for decades. The experts at these nonprofits radiated an inspiring commitment to their work. But in many cases, the hardest thing for them to recognize was when something *wasn't working*—not because they couldn't see it, but because their lifelong investment in the work made it hard to accept that some of what they were doing wasn't having the desired effect.

That's a very human reason why impact evaluation can be difficult—we have a one-sided bias toward seeing the outcomes we desire, rather than a dispassionate acceptance of both encouraging and disappointing results. But there's more that makes impact evaluation so difficult. And that has to do with the difficulty in imputing cause and effect to things that happen in the real world.

One needn't look far to uncover the nearly impenetrable tangle of causes and effects that characterizes the workings of our complex world. It is well beyond most of our abilities to infer causes from distant and indirect observations of complex phenomena like climate change and economic development. It is for this reason that we simply must rely to some extent on expert opinion to make sense of these systems. Increasing public distrust of experts is a first-order problem facing the world as it tackles these issues.[9]

The effects of government, nonprofit, and private interventions to alter income, employment, or wealth outcomes are notoriously difficult to suss out. The world does not stand still immediately following an intervention, so that one can easily impute any subsequent changes to effects of the intervention. Instead, a host of global, national, and local factors continue to bombard individuals' economic lives, altering incomes, employment, and wealth for reasons unrelated to the intervention. Employment might well rise following the introduction of a new tax policy, but can we be sure it rose for that reason? Perhaps it was instead a simultaneous rise in foreign incomes that increased demand for US-exported goods, eliciting an increase in the demand for labor. In general, how are we to know if well-designed and well-intentioned actions taken to improve outcomes for low-income populations are having the effect we hope for?

The answer is that we perform careful studies of interventions, employing the most accurate research and evaluation techniques available to determine as best we can what effect policies and programs are having. One high-quality method is a randomized controlled trial (RCT), which randomly assigns an intervention to one part of a population and withholds it from another part. Because all other differences between the "treated" and "untreated" populations are assumed to be random, any difference in outcomes between the two groups may reasonably be attributed to the intervention. But it is only occasionally possible to conduct a true RCT. In the absence of the RCT, one can attempt to control for nonintervention influences on the outcomes of interest, using statistical methodologies to parse the variations in an outcome. And in some cases, a "natural experiment" will present itself, providing a variation in policies that is plausibly uncorrelated with other features of the environment. Such a natural experiment was exploited by David Card and Alan Krueger, who analyzed the effect of a 1990 New Jersey minimum wage increase by comparing employment rates at the state's fast-food restaurants to employment rates at fast-food restaurants in neighboring eastern Pennsylvania, where no minimum wage increase was enacted.[10]

An important lesson to draw from decades of collective experience in economic development is that it is easier to build in an evaluative framework during the design phase than after the fact. Many programs start with no funding for or focus on evaluation; only after years of implementation do program organizers ask whether what they've done has had an effect. If instead they collected data from the start, and if instead they built into their projects methods for using that data to establish impact, the task of evaluating outcomes would be easier—not easy, but easier. Scrambling after the fact to see what data might be available is far from ideal, and less likely to reveal impact.

A systemic dearth of evaluation is understandable. Evaluation is costly, and many smaller nonprofits simply don't have the resources to include evaluation as part of their programs. But we need to do more here if we are to succeed in the way we hope. Too often in my work at the Federal Reserve, I heard the phrase, "There are a lot of good stories," as a proxy for evaluating one program or another. Those stories can indeed help humanize the impact of an intervention, but they need to be backed up by careful evaluation, given the endemic challenges in imputing causation.

Data

As mundane as it seems, we need access to data that allows us to track key outcomes for populations who have been left behind. This is a critical aspect of evaluation. Some programs can be designed with data collection in mind, so that program organizers have relevant data at their disposal throughout implementation and of course afterward. But in many cases, the effects of programs that hope to improve income, employment, education, financial stability, health outcomes, incarceration, or wealth-building can only be determined after the fact, from studies of the populations involved. Such studies often rely on data that tracks individuals *over time* (so-called longitudinal data) to see how their outcomes change following interventions. The data do not by themselves solve the problem of disentangling causality. But without those data, in many cases, it is much more difficult to evaluate the effectiveness of programs and interventions.

A key challenge is that relevant data are most often stewarded by government agencies that are charged with protecting confidentiality. That pledge of confidentiality is critical, as income, employment, health, incarceration, and other data concerning individuals are inherently sensitive. Researchers and government agencies arrange to use data for program evaluation while maintaining appropriate confidentiality, but most of these agreements are one-offs; there are but a few instances of a standing arrangement.[11] Making secure access to sensitive data more routine for evaluation purposes is an important if somewhat dull step on the way forward.

*   *   *

The way forward as I have described it is not a matter of shifting success from one population to another. It is not a zero-sum game. Instead, what I am proposing promises improvements for everyone, because it focuses on shoring up the foundations of economy-wide growth and prosperity by providing equal opportunity to build human and financial capital. People will benefit not because they are given a slice of the economic pie which used to belong to someone else. They will benefit because the size of the pie will grow dramatically.

It may seem as if our country has been working on these issues for decades, and indeed it has. But despite our efforts to date, we have seen little improvement in outcomes for low-income communities and communities of color. As Ms. P. from Lowell put it, "Growing up in . . . the family that I did, you know, the struggles that I did, I grew up seeing that then and I still see that now. . . . I'm almost forty. You know, I've been here since I was three years old, and . . . it still feels like it's still the same problems."[12]

With a reshaped narrative, we can focus on building systems that appropriately support rather than impede opportunity to build human and financial capital, relying on research-proven policies and programs. We must commit to learning as we go, with promising programs supplemented by careful impact assessment.

These commitments entail clearing significant hurdles—political, psychological, and economic. But the rewards to making and following through on these commitments are enormous. The gains to restructuring our economy dramatically outweigh the costs of getting there. In economic terms, the cost-benefit analysis slants overwhelmingly toward benefits: equality of opportunity is a great investment.

In human terms, the full realization of our people's potential would change not just the head but also the heart and soul of the country.

Conclusion: A Vision of Opportunity

People, you know, people think that we don't try. I tried.
—Pam A., Lowell[1]

Surveying the economic landscape through the window of data or hearing it in the voices of low-income residents, you would think we'd all leap to our feet with a deep sense of alarm spurred by the recognition that something has gone terribly wrong with our country. We must do something!

And yet instead the fortunate survey this wreckage from afar, ho-humming in response to another report of economic brokenness. Distance allows the privileged to say, "I'm OK." This wreckage is about *them*, someone else, someone who's made bad decisions or failed to put in the required effort. "They don't live in my neighborhood or attend my children's schools. They don't shop at my grocery store. I am comfortably isolated from the problem, if there is one. I have other things to worry about."

If you take one thing away from this book, I hope it is this: there is no them, there is only us. Every low-income resident I have spoken to over the past twenty years embraces the same aspirations as those with economic privilege: a reasonable measure of economic and financial security; a better future for their children; some time to live, not endlessly toil.

But tens of millions simply will not get there. Why? Not because life is unavoidably hard and making it in a free-market capitalist world is tough, although that's true to some extent. And certainly not because they didn't try.

The reason is that instead of providing onramps to prosperity, our nation has thrown roadblocks in the way of everyone who is not white, wealthy, and well-connected. We have simultaneously constructed express lanes for the latter groups. We have justified doing so in the name of individual sovereignty, meritocracy, free markets, small government—you name it, we have a readymade philosophy to rationalize our hard-heartedness and stinginess, to say nothing of outright racism. Ironically, we claim that we live in a land of opportunity, when in fact we have systematically denied opportunity for centuries.

It is well past time to cast aside false and hollow narratives, especially our ignorant narratives about who the poor are and how they got that way, and about why people of color fall disproportionately among the ranks of the low-income and low-wealth. Coming to grips with reality, recognizing our role in creating it, acknowledging all our history and its effects today may be dispiriting, but it is simultaneously empowering.

We broke this, we can fix it.

Acknowledgments

First and most obviously, I thank Mary Babson Fuhrer, my soul mate and forty-two-year life partner. She provided unconditional moral support throughout, which for a first-time book author is invaluable. She also gave me the gift of a careful read of the complete draft of the book, weeding out places where I lapsed into economics- or statistics-speak and encouraging me to bring more of my voice to the book. A historian of the early republic, she also pointed me to relevant references for the origins of The Myth and made sure I was representing them in a way that respectable historians might accept. You should read her book if you haven't already! (See the bibliography under Fuhrer, Mary.) Her story about the array of pressures that transformed early New England communities is fascinating. And she's a fluid and accessible writer (unlike many historians and economists)!

I also am grateful to my adult children, Margaret, John, and Jeffrey, for reading through the book and providing thoughtful and helpful noneconomist perspectives. They helped keep my inner nerd in check.

Eastern Bank Foundation

I am grateful to the Eastern Bank Foundation for funding my writing. As I have told them many times, I would have written this book anyway, but they chose to pay me to do it. That's hard to turn down. The statement from the foundation at the beginning of the book explains their commitment to this kind of work. Thanks especially to Nancy Stager, CEO of the foundation, for general support, for reading multiple drafts, and for ongoing encouragement.

Colleagues, Friends

Thanks to Eric Lupfer, my agent (I've never had one of those before), for help in the early development of the book proposal, for marketing it to many potential publishers, and for landing a contract with the MIT Press. He clearly has a natural talent for developing nascent book ideas, and his many suggestions helped shape the book. Thanks to Emily Taber, my editor at the MIT Press. She made numerous suggestions about language and organization and was patient and professional throughout. She was succeeded in midsummer 2022 by Laura Keeler, who ably saw the project to its conclusion. I am also grateful to Simon Waxman, who provided quite thorough and constructive editing.

I owe a deep debt of gratitude to Richard Walker, my former colleague and mentor at the Federal Reserve Bank of Boston, for our early discussions and collaboration on economic development and racial injustice work. I am indebted to Richard first for his friendship, but also for teaching me about community development, making clear to me the importance of keeping racial justice in the foreground of development efforts, and introducing me to some of the history of systemic racism.

Many thanks are due to Ben Friedman of Harvard University, my former graduate school advisor, for early conversations on refining the direction of the book, subsequent conversations on the content and focus of the book, and for support throughout. He has been a consistent supporter throughout my career, for which I am deeply grateful. Though we both started out as macroeconomists, we have both evolved and now share a new set of common interests. His work is cited significantly in the book.

Special thanks to William A. Darity Jr. for his suggestions on incorporating recent research concerning the psychology of misperceptions, barriers to changing them, and how to correct them. Thanks also for his suggestions on how best to frame the discussion of baby bonds and reparations, and for his support as an (identified) reviewer of the book proposal.

Thanks to Darrick Hamilton, who persuaded me to reconsider my priors about the causes of wealth discrepancies. As I say in the main text, he was right and I was wrong, and I thank him for accepting my questions with grace and good humor.

Many thanks to Richard Smith, my nearly lifelong friend, who provided early encouragement to take on this project, and who was gracious in reading and commenting on early section drafts as well as a complete draft of the book.

Thanks to my college friend Gary Krist, a highly regarded writer who helped connect me to my agent. He says this was a first for him. He also provided a number of helpful comments on a late draft of the book. His writing has recently focused on exploring the unknown stories of cities. His research is meticulous and his books are informative and engaging. You should check them out!

Thanks to Jim Wood, a gifted historian and good and dear friend who spent hours reading a draft of the book and provided many helpful comments—and much-appreciated moral support!

Thanks to highly regarded historian and longtime family friend Ellen Rothman, for helping in my early search to find an agent willing to take on the project and for providing insightful comments on the complete draft of the book.

Thanks to my old Fed buddies Chris Foote and Paul Willen, who graciously offered advice on the proper interpretation of the mortgage crisis. My graduate school classmate David Neumark pointed me to his work on employer tax credits for higher wages, an important substitute for (or complement to) minimum wage increases, depending on how one feels about all that. Thanks to Fed economist Dan Sullivan for advice on income distribution and the safety net and for helpful comments on the introduction. Thanks as well to Rob Stavins, a longtime friend and economics colleague who provided a thoughtful read of the introduction, which helped improve it.

Thanks to Michael Curry of Neighborhood Health Centers for early discussions about the importance of narratives, an interest that Michael and I share. Thanks to my former colleagues Lauren Liss, Bob Ruzzo, Jessica Strunkin, and Laura Canter, who provided early encouragement to speak on these subjects, while we were all working together at Mass Development. Thanks to Kaili Mauricio of Brandeis University for pointers on literature about community colleges and pipeline programs. Thanks to Tom Hopper of the University of Massachusetts for sharing his expertise on transit-oriented development and to Alicia Sasser Modestino, my former RA and now a very successful economist, for connecting me to Tom. Thanks to my old friend from my days at the Federal Reserve Board, Eileen Mauskopf, for discussions about the book's direction and for a critical reading of an early draft of the manuscript. Thanks to Debbie Kleitsch at Viking Pumps for generously tracking down and providing historical materials about my grandfather's career.

The Interviews

I am profoundly grateful to the interviewees—Pam, Ashley, Pedro, Mariela, Rosada, Brenda, Ms. P., Carlos, Dalida, Ann, Mattie, Janet, Tasha, and Tierra. All were so forthcoming and generous with their time and their life stories. Some of the episodes they relayed were both painful and poignant. All were instrumental in bringing to life the reality behind the data that the book rests on. Thanks to Carolina Trujillo, formerly of the Eastern Bank Foundation, for serving as translator for interviews conducted in Spanish, and for her suggestions for improving the phrasing of some of the interview questions.

Thanks to Jess Andors of Lawrence Community Works and Phyllis Barajas, CEO of *Conexion*, for connecting me to interviewees from Lawrence. Thanks to Turahn Dorsey from Eastern Bank Foundation for making connections to Boston-area residents for interviews. Thanks to Gladys Vega and Dinanyili Paulino from La Colaborativa for connecting me to residents from Chelsea. I am further indebted to Christina Gonzalez and Andy Ramon of La Colaborativa for serving as translators for the interviews conducted at their building. Thanks to Beth Chandler, CEO of YW Boston, for connecting me to Eric Leslie and Dennis Patrick of Union Capital Boston and to Matthew Parker of Union of Minority Neighborhoods for connecting me with Boston residents for interviews. Many thanks to Nia Evans of Boston Ujima for connecting me to Boston residents for interviews. Thanks to Yun-Ju Choi of the Lowell Coalition for a Better Acre for making the connections with Lowell residents. Finally, thanks to Rita Lara of Maverick Landing Community Services, East Boston, who worked hard to make connections to East Boston residents. In the end her contacts were undergoing personal and financial trauma, making it impossible for them to be interviewed. Such is life for families living on the economic edge.

Harvard Kennedy School Colleagues

Thanks to Aparna Mathur for conversations on elements of the safety net, including the problem of low participation rates. Her work is cited in the book. Thanks to Patrick Okigbo, Ajmal Ahmady, and Wake Smith, for encouraging me to interview residents to get a "lived-experience" perspective. I believe that was a critical addition to the book. And thanks to the other senior fellows at Harvard's Mossavar-Rahmani Center for Business and Government—Marlene Amstad, Edoardo Campanella, George Chouliarakis, Connie Friesen, Megan Greene, Michal Halperin, Sajid Javid, Joe Johnson, Ranch Kimball, Uche Ewelukwa Ofodile, Ioana Petrescu, Omar Robles, Christof Rühl, Eric Salama, Alexandra Schweitzer, Chris Skidmore, Philippe Tordoir, Ted Truman, and Longmei Zhang—and to faculty advisor Karen Dynan and program directors Richard Zeckhauser and John Haigh for questions, comments, and support for the project as I presented progress reports during my tenure as a senior fellow.

Notes

Introduction

1. Varian, *Microeconomic Analysis*, 1.

2. Friedman, "The Social Responsibility of Business."

3. See Heim, "Teaching America's Truth" and "Teaching the 1619 Project."

4. See Hicks et al., "Still Running Up the Down Escalator."

5. See Baker, *Rigged*, and Bivens, *Failure by Design*, for other takes on the notion that the US economy is designed to fail many Americans.

6. Federal Reserve Bank of Minneapolis, "Racism and the Economy," https://www.minneapolisfed.org/policy/racism-and-the-economy.

7. The White House, "President Biden Announces," https://www.whitehouse.gov/briefing-room/statements-releases/2021/10/28/president-biden-announces-the-build-back-better-framework/.

8. Darity and Mullen, *From Here to Equality*, 34.

9. See McGhee, *The Sum of Us*, for an enlightening discussion of ways in which racism harms both whites and people of color.

10. The International Monetary Fund's *World Economic Outlook provides a ranking of world economies*.

11. OECD, "Level of GDP per Capita." See bibliography for details.

12. Sovereign Wealth Fund Institute, "Top 100 Largest Financial Hold Company Rankings."

13. See Galea et al., "Estimated Deaths," for an estimate of the number of annual deaths linked to poverty, poor education, racial inequality, and segregation.

14. These losses correspond to estimates of losses due to childhood poverty (see Holzer et al., "The Economic Costs of Childhood Poverty" and McLaughlin and Rank, "Estimating the Economic Cost of Childhood Poverty"); deaths due to poverty, low education, racial inequality, and segregation (see Galea et al., "Estimated Deaths"); and the cumulative losses of wealth due to slavery (see Darity and Mullen, *From Here to Equality*). Darity and Mullen provide a wide range of estimates employing several different methodologies.

15. See Mishel and Kandra, "CEO Pay Has Skyrocketed."

16. King, *Where Do We Go from Here*, 197. The reference is to the biblical story of Dives (from the Latin *dives* for "rich"), a rich man who lives a "sumptuous" life, blissfully ignorant of the plight of Lazarus, who is "covered with sores, who longed to satisfy his hunger with what fell from the rich man's table." From Luke 16:19–31, BibleGateway, New Revised Standard Version (Anglicized).

Part I

1. The psychology of human decision-making is far from completely understood. Beach, "Decision Making" outlines "Narrative-Based Decision Theory," in which narratives—"the natural language of thought"—are linked strongly to decision-making and strategic action. Kahneman and Tversky, "Prospect Theory," and Tversky and Kahneman, "Judgment under Uncertainty," and "The Framing of Decisions" explore the simplifications that humans use in making decisions.

Chapter 1

1. Wood, "10 Billionaires Like Oprah Winfrey."

2. Markovits, *The Meritocracy Trap*, discusses aspects of the role that meritocracy plays in the US economy.

3. Friedman, "The Social Responsibility of Business."

4. A case in point was the summer 2021 discussion surrounding when to end unemployment benefits in the wake of the pandemic-induced recession. The underlying logic was that those receiving benefits were able to work but chose not to because receiving benefits was easier. Evidence bearing on this proposition suggests this was far from the case. See Coombs et al., "Early Withdrawal of Pandemic Unemployment Insurance."

5. Darity and Mullen, *From Here to Equality*, chapter 2, cites three key misperceptions with respect to race: racism and discrimination no longer exist in the United States; there are no significant economic disparities between blacks and whites; and any residual disparities must be due to "dysfunctional behavior on the part of blacks."

6. Chapter 9 provides evidence by way of international comparisons to show that many other democratic, free market, capitalist countries produce better outcomes in a variety of dimensions.

7. Hartman, "Every Student at Five Chicago High Schools."

8. See Hicks et al., "Still Running Up the Down Escalator" for a discussion of the role of false narratives in explaining racial and ethnic wealth gaps.

9. While Massachusetts is a relatively high-income state with good benefits for lower-income residents, the experiences of these interviewees should generally reflect those of low-income people around the country. Incomes for the interviewees range from below $10,000 annually to near-median US income.

10. Mariela, Rosada, and Brenda, interview with author, March 21, 2022. Interviewees' surnames purposely withheld.

11. Lazarus, "The New Colossus."

12. By way of contrast, Sana, "Public Opinion on Refugee Policy," documents a rise in support for admission of refugees since the turn of the century.

13. See Nowrasteh, "The 14 Most Common Arguments."

14. Loh, Coes, and Buthe, "The Great Real Estate Reset," fig. 2.

15. Loh, Coes, and Buthe, "The Great Real Estate Reset." See also Reardon et al., "Has Income Segregation Really Increased?"

16. Merriam-Webster.com Dictionary, "Trickle-Down Theory."

17. Rogers, "And Here's How It All Happened."

18. Rosenmann referred disparagingly to "the philosophy that . . . the object of government was to provide prosperity for those who lived and worked at the top of the economic pyramid, in the belief that prosperity would trickle down to the bottom of the heap and benefit all." Quoted in Sowell, *Trickle Down Theory*. Galbraith writes in "Recession Economics," "[Director of the Office of Management and Budget] David Stockman has said that supply-side economics was merely a cover for the trickle-down approach to economic policy—what an older and less elegant generation called the horse-and-sparrow theory: If you feed the horse enough oats, some will pass through to the road for the sparrows."

19. The research dates back at least to Mincer, "Investment in Human Capital," and includes novel empirical approaches such as that of Ashenfelter and Krueger, "Estimates of the Economic Return to Schooling."

20. See Komlos, *Foundations of Real-World Economics*, chapter 7, for a discussion of the difficulties inherent in using marginal theory to determine wages and assess other factors of production.

21. In an interesting development, some companies have raised wages for entry-level and lower-skilled workers in the wake of the pandemic. In the "The Revolt of the American Worker," Paul Krugman describes this as compensation for years of low wages. Still, the increases enjoyed to date by lower-wage workers have generally been outpaced by increases in the cost of living, so that they, like other workers, have lost ground in inflation-adjusted terms.

22. Mishel and Kandra, "CEO Pay Has Skyrocketed."

23. On the value of CEO networks, see Engelberg, Gao, and Parsons, "The Price of a CEO's Rolodex." On changing job skills required of CEOs, see Tyler Cowen, "Why CEOs Actually Deserve Their Gazillion Dollar Salaries." For the effect of increasing firm size on CEO compensation, see Gabaix and Landier, "Why Has CEO Pay Increased So Much?"

24. For research on boardroom relationships and their effect on CEO compensation, see O'Reilly and Main, "Economic and Psychological Perspectives on CEO Compensation."

25. See Nackenoff, "The Horatio Alger Myth" and Scharnhorst and Bales, *Horatio Alger Jr.: An Annotated Bibliography*.

26. Horatio Alger Society, "Bylaws."

27. Alger, *Ragged Dick*.

28. "President-Elect Obama," *Wall Street Journal*. In "Reality or Rhetoric?" Love and Tosolt provide a fascinating take on President Obama's place in the racial and political landscape.

29. Mattie, interview with author, June 30, 2022. Interviewee's surname purposely withheld.

30. Hall and Soskice eds., *Varieties of Capitalism*, explores capitalism in transnational comparison, distinguishing broadly between "liberal market economies" such as those of the United States and United Kingdom, and "coordinated market economies" such as those of Germany and Sweden.

31. As John Kenneth Galbraith puts it, "The experience of the countries for whom public ownership became policy [does not] suggest that it enlarges the liberties of the citizen. On the contrary. Accordingly, the principal case for socialism has dissolved. This is recognized." *The Good Society*, 17.

32. Reagan, Remarks at the Annual Meeting of the National Alliance of Business.

33. Gordon, "Perspectives on the Rise and Fall of American Growth," briefly summarizes some of the relevant advances.

34. Friedman, "The Social Responsibility of Business."

35. Wartzman, *The End of Loyalty*, Stiglitz, *The Price of Inequality*, and Krugman, "The Revolt of the American Worker," among others, highlight the damage done by strict adherence to Friedman's maxim.

36. Shiller, "Do Stock Prices Move Too Much," for example, examines the link between dividends—cash from profits that is distributed to investors rather than reinvested in the firm—and stock prices.

37. The share of national income going to labor is defined as the sum of compensation paid to employees plus proprietors' income. Federal Reserve Bank of St. Louis "FRED Economic Data," series A4002E1A156NBEA plus series A041RE1A156NBEA.

38. See Baker, *Rigged*, 30–33.

39. See Manyika et al., "A New Look."

40. Business Roundtable, "Business Roundtable Redefines the Purpose of a Corporation."

41. Hart and Zingales, "Companies Should Maximize Shareholder Welfare."

42. See Reich, *The System*, chapter 3, for a discussion of Dimon's and his peers' lack of commitment to act on the ideals espoused in Dimon's words.

43. Tierra, interview with author, July 26, 2022. Interviewee's surname purposely withheld.

44. Fuhrer, Invalid Bed (US Patent), 1956. Apparently the device was never put into manufacture.

Chapter 2

1. Pew Economic Mobility Project, "Findings from a National Survey & Focus Groups on Economic Mobility." Pew surveys cited in this chapter all draw from the American Trends Panel, with over ten thousand respondents. The margin of sampling error for the full sample is plus or minus 1.5 percentage points, so that all of the differences highlighted in the text are statistically significant at better than the 1 percent level.

2. See Shiller, *Narrative Economics*.

3. Pew Economic Mobility Project, "Findings from a National Survey & Focus Groups on Economic Mobility," 2.

4. Some homeowners suffered from arguably poor mortgage choices, although the lender surely bears a significant share of the responsibility in such cases.

5. Pew Research Center, "Views of the Economic System."

6. Pew Research Center, "Views of the Economic System."

7. Horowitz, Igielnik, and Kochhar, "Most Americans Say There Is Too Much Economic Inequality in the U.S."

8. Pew Research Center, "Most Americans Point to Circumstances."

9. Chapter 3 discusses the historical origins of the notion that success is a product of hard work and poverty of laziness.

10. Pew Research Center, "Partisans are Divided" (2018 survey). The reported results are from the phone survey, which has been conducted consistently since 2014. The Republican share responding that the wealth obtained their riches due to "more advantages" also rose from 2018 to 2020, but the share in 2020 was no higher than it had been in 2014 and 2015.

11. Gallup Polls, "Most Important Problem." This monthly poll has registered a significant decline in concerns about immigration, which was number-three behind poor government leadership and COVID-19 in October 2021. Note that some totals can add up to greater than 100 percent due to "multiple mentions," i.e. some respondents cite more than one "most important problem."

12. Dua et al., "Unequal America."

13. Note that surveys often find that employees believe they are paid below-market rates, even when they in fact earn more than the prevailing market wage. See Smith, "Most People Have No Idea." Of course this is not the same as being paid fairly, as markets undervalue many professions at the low end of the wage scale.

14. Infield, "Deep Divisions in Views of America's Racial History."

15. See Kraus, Rucker, and Richeson, "Americans Misperceive Racial Economic Inequality."

16. See Kraus et al., "The Misperception of Racial Economic Inequality." The psychological reasons behind these misperceptions, which Kraus et al have researched, are discussed in Part VI.

17. Pew Research Center, "On Views of Race and Inequality." Some of these statistics are cited in Darity and Mullen, *From Here to Equality*, chapter 2.

18. Pew Research Center, "Americans' Views of Government." Mistrust of the government is echoed in Newport, "Five Questions about Views of Business."

19. Pew Research Center, "Americans' Views of Government."

20. Pew Research Center, "Religious Landscape Study: Views About Government Aid." See also Benjamin Friedman, *Religion and the Rise of Capitalism*, chapter 15.

21. Pew Research Center, "Religious Landscape Study: Political Affiliation."

22. Porter and Kramer, "Shared Value," 77.

23. Porter and Kramer, "Shared Value," 75.

24. Malhotra, "Should Corporations Simply Maximize."

25. Rainie, Keeter, and Perrin, "Trust and Distrust in America." Gallup, "Confidence in Institutions."

26. Gallup Polls, "Confidence in Institutions."

27. Pew Research Center, "The Partisan Divide on Political Values," section 2.

28. Gallup Polls, "Big Business."

29. See Vogels, "56% of Americans Support More Regulation."

30. "Don't know" responses were not included in the chart data. For reasons that aren't completely clear, respondents from France, Germany, and the United Kingdom were not polled.

31. Inglehart et al., "World Values Survey, Wave 3 (1995–1998)."

32. Haerpfer et al., "World Values Survey, Wave 7 (2017–2021)."

33. This response was rated among the top three by eight of ten countries, and received the most number one and number two rankings across all ten countries.

34. See Gray and Hannah, "Modeling Democracy."

35. Reeves, *Dream Hoarders*, 59.

Chapter 3

1. Ben Friedman, *Religion and the Rise of Capitalism*, chapter 9, emphases in original.

2. Anderson and Martin, "The Public Domain," 906–908.

3. Appleby, *Inheriting the Revolution*, 64–66. Most sold their land to speculators who in turn sold it to other settlers and speculators.

4. Appleby, *Inheriting the Revolution*, 90.

5. Tocqueville, *Democracy in America*, 2:32.

6. Appleby, *Inheriting the Revolution*, 198.

7. Conwell, *Acres of Diamonds*, 15–16.

8. See for example the autobiographies collected in Appleby, *Recollections of the Early Republic*.

9. Appleby, *Inheriting the Revolution*, 65.

10. Chudacoff, "Success and Security," 106.

11. The record of displacement and murder of Indigenous people is well-documented. See, for example, Wilson, *The Earth Shall Weep*, and Saunt, *Unworthy Republic*.

12. Tocqueville, *Democracy in America*, 2:372.

13. Lee, "Public Poor Relief," 572.

14. Franklin, "On the Price of Corn," emphases in original.

15. Huang, "Financing Poor Relief," 76, emphasis added.

16. Nellis and Cecere, *The Eighteenth Century Records of the Boston Overseers*, 18.

17. Quincy, *Report to the Commonwealth of Massachusetts*.

18. On individualism, see Fuhrer, *Communities in Crisis*, and Stiglitz, *People, Power and Profits*, 225.

19. A 2020 Gallup poll found that 45 percent of Americans would vote for a qualified socialist for president. Saad, "Socialism and Atheism Still U.S. Political Liabilities."

20. Horowitz, Igielnik, and Kochhar, "Most Americans Say There Is Too Much Economic Inequality."

Part II

1. W. Kamau Bell, "Few Things Say 'the US Economy Is Broken' More Than This."

2. In 2019 the United States ranked second, behind China, in patent and trademark applications, and fourth in industrial-design applications. See *World Intellectual Property Indicators 2020*.

3. The United States has the most wealth of any country, and the second-highest wealth per capita, according to Shorrocks, Davies, and Lluberas, *Global Wealth Databook 2021*.

Chapter 4

1. Ashley T., interview with author, February 10, 2022. Interviewee's surname purposely withheld.

2. Ann J., interview with author, June 8, 2022. Interviewee's surname purposely withheld.

3. Pam A., interview with author, February 9, 2022. Interviewee's surname purposely withheld.

4. See Piketty and Saez, "Income Inequality in the United States" and Piketty, Saez, and Gabriel Zucman, "Distributional National Accounts." Earlier work includes Kuznets, "Shares of Uppers Income Groups"; Williamson and Lindert, *American Inequality*; Feenberg and Poterba, "The Income and Tax Share"; and Katz and Autor, "Changes in the Wage Structure," among others. The Hamilton Project has an excellent collection of tools for visualizing income inequality and related issues. See https://www.hamiltonproject.org/charts/filter/economic_security_poverty/all_paper _types.

5. Bureau of Economic Analysis, "Personal Income and Its Disposition." Data for the fourth quarter of 2021. Personal income includes compensation that individuals receive for providing the labor, land and capital that go toward current production of goods and services, along with transfer payments from business and government to individuals.

6. Saez, "Striking It Richer," which updates Piketty, Saez, and Zucman, "Distributional National Accounts," with 2019 data.

7. Saez, "Striking It Richer."

8. The World Bank, *World Bank Open Data*.

9. In 1964, the multiple was three times the estimated subsistence food budget. Since then, the poverty level has been adjusted for increases in the consumer price index. Debate continues over how to define the poverty line—should it be measured in terms of resources available to the family (an income measure), or in terms of expenditures required for basic necessities (a consumption measure)? If an income measure, should we include government supports, both cash payments and in-kind transfers? For an excellent summary of the issues, see Blank, "How to Improve Poverty Measurement." Meyer and Sullivan, "Identifying the Disadvantaged," argues for a consumption-based measure. Their findings suggest that the poor, as designated by their expenditures, exhibit significantly worse outcomes (lower overall spending, lower likelihood of having health insurance, reduced consumption of housing services, larger family size, lower educational attainment) than those designated as poor by income measures.

10. Census Bureau, "Poverty Thresholds," https://www.census.gov/data/tables/time -series/demo/income-poverty/historical-poverty-thresholds.html.

11. Census Bureau, "People in Poverty by Selected Characteristics," table A-1.

12. Census Bureau, "Poverty Status of People by Family Relationship, Race, and Hispanic Origin."

13. See estimates of monthly poverty rates from the Center on Poverty and Social Policy, "Monthly Poverty Data."

14. Han, Meyer, and Sullivan, "The Consumption, Income and Well-being," notes the prevalence of underreporting of income, especially for the lowest-income families. The authors find that, for people in the lowest 5 percent of incomes, consumer expenditures exceed income by 48 percent, a clear indication that their incomes are underreported. For the tenth percentile of incomes, spending exceeds income by about 8 percent. While this is clearly an issue for the poorest, it does not change the statements about the fraction of families below the poverty level, or any other threshold. It does say that the lowest-income families may not be as far below thresholds as the reported data might indicate. Fifth percentile incomes are around $10,000 in recent years, so if properly measured, they might rise to $15,000 or so.

15. Economic Policy Institute, "Family Budget calculator."

16. These most recent budget data are for 2018. The federal poverty level for a four-person family in 2018 was $25,100, a bit lower than it is today, due to the rise in the cost of living since then.

17. Internal Revenue Service, "EITC Assistant."

18. Family sizes are smaller for the lowest incomes. In 2020, the median number of persons in households with incomes of $50,000 or less was 2 and the average was 2.6. For families above that level, the median was 3, and the average was 3.6. The official poverty threshold increases with family size.

19. University of Minnesota Population Center. "Current Population Survey Data"; author's calculations.

20. University of Minnesota Population Center. "Current Population Survey Data"; author's calculations. About 10 percent of low-income workers work 50 hours or more per week.

21. University of Minnesota Population Center. "Current Population Survey Data"; author's calculations.

22. Reagan quoted in the *New York Times*, February 15, 1976.

23. Levin, "The Welfare Queen."

24. US Department of Agriculture, "SNAP Work Requirements."

25. Hahn, Kassabian, and Zedlewski, "TANF Work Requirements and State Strategies to Fulfill Them."

26. US Department of Agriculture, "What Can SNAP Buy?"

27. The history of the 1996 welfare reform is discussed in detail in chapter 10.

28. Center for Budget and Policy Priorities, "Policy Basics: Temporary Assistance for Needy Families." Participation rates are defined as program recipients divided by families with children in poverty, or child recipients divided by children in poverty.

29. Congressional Research Service, "The Temporary Assistance for Needy Families Block Grant," Appendix Table A.1. TANF caseload data from U.S. Department of Health and Human Services, "TANF Caseload data 1996–2020." Population under poverty line from Census Bureau, "Number of Poor and Poverty Rate by State." This measure is also employed by Shrivastava and Thompson, "TANF Cash Assistance."

30. See Mathur, "Frayed Protection," for a discussion of low participation rates. See also Shrivastava and Thompson, "TANF Cash Assistance," recommending state- and federal-level improvements to TANF.

31. Maximum benefits and gross income limits from Mississippi Department of Human Services, "Temporary Assistance for Needy Families Eligibility Guidelines." Participation rate from Gates, "Most Participants."

32. US Department of Agriculture, "SNAP participation rates 2002–2014"; Cunnyngham, "Reaching Those in Need." Here the participation rates are based on estimates of the *eligible* population, which is not the same as all those in poverty. The participation rate for all individuals was 54 percent in 2002, and 73 percent for children.

33. Andrews and Smallwood, "What's Behind the Rise." Restoring benefits to legal immigrants could raise or lower the participation rate, depending on whether their participation rate is higher or lower than other eligible populations.

34. Office of Management and Budget, "Historical Tables," Table 8.5.

35. Kearney, "Welfare and the Federal Budget."

36. Janet, interview with author, June 30, 2022. Interviewee's surname purposely withheld.

37. Carlos P., interview with author, June 2, 2022. Interviewee's surname purposely withheld.

38. Tasha, interview with author, July 12, 2022. Interviewee's surname purposely withheld.

39. Ashley T. interview.

40. Pedro A., interview with author, April 19, 2022. Interviewee's surname purposely withheld.

41. Author's calculations from Board of Governors of the Federal Reserve System, "Survey of Consumer Finances," 2019 data.

Chapter 5

1. Pedro A., interview with author, April 19, 2022. Interviewee's surname purposely withheld.

2. Rosada S., interview with author, March 21, 2022. Interviewee's surname purposely withheld.

3. Janet, interview with author, June 30, 2022. Interviewee's surname purposely withheld.

4. See, for example, the indicators of short-term fragility among community college students in Savage and Graves, "Promoting Pathways." See also Desmond, *Evicted*.

5. Board of Governors of the Federal Reserve System, "Economic Well-Being of U.S. Households in 2021."

6. See Thompson and Volz, "A New Look at Racial Disparities" and Sabelhaus and Thompson, "Racial Wealth Disparities."

7. Mitchell, "Worker Knowledge of Pension Provisions," finds widespread ignorance of pension plan attributes, with unionized, high-income, and better-educated workers better informed than others. Starr-McCluer and Sundén, "Workers' Knowledge of their Pensions Coverage," finds somewhat better knowledge in a study that merges Fed Survey of Consumer Finances data and a pension-fund survey, allowing them to match household perceptions with actual plan provisions. More recently Kim, "Worker Retirement Responses," surveys a number of other papers, concluding, "A growing body of research [shows] that workers have imperfect knowledge of their pension benefits and they use imprecise information to make retirement timing decisions."

8. Ms. P., interview with author, May 16, 2022. Interviewee purposely anonymized.

9. See Melvin and Shapiro, *Black Wealth, White Wealth*.

10. See Hamilton et al., "Umbrellas Don't Make It Rain" and Darity et al., "What We Get Wrong."

11. Thompson and Volz, "A New Look at Racial Disparities."

12. "Strong" statistical significance corresponds to significance at the 1 percent level, "moderate" significance corresponds to the 5 percent level, and "weak" significance to the 10 percent level. The NASCC studies include Muñoz et al., "The Color of Wealth in Boston"; Kijakazi et al., "The Color of Wealth in the Nation's Capital"; De La Cruz-Viesca et al., "The Color of Wealth in Los Angeles"; Aja et al., "The Color of Wealth in Miami"; and Biu et al., "The Color of Wealth in Tulsa, Oklahoma."

13. See, for example, Thompson and Suarez, "Accounting for Racial Wealth Disparities"; Shapiro, Meschede, and Osoro, "The Roots of the Widening Racial Wealth Gap"; Scholz and Levine, "U.S Black-White Wealth Inequality."

14. Darity et al., "What We Get Wrong," figure 1.

15. Sabelhaus and Thompson, "Racial Wealth Disparities."

16. Aliprantis, Carroll, and Young, "The Dynamics of the Racial Wealth Gap."

17. Darity et al., "What We Get Wrong."

18. Asante-Muhammad et al., "Black Entrepreneurship's Lethal Pre-Existing Condition."

19. Perry, Rothwell, and Harshbarger, "Five-Star Reviews, One-Star Profits."

20. Census Bureau, "Historical Income Tables: Households."

21. Carroll and Chen, "Income Inequality Matters."

22. Mazumder, "Fortunate sons."

23. Chetty et al., "The Fading American Dream," figure 1b.

24. Carroll and Hoffman, "New Data on Wealth Mobility," presents a wealth mobility matrix from 1984 to 1994, based on data from the Panel Study of Income Dynamics. Sixty-three percent of those in the lowest quintile in 1984 remain there ten years later. Another 23 percent make it to the next lowest quintile. Only 4 percent make it to one of the top two quintiles. Johnson and Fisher, "Inequality and Mobility," similarly finds low wealth mobility from 1984 to 2015—lower than income mobility—and like income mobility, declining over time.

25. Carroll and Hoffman, "New Data on Wealth Mobility."

26. Pfeffer and Killewald, "Intergenerational Wealth Mobility." Pfeffer and Kille-wald have created an animation that makes the point about wealth mobility in a visually compelling format. See https://viz.theinequalitylab.com/Animations/1-mo bility-rates.html.

Chapter 6

1. Ann J., interview with author, June 8, 2022. Interviewee's surname purposely withheld.

2. See Wartzman, *The End of Loyalty* and Greenhouse, *Beaten Down, Worked Up*.

3. Ton, "Why 'Good Jobs' Are Good for Retailers" and Ton, "The Case for Good Jobs."

4. Ton, "Why 'Good Jobs' Are Good for Retailers."

5. Friedman, "The Social Responsibility of Business."

6. Bureau of Labor Statistics, "Median Weekly Earnings"

7. Bureau of Labor Statistics, "Median Usual Weekly Earnings by Occupation."

8. Bureau of Labor Statistics, "Employee Benefits in the United States."

9. Cited in Glynn et al., "Fast Facts on Who Has Access."

10. Bureau of Labor Statistics, "67 Percent of Private Industry Workers." The figure for the 1990s is from Wiatrowski, "The Last Private Industry Pension Plans," 4.

11. See Boushey and Ansel, "Working by the Hour," 4–5.

12. Studies cited in Boushey and Ansel, "Working by the Hour." Harknett and Schneider's "The Shift Project" documents the prevalence of scheduling uncertainty, along with examples of businesses that take the high road.

13. See Zundl et al., "Still Unstable," figure 1 and table 1.

14. Child Care Aware of America, "The U.S. and the High Price of Child Care."

15. ChildCare.gov, "See Your State's Resources," provides details on state programs and eligibility criteria across the United States.

16. Malik, "Working Families Are Spending Big Money," table 1.

17. Pew Research Center, "The State of American Jobs."

18. Irwin, "To Understand Rising Inequality."

19. Kaiser Family Foundation, "2020 Employer Health Benefits Survey."

20. Rae, Copeland, and Cox, "Tracking the Rise in Premium Contributions."

21. Kaiser Health Network, "As Health Care Costs Rise."

22. Federal Reserve Bank of St. Louis, "FRED Economic Data," series JTSQUR. The data have been collected only since 2000, so it is difficult to compare quit rates over long spans of time. The rate of quits declined modestly in early 2022.

23. Krugman, "Revolt of the American Worker." Earnings data from Federal Reserve Bank of St. Louis, "FRED Economic Data," series CES7000000008. For an update on the "revolt," which appears to have been less a revolt than a spate of job-switching, see Krugman, "What Ever Happened to the Great Resignation."

Chapter 7

1. See Desmond, *Evicted*.

2. See the Eviction Lab, "Research," for updated research on effects of eviction on children, from newborns to school-age.

3. The Eviction Lab, "National Estimates."

4. The Eviction Lab, "Eviction Tracker."

5. Census Bureau, "American Housing Survey, Housing Cost Data."

6. Census Bureau, "American Housing Survey, Housing Quality Data."

7. US Department of Housing and Urban Development, "PIT and HIC Data since 2007."

8. Rothstein, *The Color of Law*, and Anderson, *White Rage*, document many of these disparate treatments. Munnell et al., "Mortgage Lending in Boston," documents the prevalence of mortgage discrimination.

9. Xu et al., "Deaths: Final Data for 2019." Hoyert, "Maternal Mortality Rates." Cairns, Ashman, and Kang, "Emergency Department Visit Rates." Arias and Xu, "United States Life Tables, 2018," table A.

10. Case and Deaton, "Mortality and Morbidity in the 21st Century."

11. Auerbach et al., "How the Growing Gap in Life Expectancy."

12. Kaiser Family Foundation, "Status of Medicaid."

13. Goldin and Katz, "Why the United States Led in Education."

14. National Assessment of Educational Progress scores collected from Brightbeam, "Racial Gaps in Academic Proficiency." New York and California display similar gaps. Texas's gaps are a bit smaller, especially at the eighth grade level.

15. Smith and Reeves, "SAT Math Scores."

16. US Department of Education, "Data Express Dashboards."

17. Andre Perry, "Students Need More Than an SAT Adversity Score."

18. US Department of Education, "Graduation Rate Data."

19. National Center for Education Statistics, "Total and Current Expenditures."

20. See Johnson and Jackson, "Reducing Inequality." Johnson, Jackson, and Persico, "The Effects of School Spending."

21. Alexander, *The New Jim Crow*, 76.

22. Institute for Crime & Justice Policy Research, "World Prison Brief Data."

23. Alexander, *The New Jim Crow*, 73–77.

24. Federal Bureau of Prisons, "Statistics on Race, Ethnicity, Gender, and Offense Type."

25. Human Rights Watch, "Who Goes to Prison for Drug Offenses?" estimated in 1999 that 89 percent of repeat drug offenders were convicted of minor crimes such as possession of, or intent to sell, "small amounts of drugs."

26. Deloitte, "Missing Pieces Report."

27. Eavis, "Board Diversity Increases in 2021."

28. Larcker and Tayan, "Diversity in the C-Suite."

29. Census Bureau, "Annual Business Survey, 2020."

30. Asante-Muhammad et al., "Black Entrepreneurship's Lethal Pre-Existing Condition."

31. Board of Governors of the Federal Reserve System, "Report on the Economic Well-Being of U.S. Households in 2021."

32. See Munnell et al., "Mortgage Lending in Boston."

33. Hamdani et al., "Unequal Access to Credit," 14.

Part III

1. The original language from *Star Wars IV: A New Hope* (1977) is: "It surrounds us and penetrates us; it binds the galaxy together."

Chapter 8

1. Ms. P., interview with author, May 18, 2022. Interviewee purposely anonymized.

2. The psychological basis for this persistent blindness is discussed in chapter 13.

3. "The Opportunity Atlas." See also Chetty et al., "The Opportunity Atlas: Mapping the Childhood Roots of Social Mobility."

4. The Census tracts are 25025110103 (Forest Hills), 20525110401 (Roslindale), 01097006702 (Fowl River), and 09097007101 (Westfield).

5. See Chetty, Friedman, and Rockoff, "Measuring the Impacts of Teachers," for evidence on effects of individual teachers on adult outcomes.

6. How those imbalances in the economy occur is a fascinating topic, one that Nobel laureate Robert Shiller has studied in detail. See Shiller, *Irrational Exuberance* and Shiller, *Narrative Economics*.

7. The financial institutions in question were Bank of America/Merrill Lynch, Bank of New York Mellon, Citigroup, Goldman Sachs, JP Morgan Chase, Morgan Stanley, State Street, and Wells Fargo. See Amadeo, "TARP Bailout Program."

8. See US Department of the Treasury, "Troubled Assets Relief Program (TARP)." One can argue that supporting the domestic auto industry prevented some job loss, which seemed essential in the months following the fall of 2008, which featured losses of 700,000 to 800,000 jobs per month from November 2008 through March 2009. These are the latest vintage of data. In real time, the employment losses over

the same period were understood to be 600,000 to 750,000 jobs per month. Federal Reserve Bank of Philadelphia, "Data Files—Real-Time Data Set (EMPLOY)."

9. Federal Reserve Board of Governors, "Factors Affecting Reserve Balances."

10. As detailed in Foote et al., "A Proposal to Help Distressed Homeowners," loan modifications were likely not the most efficient way to address the housing crisis. See also US Department of the Treasury, "Troubled Assets Relief Program (TARP). See also Amadeo, "TARP Bailout Program."

11. See Foote, Gerardi, and Willen, "Why Did So Many People."

12. See "After the Fall." See also Brand, "Yale Professor Predicts."

13. The first financial intervention bill—the Emergency Economic Stabilization Act of 2008—failed to pass in the House on September 29, 2008, with a vote of 228-205 against. Republican opposition to the bill cited "ideological objections to government intervention." Hulse and Herszenhorn, "Defiant House Rejects Huge Bailout." The Dow Jones stock index closed down that day by 778 points, or 7 percent. An amended version passed on October 3, 2008. For daily historical Dow Jones data, see Yahoo! Finance's tool: https://finance.yahoo.com/quote/%5EDJI/history?p=%5EDJI.

14. Unemployment rate from Federal Reserve Bank of St. Louis, "FRED Economic Data," series UNRATE.

15. Federal Reserve Bank of St. Louis, "FRED Economic Data," series DFF.

16. Congressional Budget Office, "Estimated Impact of the American Recovery and Reinvestment Act." Estimates total effects over ten years.

17. For a discussion of "shovel-ready projects," see Naylor, "Stimulus Bill."

18. The US economy is not alone in this respect, as Reinhart and Rogoff's *This Time is Different*, a history of economic crises spanning countries and centuries, very clearly demonstrates.

19. Komlos, *Foundations of Real-World Economics*, chapter 8, discusses departures from the ideal conditions under which regulation might not be required.

20. Rappeport and Flitter, "Congress Approves First Bid Dodd-Frank Rollback."

21. Profits for financial firms fell steeply in the second half of 2008, but by the third quarter of 2009, they had risen above their level at year-end 2006. Federal Reserve Bank of St. Louis, "FRED Economic Data," series N398RC1Q027SBEA.

22. See Friedman, "Is Our Financial System Serving Us Well?" on the appropriate role of the financial sector.

23. See Foote et al., "A Proposal to Help Distressed Homeowners," for a simple proposal for foreclosure relief.

24. The Brookings Institution, "Responding to the Global Financial Crisis," 11.

25. Bernanke, *The Courage to Act*, 490.

26. Debates about how long to extend unemployment benefits—and how gener-ous those benefits should be—arise in every recession, including the most recent COVID-induced recession. Conservative politicians tend to worry that benefits will reduce the incentive to work. The evidence on this is scant. For example, the cessa-tion of unemployment benefits in some states in mid-2021 did not result in a surge of returns to work. Coombs et al., "Early Withdrawal of Pandemic Unemployment Insurance." The position seems to reflect a basic mistrust of those in lower income brackets, as if they are looking for ways not to work, a powerful and damaging ele-ment of The Myth.

27. Smith, *The Theory of Moral Sentiments*, 70.

28. John Kenneth Galbraith, "Recession Economics."

29. Stiglitz, *The Price of Inequality*, 6.

30. Kopp et al., "U.S. Investment Since the Tax Cuts and Jobs Act of 2017."

31. See Gale, "Did the 2017 Tax Cut." See also Gale and Haldeman "The Tax Cuts and Jobs Act."

32. Slemrod, "Is This Tax Reform, or Just Confusion?" 88.

Chapter 9

1. For instance, Rutz, "Twitter Erupts," reports: "In 2018, the top 1% of taxpayers . . . earned 20.9% of all adjusted gross income . . . and paid 40.1% of all federal income taxes, according to data from the Tax Foundation."

2. Institute on Taxation and Economic Policy, "Who Pays Taxes in America in 2019?"

3. OECD Data, "Tax on Corporate Profits."

4. Federal Reserve Bank of St. Louis, "FRED Economic Data," series A054RC1Q027S-BEA divided by series GDP.

5. OECD Data, "Income Inequality." Data for OECD countries reporting in 2020.

6. Shorrocks, Davies, and Lluberas, *Global Wealth Databook 2021*, 115–118.

7. WID.World, "World Inequality Database" (net personal wealth, top one percent share, adults, equal split). See Zucman, "Global Wealth Inequality," for a discussion of recent international developments in wealth inequality.

8. Tikkanen and Abrams, "US Health Care from a Global Perspective."

9. See, for example, Marmot, "Social Determinants of Health Inequalities."

10. Tikkanen and Abrams, "US Health Care from a Global Perspective," 15.

11. OECD, "Public spending on childcare and early education," chart PF3.1.B.

12. Davis and Sojourner, "Increasing Federal Investment."

13. OECD Data, "Education Spending."

14. Pew Economic Mobility Project, "Does America Promote Mobility as Well as Other Nations?"

15. See Isaacs, "International Comparisons of Economic Mobility."

Part IV

1. See generally Bivens, *Failure by Design*.

2. Stiglitz, *The Price of Inequality*, 34, emphasis in original. Stiglitz's other books on inequality—*Rewriting the Rules of the American Economy* and *People, Power, and Profits*—are equally forceful on these points.

3. Krugman, "Doing Economics as if Evidence Matters."

4. Semuels, "Severe Inequality Is Incompatible with the American Dream."

5. Corak, "How to Slide Down the 'Great Gatsby Curve,'" 4.

6. Pope Francis, "Evangelii Gaudium," 23.

Chapter 10

1. Muñoz et al., "The Color of Wealth in Boston." See the summary of the work group's process and shared agenda in Bryant et al., "Reducing Racial Wealth Inequalities in Greater Boston."

2. Anderson, *White Rage*, 9, quoting Vorenberg, "Abraham Lincoln and the Politics of Black Colonization," 33.

3. See Anderson, *White Rage*, 18.

4. See Anderson, *White Rage*, 18–20.

5. United States Senate, Senate Historical Office, "The Enforcement Acts of 1870 and 1871."

6. See Anderson, *White Rage*, 33–38.

7. Rothstein, *Color of Law*, 39.

8. The Jim Crow Museum maintains a detailed and useful timeline of the era: https://www.ferris.edu/htmls/news/jimcrow/timeline/jimcrow.htm.

9. Bureau of Labor Statistics, "Databases, Tables & Calculators by Subject"; Greenhouse, *Beaten Down, Worked Up*, 74.

10. Rothstein, *Color of Law*, 155.

11. Rothstein, *Color of Law*, 19.

12. See U.S. Department of Labor, Wage and Hour Division, "Handy Reference Guide." See also Greenhouse, *Beaten Down, Worked Up*, 78.

13. Solomon, Maxwell, and Castro, "Systematic Inequality and Economic Opportunity."

14. Rothstein, *Color of Law*, chapter 6. See also Price, "Doing 'The Right Thing'" for a powerful account of redlining's effect on one of her forbears' ability to accumulate wealth.

15. Katznelson, *When Affirmative Action Was White*, 140.

16. Herbold, "Never a Level Playing Field."

17. Turner and Bound, "Closing the Gap or Widening the Divide."

18. Rosales, "Fighting the Peace at Home," table 3.

19. Fernández, "Of Immigrants and Migrants" and Aiken, Reina, and Culhane, "Understanding Low-Income Hispanic Housing Challenges" document migration and housing patterns among low-income Hispanics during this period.

20. Rothstein, *Color of Law*, chapter 10.

21. The full text of the 1964 Civil Rights Act is available via the National Archives: https://www.archives.gov/education/lessons/civil-rights-act.

22. See Bertrand and Mullainathan, "Are Emily and Greg More Employable."

23. Quillian et al., "Meta-analysis of Field Experiments."

24. US Equal Employment Opportunity Commission, "EEOC Budget and Staffing." Population and inflation adjustment from Federal Reserve Bank of St. Louis, "FRED Economic Data," series POPTHM and CPIAUCSL, respectively. Backlogs are reported in US Equal Employment Opportunity Commission, "Annual Performance Report, Fiscal Year 2020," 31. Backlogs have improved modestly since 2018.

25. King, April 1968 speech at unknown location.

26. Komlos, *Foundations of Real-World Economics*, 19, emphasizes that markets "are not created by divine power."

27. Baker, *Rigged*, 9.

28. See Barro, *Determinants of Economic Growth* and Knack and Keefer, "Institutions and Economic Performance."

29. International Trade Administration, "China-Country Commercial Guide."

30. Heritage Foundation, "Index of Economic Freedom: United States."

31. Roth, "The Art of Designing Markets." For purists, the official name of the economics Nobel is the Sveriges Riksbank Prize in Economic Sciences in Memory of Alfred Nobel.

32. Roth, "The Art of Designing Markets."

33. Drucker and Hakim, "Private Inequity."

34. Kaiser-Schatzlein, "This is How America's Richest Families Stay That Way."

35. See Drucker and Hakim, "How Accounting Giants"; Kaiser-Schatzlein, "This Is How America's Richest Families Stay That Way." Richter, Samphantharak, and Timmons, "Lobbying and Taxes" and Chirinko and Wilson, "Can Lower Tax Rates Be Bought?" provide estimates of the effectiveness of campaign contributions and lobbying expenses in reducing effective tax rates.

36. Guyton et al., "Tax Evasion at the Top."

37. Sarin, "The Case for a Robust Attack on the Tax Gap."

38. Drucker and Hakim, "Private Inequity."

39. Sarin, "The Case for a Robust Attack on the Tax Gap"; Rappeport, "The Top 1 Percent."

40. For more evidence on the performance of private equity firms relative to public equity indexes, and the fees collected by the relatively small number of owners, see Phalippou, "An Inconvenient Fact."

41. Faturechi and Elliot, "How the Trump Tax Law Created a Loophole."

42. Moffitt, "The Deserving Poor."

43. Moffitt, "The Deserving Poor." Note that these calculations omit the Medicaid program, as Medicaid spending on individual families cannot be obtained from the household survey used for these calculations.

44. Shrider et al., "Income and Poverty in the United States: 2020."

45. López-Santana and Núñez, "Most Americans Support Biden's Expanded Child Tax Credit."

46. Friedman, *Capitalism and Freedom*, chapter 12. "There is every reason to help the poor man who happens to be a farmer, not because he is a farmer but because he is poor," Friedman wrote (230).

47. Council of Economic Advisers, "Economic Report of the President" (1964), 77. Elsewhere, the report is more effusive: "Let us, above all, open wide the exits from poverty to the children of the poor" (15).

48. Ventry, "The Collision of Tax and Welfare Politics," 985.

49. Ventry, "The Collision of Tax and Welfare Politics," 988.

50. Ventry, "The Collision of Tax and Welfare Politics," 984.

51. Joint Economic Committee, Subcommittee on Fiscal Policy, *Income Security for Americans*, 76.

52. Ventry, "The Collision of Tax and Welfare Politics," 996.

53. Ventry, "The Collision of Tax and Welfare Politics," 1002.

54. Ventry, "The Collision of Tax and Welfare Politics," 1003.

55. Personal Responsibility and Work Opportunity Reconciliation Act of 1996, Title I, Section 101.

56. Personal Responsibility and Work Opportunity Reconciliation Act of 1996, Title IV, Section 401.

57. See Blank, "Evaluating Welfare Reform," for a summary of the program changes and analysis of their effects.

58. Blank, "Evaluating Welfare Reform," table 2. State personal income from Bureau of Economic Analysis Regional Data, https://www.bea.gov/data/income-saving/personal-income-by-state.

59. Moffitt, "Explaining Welfare Reform."

60. Weaver, *Ending Welfare as We Know It*, figure 7-1, 173.

61. See Weaver, *Ending Welfare as We Know It*, chapter 6.

62. Blank, "Evaluating Welfare Reform."

63. Bitler, Gelbach, and Hoynes, "Some Evidence on Race."

64. See Liebman et al., "Chelsea Eats Study," for evidence on how poor families spend cash aid.

65. Janet, interview with author, June 30, 2022. Interviewee's surname purposely withheld.

66. Dalida R., interview with author, May 9, 2022. Interviewee's surname purposely withheld.

67. See Wartzman, *The End of Loyalty*, and Greenhouse, *Beaten Down, Worked Up*.

68. Wartzman, *The End of Loyalty*, 12.

69. Wartzman, *The End of Loyalty*, 24.

70. Wartzman, *The End of Loyalty*, 104. Boulware wrote a book, *The Truth about Boulwarism: Trying to Do Right Voluntarily*, whose title suggests that at least part of his motivation in augmenting workers' benefits and compensation was to do well by the workers.

71. Wartzman, *The End of Loyalty*, 86.

72. Wartzman, *The End of Loyalty*, 46, 160–162.

73. Wartzman, *The End of Loyalty*, 49, 61.

74. Initial Labor Department funding for the first decade of the NAB was $8 million, while "more than double that amount" was contributed by private industry. Mullaney, "Alliance of Businessmen."

75. Humphrey, Remarks to the National Alliance of Businessmen.

76. Greenhouse, *Beaten Down, Worked Up*, provides an excellent summary of the history of the PATCO strikes.

77. Greenhouse, *Beaten Down, Worked Up*, chapters 9–10.

78. Reagan, Remarks on the Air Traffic Controllers Strike.

79. Quoted in Greenhouse, *Beaten Down, Worked Up*, 133.

80. Greenhouse, *Beaten Down, Worked Up*.

81. Willis J. Nordlund quoted in Greenhouse, *Beaten Down, Worked Up*, 136. See also Shiller, *Narrative Economics*, 20–21.

82. Western and Rosenfeld, "Workers of the World Divide."

83. Baker, *Rigged*, chapter 3.

84. Includes both private- and public-sector workers. The share of private-sector workers represented in a union is 6.3 percent. Bureau of Labor Statistics, "Union Members Summary," and OECD "Trade Union Dataset."

85. See Gallup, "Labor Unions."

86. Gelles, *The Man Who Broke Capitalism*, places much of the blame for US capitalism's problems on Jack Welch.

87. Quoted in Wartzman, *The End of Loyalty*, 252–253.

88. See Kodrzycki and Muñoz, "Reinvigorating Springfield's Economy," for a discussion of the history of postindustrial cities, with lessons for successful redevelopment.

89. Wartzman, *The End of Loyalty*, 245–247.

90. This witticism may have originated with economist Jagdish Bhagwati. Wildasin, "What's So Funny about Economics?"

91. "Occupy Boston Timeline."

92. See Federal Reserve Bank of Boston, "Working Cities Challenge." Eric Rosengren, who was president of the Boston Fed when it launched the Working Cities Challenge, deserves much credit for supporting an effort that was both riskier than most Feds were willing to undertake and novel in engaging many community partners to effect change. I was a member of the original steering committee for the project and was responsible for the department in which the work took place. Key contributors early on included Rosengren, Senior Vice President Richard Walker, Vice President Prabal Chakrabarti, and Tamar Kotelchuck.

93. The expanded Working Communities program extends its focus to rural areas of northern New England.

94. Senior Vice President Richard Walker was one of the strongest advocates for focusing on racial equity.

95. See Board of Governors of the Federal Reserve System, "Statement on Longer-Run Goals." See Baker, *Rigged*, chapter 3.

96. Unemployment rate: Federal Reserve Bank of St. Louis, "FRED Economic Data," series UNRATE. Natural rate: Federal Reserve Bank of St. Louis, "FRED Economic Data," series NROUST.]

97. According to the personal consumption expenditures chain-type price index, the Fed's preferred measure of inflation, inflation averaged 1.79 and 1.78 percent, respectively, for the twenty- and twenty-five-year periods leading up to the pandemic. (Federal Reserve Bank of St. Louis, "FRED Economic Data," series PCEPI.)

98. Note that the inflation measure in this figure is the consumer price index, because the Bureau of Economic Analysis did not begin compiling the personal consumption expenditures chain-type price index until 1959.

99. The labor force averaged about 164 million during 2022. Federal Reserve Bank of St. Louis, "FRED Economic Data," series CLF16OV.

100. Federal Reserve Bank of St. Louis, "FRED Economic Data," series LNS14000003 (white unemployment rate), LNS14000006 (Black unemployment rate), and LNS14000009 (Hispanic) unemployment rate.]

101. See Board of Governors of the Federal Reserve System, "Review of Monetary Policy Strategy."

102. Ellen Meade, then a special advisor to Fed Vice-Chair Richard Clarida, led the effort.

103. Board of Governors of the Federal Reserve System, "FedListens," 6.

104. Board of Governors of the Federal Reserve System, "FedListens," 105–107.

105. This discussion refers to inflation expectations data from financial markets (inferred from Treasury inflation-protected securities, such as the implied inflation rate for the five years beginning five years from now, Federal Reserve Bank of St. Louis, "FRED Economic Data," series T5YIFR), University of Michigan Survey Research Center "Survey of Consumers" (consumers' expectations over the next year or the next five years), and the Federal Reserve Bank of Philadelphia's "Survey of Professional Forecasters" (Median CPI and PCE inflation forecasts over the next four quarters and over the next ten years).

106. Federal Reserve Bank of Atlanta, "Wage Growth Tracker."

107. The employment cost index rose 3.9 percent in 2021, while average hourly earnings rose 5.2 percent. Federal Reserve Bank of St. Louis, "FRED Economic Data," series ECIALLCIV and CES0500000003, respectively. Corporate profits exceeded 10 percent of GDP, just shy of the highest percentage since data were first collected in 1947. Federal Reserve Bank of St. Louis, "FRED Economic Data," series CPATAX as a percentage of series GDP.

108. Owens, "I Listened In on Big Business," examines some evidence supporting the proposition that inflation is a result of profiteering.

109. Unemployment exceeded 25 percent during the Great Depression versus about 14 percent in the wake of the pandemic. However, the speed with which unemployment surged and rebounded in 2020 is unmatched since official estimates of the unemployment rate began in 1929. Federal Reserve Bank of St. Louis, "FRED Economic Data," series for unemployment M0892AUSM156SNBR (1929-1942) and UNRATE (1948 to present).

110. Internal Revenue Service, "Filing Season 2021 Child Tax Credit."

111. Unofficial estimates using Center on Poverty and Social Policy, "Monthly Poverty Data" and "Columbia Monthly Poverty Tracker." The methodology is detailed in Parolin et al., "Estimating Monthly Poverty Rates." Zippel, "Tax Credits to Pay for Necessities, Education," finds that 91 percent of families with low incomes used their child tax credit payments for "the most basic household expenses—food, clothing, shelter, and utilities—or education."

112. Autor et al., "The $800 billion Paycheck Protection Program."

113. Zundl, et al., "Still Unstable."

114. Goldhaber et al., "The Consequences of Remote and Hybrid Instruction." The authors conclude that in order to compensate for the losses suffered during the pandemic, high-poverty school districts will need to spend "nearly all of their federal aid on academic recovery" (7).

115. Census Bureau. "Week 42 Household Pulse Survey," tables 1, 3; Coleman-Jensen et al., "Household Food Security in the United States in 2019," table 2.

116. Horowitz, "Support for Black Lives Matter." As of September 2021, support varied from a low of 47 percent among whites to 83 percent among Black respondents. Support fell monotonically with age and rose with education. Most striking was the political divide: 85 percent of Democrats supported the movement, compared to just 19 percent of Republicans.

Part V

1. An expansive literature documents our nation's mistreatment of Indigenous peoples. See, for example, Wilson, *The Earth Shall Weep*, and Saunt, *Unworthy Republic*.

Chapter 11

1. Estimates of Native American net worth are scarce, but one, from 2000, found that median net worth of Native Americans was about 9 percent that of of whites, similar to the results for Blacks and Hispanics. Zagorsky, "Native Americans' Wealth." If that percentage holds today, then the aggregate wealth gap for Native Americans is about $900 billion. The Color of Wealth survey for Tulsa, Oklahoma, shows a wide range of net worth estimates for different tribes, all of which fall below median net worth for white families. However, the samples are too small to be statistically significant. Akee et al., "The Role of Race."

2. First Nations Development Institute, "Stewarding Native Lands."

3. Bureau of Indian Affairs, "What Is a Federal Indian Reservation?" Currently 56.2 million acres are held in trust as reservations, out of a total of roughly 2.43 billion acres of US land.

4. See Larson, "New Estimates of Value of Land."

5. The Case-Shiller house price index rose 90 percent from December 2009 to December 2021 (Federal Reserve Bank of St. Louis, "FRED Economic Data," series CSUSHPISA). Only a very small percentage of the rise in prices may be attributed to increased costs of construction. The Financial Accounts of the United States (formerly the Flow of Funds Accounts) shows $41 trillion of real estate assets on the

balance sheet of households in the third quarter of 2021. An additional $32 trillion of real estate assets are owned by corporate and noncorporate business. These values include the value of the structures that sit on the land but still provide a rough check on the total value of land. Board of Governors of the Federal Reserve, "Financial Accounts of the United States," tables B.101–B.103.

6. Darity and Mullen, *From Here to Equality*, chapter 13.

7. Darity and Mullen, *From Here to Equality*, chapter 13; Darity and Mullen, "Direct Payments to Close the Racial-Wealth Gap."

8. This estimate uses the Census Bureau's definition of the household by "race of the reference person." Census Bureau, "Households by Race and Hispanic Origin."

9. Total household net worth from the Financial Accounts of the United States, 2019. Black population share from Census Bureau, "American Community Survey," 2019. Current holdings of net worth by Black households from Survey of Consumer Finances, 2019.

10. Civil Liberties Public Education Fund Network, "Historical Overview of the Japanese-American Internment."

11. *Densho Encyclopedia*, "Civil Liberties Act of 1988." This reference cites the Act of 1988, the date on which the Civil Liberties Act of 1987 was signed into law.

12. US Congress, "Civil Liberties Act of 1987"; Civil Liberties Public Education Fund Network, "Historical Overview."

13. Average hourly earnings of production and nonsupervisory employees in manufacturing (Federal Reserve Bank of St. Louis, "FRED Economic Data," series CES3000000008). Income in 1945 dollars is inflated to 1988 using ten-year Treasury yields (Federal Reserve Bank of St. Louis, "FRED Economic Data," series DG10, augmented by historical yields from US Government Publishing Office, "Bond Yields and Interest Rates").

14. See Howard-Hassman and Lombardo, "Framing Reparations Claims," for a summary.

15. Darity and Frank, "The Economics of Reparations." The Conference on Jewish Material Claims Against Germany was established in 1951 by representatives of twenty-three international Jewish organizations. The conference "negotiates for and disburses funds to individuals and organizations and seeks the return of Jewish property stolen during the Holocaust." See https://www.claimscon.org/about.

16. Sebba, "The Reparations Agreements," 208.

17. Gribetz, "Holocaust Compensation."

Chapter 12

1. Holzer et al., "The Economic Costs of Childhood Poverty," 43.

2. Holzer et al., "The Economic Costs of Childhood Poverty," 43; McLaughlin and Rank, "Estimating the Economic Cost of Childhood Poverty." Estimates are converted to 2021 dollars, assuming that shares of nominal GDP remain constant.

3. Census Bureau, "Income Summary Measure," table A-1.

4. I reduce spending on transportation and other necessities by 50 percent. It would be difficult for these families to reduce spending on food, housing, health care, or childcare. The resulting budgets are about 85 percent as large as the original budgets.

5. University of Minnesota Population Center, "IPUMS/CPS Data." Using data from IPUMS, I tabulate family income by percentile from the SPM measure and calculate averages below the threshold from this tabulation. Each percentile of the family income distribution accounts for 1 percent of the families in the US (by definition), or 1.26 million families.

6. University of Minnesota Population Center, "IPUMS/CPS Data." Author's calculations using IPUMs supplemental poverty measure of income by race, ethnicity, and gender, 2020 data.

7. Card, "Estimating the Return to Schooling," table 2.

8. Census Bureau, "Educational Attainment in the United States: 2019," tables 1-1 through 1-6.

9. Author's calculations from Census Bureau, "Educational Attainment in the United States: 2019," tables 1-1 through 1-6, and Bureau of Labor Statistics, "Median Usual Weekly Earnings by Educational Attainment." The loss for the associate's degree benchmark is so much larger primarily because there are many more adults who have received a high school degree or some college credits than there are adults who have not completed high school. Of course, average earnings for those with some college credits are also higher than those without a high school degree.

10. Hanushek and Woessmann, "Universal Basic Skills," 18.

11. Hanushek and Woessmann, "Economic Impacts of Learning Losses," table 3. These are eighty-year lifetime effects, discounted back to the present at a rate of 3 percent per year.

12. See Galea et al., "Estimated Deaths."

13. See US Department of Transportation, "Departmental Guidance on Valuation of a Statistical Life"; US Environmental Protection Agency, "Mortality Risk Evaluation"; and Merrill, "No One Values Your Life," which provides a summary of valuations

across government agencies. The values of children's lives are higher, often assessed a multiple of 1.5 or greater.

14. Ten million dollars is also—and not coincidentally—the value of a statistical life recommended by W. Kip Viscusi, a leading expert in the valuation of life. See Viscusi, *Pricing Lives*, 38.

15. Author's calculations from Board of Governors of the Federal Reserve System, "Survey of Consumer Finances," 2019 data. These data include only the asset side of households' balance sheets. The debt that many lower-income households carry would of course impose an additional constraint on their ability to use these assets for stabilization or wealth-building.

16. Hunt et al., "Diversity wins," exhibit 3.

17. The loss from childhood poverty alone is estimated at $0.9–$1.2 trillion annually. The loss from below-subsistence wages, which is computed as the loss in excess of the losses from childhood poverty (but almost surely includes losses due to subpar educational attainment), is $1.3–$1.9 trillion per year. The cost of the roughly 1 million deaths and other effects of poverty, each year, is $10 trillion annually, using standard government assessment of the value of a lost life—and that of course is in addition to wages and wealth not accrued. Looking backward, the losses from lack of wealth accumulation are staggering, totaling at least $30–$40 trillion, equivalent to a stream of income going forward of $0.9–$2 trillion annually, indefinitely, depending on the rate of return assumed for this missing wealth. The land theft from Indigenous Peoples has an estimated value of $40 trillion, equivalent to a stream of income going forward of $1.2–$2 trillion annually. The loss of opportunity due to little or no wealth is harder to measure but likely large. Altogether, these losses sum to $14.3–$17.1 trillion.

Part VI

1. The question posed in this part's title comes from *The Untouchables* (1987).

Chapter 13

1. Dalida, interview with the author, May 9, 2022. Interviewee's surname purposely withheld.

2. Hicks, et al., "Still Running Up the Down Escalator," 24–25.

3. Bhattacharya and Price, "The Power of Narrative," discusses the role of public adherence to the personal responsibility and "toxic individualism" narratives in impeding progress toward systemic change.

4. Kraus, Rucker, and Richeson, "Americans Misperceive Racial Economic Inequality," 10324–10325. Respondents' views are further examined by experimental evidence that altered the framing of the questions about equality, by "inducing participants (mostly white) to think about Black individuals and families that are similar to themselves," a framing that increased their tendency to overestimate racial equality.

5. Quoted in Kraft, Lodge, and Taber, "Why People Don't Trust the Evidence," 123.

6. Kraus et al., "The Misperception of Racial Economic Inequality," 906.

7. Kraft, Lodge, and Taber, "Why People Don't Trust the Evidence," discuss the role of motivated reasoning in public distrust of evidence in the political context.

8. Jost, Banaji, and Nosek, "A Decade of System Justification Theory," 881.

9. Jost et al., "Belief in a Just God," 66. The study focuses on differences between "religious" and other respondents, but overall belief in free market ideology is high across all categories. Those with stronger religious attachments—especially Catholics and Protestants and to some extent Buddhists—hew even closer to this philosophy.

10. Jost et al., "Belief in a Just God," 63, citing Jost et al., "Fair Market Ideology."

11. See Ian Haney López, *Dog Whistle Politics*, for a complete discussion of the use of "dog whistles" to successfully cast "whites as victims of an activist government that rains gifts on grasping minorities" (6), as part of a campaign to dismantle the safety net, voting rights, and the economic stability of the broader middle class. López contends that dog-whistlers use the phrases "government benefit abusers," "illegal aliens," and "terrorists" as stand-ins for "Black," "Hispanic," and "Muslim" to garner support among white voters who would otherwise reject overtly racist language or intent. López's thesis is that right-wing business and political interests have used racial division to "distract low-income and middle-class people of all colors from their shared economic interests." Lempinen, "Ian Haney López: To Combat Racism."

12. Hicks, et al., "Still Running Up the Down Escalator," esp. 10–12. With apologies to *The Wizard of Oz* (1939).

13. See Paluck et al., "Prejudice Reduction," for a discussion of difficulties in measuring the effects of efforts to reduce prejudice.

14. Paluck and Clark, "Can Playing Together Help Us Live Together?" The research tests the "contact hypothesis," which predicts that "prejudice can be reduced when rival groups come together under optimal circumstances of cooperation and equal status" (769). The researcher found that changes in *behavior* were more common than changes in *attitude*. This conflicts with some psychological theories that argue that change in attitude is a prerequisite for behavioral change. However, change in behavior is arguably more important. And the causality may run (at least in part) the other way: consistent behavioral change may well foster attitudinal change.

15. Prentice and Paluck, "Engineering Social Change Using Social Norms," 140.

16. Paluck and Starck, "Perspective Getting In a Democracy," 178.

17. Norton and Ariely, "Building a Better America," figure 2. Respondents believed that the bottom two-fifths of the distribution owned about 10 percent of wealth, whereas the actual figure at the time was about 0.3 percent. Respondents correspondingly underestimated the share held by the top one-fifth at about 60 percent, whereas the actual share was over 80 percent.

18. Norton and Ariely, "Building a Better America," figures 2 and 3.

Chapter 14

1. Goolsbee, Hubbard, and Ganz, "A Policy Agenda," advances a related agenda focused on human capital.

2. Currie and Rossin-Slater, "Early-Life Origins," summarizes adult health, educational, labor-market, and other socioeconomic-success measures associated with early childhood experiences.

3. See Davis and Sojourner, "Increasing Federal Investment," for discussion of data and issues surrounding early childhood education.

4. See Council of Economic Advisers, "Economic Report of the President" (2016), chapter 4.

5. Council of Economic Advisers, "Economic Report of the President" (2016), figures. 4.3, 4.4, 4.6.

6. Isaacs, "International Comparisons of Economic Mobility," figs. 6–10.

7. See García et al., "Benefits of an Influential Early Childhood Program," for analysis of two programs in North Carolina, and Elango et al., "Early Childhood Education," for analysis of four programs that span the 1960s through the mid-1980s.

8. Elango et al., "Early Childhood Education."

9. Elango et al.

10. The programs are the Perry Preschool Project and the Carolina Abecedarian Project, described in Elango et al., table 8.

11. García, Heckman, and Ronda, "Boosting Intergenerational Mobility."

12. The two programs are the Carolina Abecedarian Project and the closely related Carolina Approach to Responsive Education. See García et al., "Benefits of an Influential Early Childhood Program."

13. Heckman, "Early Childhood Education: Quality and Access Pay Off," 2.

14. One summary of key early education characteristics is Heckman, "ABC/CARE."

15. See Hilger, *The Parent Trap*, for additional discussion of these issues.

16. Garcia et al., "Benefits of an Influential Early Childhood Program," section 4.4. Their estimate is $18,514 in 2014 dollars. Inflating this estimate to 2021 dollars using the consumer price index (Federal Reserve Bank of St. Louis, "FRED Economic Data," series CPIAUCSL) yields the figure in the text.

17. Census Bureau, "American Community Survey, 2020."

18. One-half is not totally arbitrary—by definition, one-half of families fall below median income, which in the United States was about $70,000 in 2021. At that level of income, taking into account the budgets presented in chapter 4, adding early childhood expenses of this magnitude would be a significant strain.

19. "Economist Says Early Childhood Education Spending Has Big Payoff."

20. American Association of Community Colleges, "Fast Facts 2021."

21. For an example of the array of offerings at a highly regarded community college in Michigan, see "Academic Pathways" at Grand Rapids Community College, https://www.grcc.edu/programs/pathways.

22. For a thoughtful discussion of the shortage of skilled workers, see Chamberlain, "Addressing the Skilled Labor Shortage."

23. Levesque, "Improving Community College Completion Rates."

24. See Van Noy and Jacobs, "Employer Perceptions of Associate Degrees."

25. See Griffin, Klempin, and Jenkins, "Using Guided Pathways."

26. See Lowe, *Putting Skill to Work*, esp. chapter 5.

27. Goolsbee, Hubbard, and Ganz, "A Policy Agenda."

28. Adapted from Heidkamp and Hilliard, "A Review of Community College-Employer Partnerships."

29. Massachusetts Business Alliance for Education, "The P-Tech Model of Early College High School."

30. See Levin et al., "Promising Practices in Community Colleges."

31. Stevens, Kurlaender, and Grosz, "Career Technical Education and Labor Market Outcomes."

32. See Backes, Holzer, and Velez "Is It Worth It?" and Jepsen, Troske, and Coomes "The Labor-Market Returns to Community College Degrees." The latter finds that net returns are sizable for degree and diplomas—$6,000 to $8,000 per year—more than compensating for the cost of obtaining these academic credentials. Even

though the earnings boost from certificates is smaller at about $1,200 per year, "the benefits to certificates likely still outweigh the costs," 98.

33. See Holzer, "A Race to the Top."

34. Tobenkin, "Employers Partner with Community Colleges."

35. Karam, "How Community Colleges Can Establish Better Partnerships."

36. Goolsbee, Hubbard, and Ganz, "A Policy Agenda," 18.

37. See Goldin and Katz, "Why the United States Led in Education."

38. See Holzer, "A Race to the Top." Holzer also offers a proposal with a variety of options for improving outcomes from community colleges.

39. As discussed in Holzer, "A Race to the Top," $5,000 stipends for students who work while attending college, coupled with competitive grants to colleges that raise completion rates and guide students into areas with better chance of employment, would cost a similar amount.

40. See Ton, "The Case for Good Jobs."

41. Economic Policy Institute, "Minimum Wage Tracker."

42. See "What Harm Do Minimum Wages Do?" for a discussion of the evolution of thinking about minimum wages. See Neumark and Wascher, "Minimum Wages and Employment," for a critique of the view that minimum wages do not lower employment. See Dube, Lester, and Reich, "Minimum Wage Effects Across State Borders," for a careful study of minimum wage effects that finds *no adverse employment effects*.

43. Meer, "Minimum-Wage Study Faces Misplaced Skepticism," concludes that the evidence overall from the Seattle wage increase suggests declines in hours and employment. Jardim et al., "Minimum Wage Increases and Employment Trajectories," subsequently found that while the minimum wage increases in Seattle led to both hours reductions and wage increases, the net result was an increase in earnings of $8–$12 weekly.

44. Derenoncourt and Montialoux, "Minimum Wages and Racial Inequality."

45. Neumark, "The Higher Wages Tax Credit."

46. See Neumark, "The Higher Wages Tax Credit" and Meer and Farren, "Subsidized—not minimum—wages should assist workers," for discussion.

47. Henderson, "The Crisis of Low Wages in the US." Jewish Vocational Services of Boston is using a Job Quality Benchmarking Index that provides smaller businesses with a tool that allows them to compare characteristics of their lower-wage jobs with those of their competitors. The hope is to "raise the floor" of lower-wage jobs.

See Johnston, "Employers Can See Where Their Wages, Benefits Stand," and Jewish Vocational Services, "The History of JVS' Job Quality Index."

48. Many analyses, including Congressional Budget Office, "Effects on Employment and Family Income" and "Budgetary Effects of the Raise the Wage Act," count increased wages as a loss in business income. However, the loss to the economy of a reduction in business profits may be relatively small. Profit rates are already quite high. And businesses have famously not been tapping into profits to finance investment in new capacity. See Krugman, "Profits Without Production"; Center for Economic Policy Research, "Higher Corporate Profits Mean Higher Investment (Not)"; and Gruber and Kamin, "The Corporate Saving Glut."

49. See Congressional Budget Office, "Effects on Employment and Family Income" and Congressional Budget Office, "Budgetary Effects of the Raise the Wage Act."

50. Komlos, *Foundations of Real-World Economics*, chapter 9 discusses the virtues of the minimum wage in the context of markets characterized by imperfect competition and robust profits.

51. See Carroll, "The Real Reason."

52. Keisler-Starkey and Bunch, "Health Insurance Coverage in the United States: 2020." Note that there is some overlap across categories, as the insured may be covered by more than one plan.

53. See the data presented in chapter 6.

54. See Davis, "Uninsured in America."

55. Coughlin, Samuel-Jakubos, and Garfield, "Sources of Payment for Uncompensated Care for the Uninsured." The authors estimate that 80 percent of uncompensated costs are offset by reimbursements from Veterans Administration programs, Medicaid, and state and local programs.

56. Institute of Medicine, "Spending on Health Care for Uninsured Americans," table 3.2.

57. Malik, "Working Families Are Spending Big Money."

58. Calcuations based on Malik, "Working Families Are Spending Big Money."

59. Schedules That Work Act, H.R. 5004.

60. Williams et al., "Stable Scheduling Increases Productivity," reports a randomized controlled trial at GAP stores, which finds that stabilizing shifts reduces worker turnover and improves sales and productivity, boosting profits.

61. Blakely-Gray, "States with Paid Family Medical Leave."

62. Bureau of Labor Statistics, "Employee Benefits Survey."

63. Based on estimated wage and salary disbursements in the forty states without PFML, using their shares of GDP to estimate their share in total wage and salary disbursements (about two-thirds). State GDP data from Bureau of Economic Analysis, "GDP by State." Total wage and salary disbursements 2021: Q3 (Federal Reserve Bank of St. Louis, "FRED Economic Data," series A576RC1).

64. Pam A., interview with author, February 9, 2022. Interviewee's surname purposely withheld.

65. Mariela, interview with author, March 21, 2022. Interviewee's surname purposely withheld.

66. Rosada, interview with author, March 21, 2022. Interviewee's surname purposely withheld.

67. Tasha, interview with author, July 12, 2022. Interviewee's surname purposely withheld.

68. See Getsinger et al., "The Housing Affordability Gap," appendix C.

69. Getsinger et al., "The Housing Affordability Gap."

70. See Popkin et al., "An Equitable Strategy for Public Housing Redevelopment."

71. See the analysis and commentary in Getsinger et al., "The Housing Affordability Gap," which employs data from the Department of Housing and Urban Development. The 2019 data for the housing gap are from Aurand et al., "The Gap: A Shortage of Affordable Homes."

72. Aurand et al, "The Gap."

73. Glaeser, Schuetz, and Ward, "Regulation and the Rise of Housing Prices in Greater Boston"; Corley et al., "From Transactional to Transformative"; and Crump et al., "Zoned Out," among many others, argue that local zoning restrictions are the primary cause of high housing prices and insufficient residential construction.

74. See, for example, Parrott and Zandi, "Overcoming the Nation's Daunting Housing Supply Shortage."

75. Parrott and Zandi, "Overcoming the Nation's Daunting Housing Supply Shortage," and Schuetz, "To Improve Housing Affordability," argue for zoning reform and point to federally led solutions.

76. Office of Management and Budget, "Historical Tables," table 12.3.

77. For description of the CDBG state program, see HUD Exchange, "CDBG State Program."

78. Office of Management and Budget, "Historical Tables," table 12.2.

79. See Badger, "How 'Not in My Backyard' Became 'Not in My Neighborhood.'"

80. Zillow, "Home Values." Typical value for homes in the 35th to 65th percentile range, in current dollars.

81. Corley et al., "From Transactional to Transformative."

82. Padeiro, Lour, and da Costa, "Transit-Oriented Development and Gentrification," reviews thirty-five articles on TOD and gentrification. The authors find significant variation in methodological rigor, so their conclusions place greater weight on studies they judge to be methodologically stronger.

83. See McKenzie, "Transit Access and Population Change," for an examination of transit access in the Washington, DC, metro area.

84. Census Bureau, "American Community Survey," 2019. That figure fell from 5 percent in the 2019 American Community Survey.

85. Burrows et al., "Commuting by Public Transportation in the United States," table 2.

86. For an accessible summary of rail and subway costs, see Levy, "Why It's So Expensive to Build Urban Rail." Above-ground rail in the United States costs between $100 million and $500 million per mile. The lower end of this range is comparable to construction costs in Europe.

87. There are dozens of electric bus manufacturers; see VentureRadar, "Top Electric Bus Companies." For an evaluation of fuel-cell bus manufacturers, see National Renewable Energy Laboratory, "Fuel Cell Electric Bus Evaluations."

88. Cannata et al., "Bus Electrification."

89. See Zuk and Carlton, "Equitable Transit Oriented Development," for a summary of the challenges to succesful TOD.

90. See Calef, "15-Minute Neighborhoods," for description of a "complete neighborhood."

91. See Cannata et al., "Bus Electrification," table 1.

92. Purchase prices for electric buses range from $650,000–$750,000, compared to $500,000 for a diesel bus. Maloney, "Electric Buses for Mass Transit."

93. This estimate provides over 90,000 new electric buses nationwide, each with an assumed service life of fifteen years. The scale of the system and the cost per capita are based on the 1,250-bus system in Boston, with population 685,000, using lifetime costs for electric buses from Cannata et al., "Bus Electrification." For number of US cities with population greater than 5,000, see "How Many Cities Are in the United States? 2022," citing Census data.

94. Budget numbers are based on Earls, "MBTA Analysis."

95. I am grateful to William A. Darity Jr. for recent discussions on baby bonds and reparations and to Darrick Hamilton for earlier discussions on the same topics.

96. William A. Darity Jr., Darrick Hamilton, and others have long advocated the use of baby bonds or the equivalent as one means to address the racial wealth gap. See Darity, Hamilton et al., "What We Get Wrong," and Hamilton and Darity, "Can 'Baby Bonds' Eliminate the Racial Wealth Gap?"

97. This recommendation follows closely the program outlined in Hamilton and Darity, "Can 'Baby Bonds' Eliminate the Racial Wealth Gap?"

98. For a summary of Children's Savings Account (CSA) programs around the United States, see Prosperity Now, "Find a Children's Savings Program." The SEED OK program in Oklahoma is one of the earliest policy-focused CSA programs in the country. See Beverly, Clancy, and Sherraden, "Universal Accounts at Birth," for a summary of research results.

99. Osterman et al, "Births: Final Data for 2020," table 1.

100. Darity and Mullen, *From Here to Equality*, chapter 13.

101. Dawson and Popoff, "Justice and Greed," reports on the 2000 survey. The 2016 poll is Marist Polls, "Exclusive Point Taken," table BM 160427. The 2021 poll is Washington Post-ABC News Poll, question 25. See Mullen and Darity, *From Here to Equality*, for a summary of these results.

102. The value of payments that are spread over time might increase if the payments were accompanied by an explicit government promise to pay. In that case, families might be able to borrow against nearly sure future payments, essentially bringing future payments forward to the present, and making them more immediately useful. Darity and Mullen consider a number of payments options, and suggest that "the aim should be at least to eliminate the racial wealth gap within a decade." Darity and Mullen, "From Here to Equality," 258–260.

103. See the discussion of Alger's work in chapter 1.

104. 100 Black Men of America, "Mentoring."

105. Conexión, "About Conexión." Robert Putnam's seminal—albeit controversial—work on social capital and the decline of community involvement is *Bowling Alone*. I have been involved as a mentor and advisor to *Conexion* for the past dozen years.

106. Lyle and Smith, "The Effect of High-Performing Mentors." Tonidandel, Averym, and Phillips, "Maximizing Returns on Mentoring," relying on a less formal methodology, echoes this conclusion.

107. Blau et al. "Can Mentoring Help Female Assistant Professors? Interim Results"; Ginther, et al., "Can Mentoring Help Female Assistant Professors?"

108. I should point out that while I was the executive in charge of the group, the expertise resided in those whose careers were formed in DEI—Marques Benton, Pamela Harris, Carole Sears, Yasin Jamal, and Nathalie Hills.

109. This estimate assumes one million new community college graduates each year, as recommended earlier in this chapter, who then earn about $8200 more per year—the average difference in earnings for those with an associate's degrees versus a high-school diploma—for the balance of their working lives. The earnings differential is taken directly from Bureau of Labor Statistics, "Median Usual Weekly Earnings by Educational Attainment."

110. See Center for Economic Policy Research, "Higher Corporate Profits Mean Higher Investment (Not)."

Chapter 15

1. See O'Mara et al., "The Effectiveness of Community Engagement," for an assessment of the effects of community engagement in public health interventions for disadvantaged groups. See Wilson, "Creative Placemaking—A Cautionary Tale," for a warning about the results of excluding community voices from community development efforts.

2. Read about Bill Traynor and his colleagues' community engagement work at "Trusted Space Partners," http://www.trustedspacepartners.com/our-work.html. See a summary of the Working Cities program (now the Working Places program, to encompass rural development as well as mid-sized cities) at https://www.bostonfed .org/workingplaces/cities-challenge.aspx.

3. Benderskaya and Dawicki, "Sparking Change in New England's Smaller Cities." See also Radcliffe, "The Art and Heart of Community Engagement."

4. Ocasio-Cortez, "Yep. Means testing = more bureaucracy . . . ," Twitter.

5. Eduardo Porter, "Patching Up the Social Safety Net." Porter also discusses arguments against means-testing, which may counter its obvious appeal.

6. Zhou, "The Case against Means Testing."

7. See Sunstein, *Sludge*, esp. chapter 5.

8. Biggs, "Means Testing and Its Limits."

9. See Jacobs, "The Downfall (and Possible Salvation) of Expertise," for a discussion of the role of public trust in experts in the context of COVID, climate change, economic policy, and "the politicization of expertise." See Simonov, et al., "The Persuasive Effect of Fox News," on the effects of the media on the public's adherence to expert advice during the pandemic. A 2022 Pew survey, "Americans' Trust

in Scientists, Other Groups Declines," found erosion in confidence in a variety of expert sources, from medical experts and scientists to public school principals, religious leaders, and elected officials. The last of these were, and have been for some time, the least trusted. Among medical experts, erosion in trust was highly politicized, with a 22 percentage point drop in confidence among Republican/ Republican-leaning respondents between early 2020 and late 2021. The drop among Democratic/Democratic-leaning respondents was 1 percentage point.

10. Card and Krueger, "Minimum Wages and Employment." The legislation was passed in November 1989 and took effect in two rounds beginning on April 1, 1990. As a validation check, Card and Krueger also studied the difference between employment changes at higher-wage New Jersey establishments and at fast-food establishments within the state.

11. Notable exceptions include the Wisconsin Administrative Data Core, a collaboration between state agencies and the University of Wisconsin's Institute for Research on Poverty (https://www.irp.wisc.edu/wadc), and California's Cradle-to-Career Data System—instituted by state law, backed by Governor Gavin Newsom, and funded out of the state budget (https://c2c.ca.gov).

12. Ms. P., interview with author, May 18, 2022. Interviewee's surname purposely withheld.

Conclusion

1. Pam A., interview with author, February 9, 2022. Interviewee's surname purposely withheld.

Bibliography

"After the Fall." *Economist*, June 16, 2005. https://www.economist.com/leaders/2005/06/16/after-the-fall.

Aiken, Claudia, Vincent J. Reina, and Dennis P. Culhane. "Understanding Low-Income Hispanic Housing Challenges and the Use of Housing and Homelessness Assistance." *Cityscape* 23, no. 2 (2021): 123–158.

Aja, Alan A., Gretchen Beesing, Daniel Bustillo, Danielle Clealand, Mark Paul, Zhaing Za, et al. "The Color of Wealth in Miami." Kirwan Institute for the Study of Race and Ethnicity, 2019. https://kirwaninstitute.osu.edu/sites/default/files/2019-02//The-Color-of-Wealth-in-Miami-Metro.pdf.

Alexander, Michelle. *The New Jim Crow: Mass Incarceration in the Era of Colorblindness.* New York: The New Press, 2010.

Alger, Horatio Jr. *Ragged Dick; or, Street Life in New York.* Digireads.com Publishing, 2009 (original publisher A. K. Loring, 1868).

Aliprantis, Dionissi, Daniel Carroll, and Eric Young. "The Dynamics of the Racial Wealth Gap." Federal Reserve Bank of Cleveland Working Paper, August 27, 2021. http://www.dionissialiprantis.com/pdfs/dynamics_RWG_August_2021.pdf.

Amadeo, Kimberly. "TARP Bailout Program: Did TARP Help You or the Banks?" *The Balance*, December 31, 2021. https://www.thebalance.com/tarp-bailout-program-3305895.

American Association of Community Colleges. "Fast Facts 2021." March 2021. https://www.aacc.nche.edu/wp-content/uploads/2021/03/AACC_2021_FastFacts.pdf.

Anderson, Carol. *White Rage: The Unspoken Truth of Our Racial Divide.* New York: Bloomsbury, 2016.

Anderson, Gary, and Dolores Martin. "The Public Domain and Nineteenth Century Transfer Policy." *Cato Journal* 6, no. 3 (1987): 9905-9923.

Andrews, Margaret, and David Smallwood. "What's Behind the Rise in SNAP Participation?" US Department of Agriculture, Economic Research Service, March 1, 2012.

https://www.ers.usda.gov/amber-waves/2012/march/what-s-behind-the-rise-in-snap-participation.

Andrews, Michelle. "As Health Care Costs Rise, Workers at Low-Wage Firms May Pay a Larger Share." Kaiser Health Network, September 25, 2019. https://khn.org/news/health-care-costs-employer-survey-workers-at-lower-wage-firms-may-have-higher-costs.

Appleby, Joyce. *Inheriting the Revolution: The First Generation of Americans*. Cambridge, MA: Harvard University Press, 2000.

Appleby, Joyce. *Recollection of the Early Republic: Selected Autobiographies*. Boston: Northeastern University Press, 1997.

Arias, Elizabeth and Jiaquan Xu. "United States Life Tables, 2018." *National Vital Statistics Reports* 69, no. 12 (2020). https://www.cdc.gov/nchs/data/nvsr/nvsr69/nvsr69-12-508.pdf.

Asante-Muhammad, Dedrick, Jared Ball, Jamie Buell, and Joshua Devine. "Black Entrepreneurship's Lethal Pre-Existing Condition: The Racial Wealth Divide during the COVID Crisis." National Community Reinvestment Coalition, April 6, 2021. https://ncrc.org/black-entrepreneurships-lethal-pre-existing-condition-the-racial-wealth-divide-during-the-covid-crisis.

Ashenfelter, Orley, and Alan Krueger. "Estimates of the Economic Return to Schooling from a New Sample of Twins." *American Economic Review* 84, no. 5 (1994): 1157–1173.

Auerbach, Alan J., Kerwin K. Charles, Courtney C. Coile, William Gale, Dana Goldman, Ronald Lee, et al. "How the Growing Gap in Life Expectancy May Affect Retirement Benefits and Reforms." NBER Working Paper 23329, April 2017. https://www.nber.org/system/files/working_papers/w23329/w23329.pdf.

Aurand, Andrew, Dan Emmanuel, Daniel Threet, Ikra Rafi, and Diane Yentel. "The Gap: A Shortage of Affordable Homes." National Low Income Housing Coalition, March 2021. https://reports.nlihc.org/sites/default/files/gap/Gap-Report_2021.pdf.

Autor, David, et al. "The $800 Billion Paycheck Protection Program: Where Did the Money Go and Why Did It Go There?" NBER Working Paper 29669, January 2022. http://www.nber.org/papers/w29669.

Backes, Ben, Harry Holzer, and Erin Velez. "Is It Worth It? Postsecondary Education and Labor Market Outcomes for the Disadvantaged." *IZA Journal of Labor Policy* 4, no. 1 (2015): 1–30.

Badger, Emily. "How 'Not in My Backyard' Became 'Not in My Neighborhood.'" *New York Times*, January 3, 2018. https://www.nytimes.com/2018/01/03/upshot/zoning-housing-property-rights-nimby-us.html.

Baker, Dean. *Rigged: How Globalization and the Rules of the Modern Economy Were Structured to Make the Rich Richer*. Washington, DC: Center for Economic and Policy Research, 2016. https://deanbaker.net/images/stories/documents/Rigged.pdf.

Barro, Robert J. *Determinants of Economic Growth: A Cross-Country Empirical Study*. Cambridge, MA: MIT Press, 1998.

Beach, Lee Roy. "Decision Making." *Narrative Inquiry* 19, no. 2 (2009): 393–414.

Bell, W. Kamau. "Few Things Say 'the US Economy Is Broken' More Than This." CNN. com, May 23, 2021. https://www.cnn.com/2021/05/23/opinions/united-shades-the -wealth-gap-kamau-bell/index.html.

Benderskaya, Kseniya, and Colleen Dawicki. "Sparking Change in New England's Smaller Cities: Lessons from Early Rounds of the Working Cities Challenge." *Communities and Banking*, April 13, 2017. https://www.bostonfed.org/publications/com munities-and-banking/2017/spring/sparking-change-new-englands-smaller-cities -lessons-from-early-rounds-of-working-cities-challenge.aspx.

Bernanke, Benjamin S. *The Courage to Act: A Memoir of a Crisis and Its Aftermath*. New York: W. W. Norton, 2015.

Bertrand, Marianne, and Sendhil Mullainathan. "Are Emily and Greg More Employable Than Lakisha and Jamal? A Field Experiment on Labor Market Discrimination." *American Economic Review* 94, no. 4 (2004): 991–1013. https://cos.gatech.edu/facul-tyres/Diversity_Studies/Bertrand_LakishaJamal.pdf.

Beverly, Sondra G., Margaret M. Clancy, and Michael Sherraden. "Universal Accounts at Birth: Results from SEED for Oklahoma Kids." Washington University at St. Louis Center for Social Development research summary 16-07, March 2016. https://open-scholarship.wustl.edu/cgi/viewcontent.cgi?article=1325&context=csd_research.

Bhattacharya, Jhumpa, and Anne Price. "The Power of Narrative in Economic Policy." Insight Center for Community Economic Development, November 8, 2019. https://medium.com/economicsecproj/the-power-of-narrative-in-economic-policy-27bd8a 9ed888.

BibleGateway, Luke 16:19–31. New Revised Standard Version, Anglicized. https://www.biblegateway.com/passage/?search=Luke+16%3A19%E2%80%9331&version =NRSVA. Accessed December 2, 2022.

Biggs, Andrew G. "Means Testing and Its Limits." *National Affairs* 9 (2011). https://www.nationalaffairs.com/publications/detail/means-testing-and-its-limits.

Bitler, Marianne P., Jonah B. Gelbach, and Hilary W. Hoynes. "Some Evidence on Race, Welfare Reform, and Household Income." *American Economic Review Papers and Proceedings* 93, no. 2 (2003): 293–298.

Biu, Ofronama, Grieve Chelwa, Christopher Famighetti, Lynn Parramore, Kate Richey, Damario Solomon-Simmons, and Darrick Hamilton. "The Color of Wealth in Tulsa, Oklahoma: The Destruction of Greenwood and the Legacy of Land Loss." Institute on Race, Power and Political Economy, The New School, December 2021. https://www.oknativeassets.org/resources/Documents/Tulsa%20Color%20of%20Wealth%20Full%20Report_December2021.pdf.

Bivens, Josh, *Failure by Design: The Story behind Americas' Broken Economy*. Ithaca, NY: ILR Press, 2011.

Blakeley-Gray, Rachel. "States with Paid Family Leave," Patriot Software, June 15. https://www.patriotsoftware.com/blog/payroll/states-with-paid-family-leave/. Accessed December 1, 2022.

Blank, Rebecca. "Evaluating Welfare Reform in the United States." *Journal of Economic Literature* 40, no. 4 (2002): 1105–1166.

Blank, Rebecca. "How to Improve Poverty Measurement in the United States." *Journal of Policy Analysis and Management* 27, no. 2 (2008): 233–254.

Blau, Francine D., Janet M. Currie, Rachel T. A. Croson, and Donna K. Ginther. "Can Mentoring Help Female Assistant Professors? Interim Results from a Randomized Trial." *American Economic Review Papers and Proceedings* 100, no. 2 (2010): 348–352.

Board of Governors of the Federal Reserve System. "Factors Affecting Reserve Balances." https://www.federalreserve.gov/releases/h41. Accessed May 24, 2022.

Board of Governors of the Federal Reserve System. "FedListens: Perspectives from the Public," June 2020. https://www.federalreserve.gov/publications/files/fedlistens-report-20200612.pdf.

Board of Governors of the Federal Reserve System. "Financial Accounts of the United States: Flow of Funds, Balance Sheets, and Integrated Macroeconomic Accounts," December 5, 2022. https://www.federalreserve.gov/releases/z1/20191212/z1.pdf.

Board of Governors of the Federal Reserve System. "Report on the Economic Well-Being of U.S. Households in 2021." 2022. https://www.federalreserve.gov/publications/files/2021-report-economic-well-being-us-households-202205.pdf.

Board of Governors of the Federal Reserve System. "Review of Monetary Policy Strategy, Tools, and Communications." 2020. https://www.federalreserve.gov/monetarypolicy/review-of-monetary-policy-strategy-tools-and-communications.htm.

Board of Governors of the Federal Reserve System. "Survey of Consumer Finances." 2019. https://www.federalreserve.gov/econres/scfindex.htm.

Boulware, Lemuel R. *The Truth about Boulwarism: Trying to Do Right Voluntarily*. Washington, DC: Bureau of National Affairs, 1969.

Bound, John, and Sarah Turner. "Closing the Gap or Widening the Divide: The Effects of the G.I. Bill and World War II on the Educational Outcomes of Black Americans." *Journal of Economic History* 63, no. 1 (2003): 145–177.

Boushey, Heather, and Bridget Ansel. "Working by the Hour: The Economic Consequences of Unpredictable Scheduling Practices." Washington Center for Equitable Growth, September 2016. https://equitablegrowth.org/wp-content/uploads/2016/09/090716-unpred-sched-practices.pdf.

Brand, Madeleine. "Yale Professor Predicts Housing 'Bubble' Will Burst." National Public Radio *Day to Day*, June 3, 2005. https://www.npr.org/templates/story/story.php?storyId=4679264.

Brightbeam. "Racial Gaps in Academic Proficiency." 2021. https://whyproficiencymatters.org.

Brookings Institution. "Responding to the Global Financial Crisis: What We Did and Why We Did It." September 12, 2018. https://www.brookings.edu/wp-content/uploads/2018/09/es_20180912_financial_crisis_day2_transcript.pdf.

Bryant, David, Ginger Haggerty, Cynthia Parker, Mimi Turchinetz, and Esther Schlorholtz. "Reducing Racial Wealth Inequalities in Greater Boston: Building a Shared Agenda." Federal Reserve Bank of Boston, May 31, 2017. https://www.bostonfed.org/publications/one-time-pubs/reducing-racial-wealth-inequalities-in-greater-boston.aspx.

Bureau of Economic Analysis. "GDP by State." https://www.bea.gov/data/gdp/gdp-state.

Bureau of Economic Analysis. "Personal Income and Its Disposition." Table 2. January 28, 2022. https://www.bea.gov/sites/default/files/2022-02/pi0122.pdf. Accessed February 7, 2022.

Bureau of Indian Affairs. "What Is a Federal Indian Reservation?" 2017. https://www.bia.gov/faqs/what-federal-indian-reservation.

Bureau of Labor Statistics. "Databases, Tables & Calculators by Subject" (annual unemployment rate data, 1929–1939). https://data.bls.gov/timeseries/LFU21000100&series_id=LFU22000100&from_year=1929&to_year=1939&periods_option=specific_periods&periods=Annual+Data. Accessed November 12, 2022.

Bureau of Labor Statistics. "Employee Benefits in the United States." Tables 1, 2, 6. March 2021. https://www.bls.gov/news.release/archives/ebs2_09232021.htm.

Bureau of Labor Statistics. "A Look at Pay at the Top, the Bottom, and in Between." May 2015. https://www.bls.gov/spotlight/2015/a-look-at-pay-at-the-top-the-bottom-and-in-between/pdf/a-look-at-pay-at-the-top-the-bottom-and-in-between.pdf.

Bureau of Labor Statistics. "Median Usual Weekly Earnings by Educational Attainment." https://www.bls.gov/charts/usual-weekly-earnings/usual-weekly-earnings-over-time-by-education.htm. Accessed December 5, 2022.

Bureau of Labor Statistics. "Median Usual Weekly Earnings by Occupation." 2021. https://data.bls.gov/PDQWeb/le.

Bureau of Labor Statistics. "Median Weekly Earnings Were $900 for Women, $1,089 for Men, in First Quarter 2021." April 23, 2021. https://www.bls.gov/opub/ted/2021/median-weekly-earnings-were-900-for-women-1089-for-men-in-first-quarter-2021.htm.

Bureau of Labor Statistics. "67 Percent of Private Industry Workers Had Access to Retirement Plans in 2020." March 1, 2021. https://www.bls.gov/opub/ted/2021/67-percent-of-private-industry-workers-had-access-to-retirement-plans-in-2020.htm.

Bureau of Labor Statistics. "Union Members Summary." January 20, 2022. https://www.bls.gov/news.release/union2.nr0.htm.

Burrows, Michael, Charlynn Burd, and Brian McKenzie. "Commuting by Public Transportation in the United States: 2019." US Census Bureau, American Community Survey Reports, April 2021.

Business Roundtable. "Business Roundtable Redefines the Purpose of a Corporation to Promote 'An Economy That Serves All Americans.'" August 19, 2019. https://www.businessroundtable.org/business-roundtable-redefines-the-purpose-of-a-corporation-to-promote-an-economy-that-serves-all-americans.

Cairns, Christopher, Jill J. Ashman, and Kai Kang. "Emergency Department Visit Rates by Selected Characteristics: United States, 2018." National Center for Health Statistics, 2021. https://www.cdc.gov/nchs/products/databriefs/db401.htm.

Calef, Anne, Luc Schuster, Tom Hopper, and Peter Ciurczak. "15-Minute Neighborhoods: Repairing Regional Harms and Building Vibrant Neighborhoods for All." Boston Indicators, September 2021. https://www.bostonindicators.org/-/media/indicators/boston-indicators-reports/report-files/15minfinal_lr_2021_11.pdf.

Cannata, Rob, et al. "Bus Electrification: Accelerating the Electrification of Bus Service in the Boston Metro Area." Sierra Club, September 2021. https://www.sierraclub.org/sites/www.sierraclub.org/files/press-room/MBTAReport_Final2.pdf.

Card, David. "Estimating the Return to Schooling: Progress on Some Persistent Econometric Problems." *Econometrica* 69, no. 5 (2001): 1127–1160.

Card, David, and Alan Krueger. "Minimum Wages and Employment: A Case Study of the Fast-Food Industry in New Jersey and Pennsylvania." *American Economic Review* 84, no. 4 (1994): 772–793.

Carroll, Aaron E. "The Real Reason the U.S. Has Employer-Sponsored Health Insurance." *New York Times*, September 5, 2017. https://www.nytimes.com/2017/09/05/upshot/the-real-reason-the-us-has-employer-sponsored-health-insurance.html.

Carroll, Daniel R., and Anne Chen. "Income Inequality Matters, but Mobility is Just as Important." Federal Reserve Bank of Cleveland, June 20, 2016. https://www.clevelandfed.org/newsroom-and-events/publications/economic-commentary/2016-economic-commentaries/ec-201606-income-inequality-and-mobility.aspx.

Carroll, Daniel R., and Nicholas Hoffman. "New Data on Wealth Mobility and Their Impact on Models of Inequality." Federal Reserve Bank of Cleveland, June 27, 2017. https://www.clevelandfed.org/en/newsroom-and-events/publications/economic-commentary/2017-economic-commentaries/ec-201709-new-data-on-wealth-mobility.aspx.

Case, Anne, and Angus Deaton. "Mortality and Morbidity in the 21st Century." *Brookings Papers on Economic Activity* (2017): 397–443.

Census Bureau. "American Community Survey." 2019. https://data.census.gov/table?tid=ACSDP5Y2019.DP05. Accessed December 5, 2022.

Census Bureau. "American Community Survey." 2020. https://data.census.gov/table?tid=ACSDP5Y2020.DP05. Accessed December 7, 2022.

Census Bureau. "American Community Survey." 2021. https://data.census.gov/table?tid=ACSDP5Y2021.DP03. Accessed January 3, 2023.

Census Bureau. "American Housing Survey, Housing Costs." 2021. https://www.census.gov/programs-surveys/ahs/data/interactive/ahstablecreator.html?s_areas=00000&s_year=2021&s_tablename=TABLE10&s_bygroup1=7&s_bygroup2=9&s_filtergroup1=3&s_filtergroup2=1. (Set filtergroup1=3 for data for Hispanics.)

Census Bureau. "American Housing Survey. Housing Quality Data." 2021. https://www.census.gov/programs-surveys/ahs/data/interactive/ahstablecreator.html?s_areas=00000&s_year=2021&s_tablename=TABLE5&s_bygroup1=9&s_bygroup2=8&s_filtergroup1=1&s_filtergroup2=1. (Set filtergroup1=3 for data for Hispanics.)

Census Bureau. "Annual Business Survey, 2020." 2021. https://data.census.gov/cedsci/table?tid=ABSCS2019.AB1900CSA02&hidePreview=true.

Census Bureau. "Educational Attainment in the United States: 2019." March 30, 2020. https://www.census.gov/data/tables/2019/demo/educational-attainment/cps-detailed-tables.html.

Census Bureau. "Health Insurance in the United States: 2019-Tables." Table A1. September 15, 2020. https://www.census.gov/data/tables/2020/demo/health-insurance/p60-271.html.

Census Bureau. "Historical Income Tables: Households." https://www.census.gov /data/tables/time-series/demo/income-poverty/historical-income-households.html. Accessed June 30, 22.

Census Bureau. "Households by Race and Hispanic Origin of Household Reference Person and Detailed Type:2021." Table H3. 2021. https://www.census.gov/data/tables /2021/demo/families/cps-2021.html. Accessed December 5, 2022.

Census Bureau. "Income Summary Measures by Selected Characteristics: 2020 and 2021" (Microsoft Excel spreadsheet). https://www2.census.gov/programs-surveys/ demo/tables/p60/273/tableA1.xlsx. Accessed December 7, 2022.

Census Bureau. "Number of Poor and Poverty Rate by State" (Microsoft Excel spreadsheet). Updated August 29, 2022. https://www.census.gov/data/tables/time-series /demo/income-poverty/historical-poverty-people.html#:~:text=Table%2019.%20 Number%20of%20Poor%20and%20Poverty%20Rate%20by%20State%20%5B%3C1 .0%20MB%5D.

Census Bureau. "People in Poverty by Selected Characteristics, Table A-1." https:// www2.census.gov/programs-surveys/demo/tables/p60/277/tableA1_pov_characteris tics.xlsx. Accessed December 9, 2022.

Census Bureau. "Poverty Status of People by Family Relationship, Race, and Hispanic Origin, 1959 to 2021, Table A-4." https://www2.census.gov/programs-surveys/demo /tables/p60/277/tableA4_hist_pov_by_family_type.xlsx. Accessed December 9, 2022.

Census Bureau. "Week 42 Household Pulse Survey: January 26–February 7." February 16, 2022. https://www.census.gov/data/tables/2022/demo/hhp/hhp42.html.

Center for Budget and Policy Priorities. "Policy Basics: Temporary Assistance for Needy Families." Updated March 1, 2022. https://www.cbpp.org/research/family -income-support/temporary-assistance-for-needy-families.

Center for Economic and Policy Research. "As the Data Show, Higher Corporate Profits Mean Higher Investment (Not)." August 31, 2017. https://www.cepr.net/as -the-data-show-higher-corporate-profits-mean-higher-investment-not.

Center on Poverty and Social Policy. "Columbia Monthly Poverty Tracker" (Google Docs spreadsheet). https://docs.google.com/spreadsheets/d/10q9eSPr2UOMw1NtJu VDDlPewTDlm8kb73WTom0uWZOI. Accessed June 1, 2022.

Center on Poverty and Social Policy. "Monthly Poverty Data." https://www.poverty center.columbia.edu/forecasting-monthly-poverty-data. Accessed March 9, 2022.

Centers for Disease Control and Prevention. "CDC WONDER: Natality, 2007-2021 Results." https://wonder.cdc.gov/natality-current.html. (Select "2020" Under "4. Select birth Characteristics.")

Chamberlain, Sarah. "Addressing the Skilled Labor Shortage in America." *Forbes*, August 21, 2019. https://www.forbes.com/sites/sarahchamberlain/2019/08/21/address ing-the-skilled-labor-shortage-in-america.

Chetty, Raj, John N. Friedman, Nathaniel Hendren, Maggie R. Jones, and Sonya R. Porter. "The Opportunity Atlas: Mapping the Childhood Roots of Social Mobility." NBER Working Paper 25147, October 2018. https://www.nber.org/papers/w25147.

Chetty, Raj, John N. Friedman, and Jonah E. Rockoff. "Measuring the Impacts of Teachers II: Teacher Value-Added and Student Outcomes in Adulthood." *American Economic Review* 104, no. 9 (2014): 2633–2679.

Chetty, Raj, David Grusky, Maximilian Hell, Nathaniel Hendren, Roberg Manduca, and Jimmy Narang. "The Fading American Dream: Trends in Absolute Income Mobility Since 1940." *Science* 356 (2016): 398–406.

Child Care Aware of America. "The U.S. and the High Price of Child Care: An Examination of a Broken System." 2019. https://info.childcareaware.org/hubfs/2019 %20Price%20of%20Care%20State%20Sheets/Final-TheUSandtheHighPriceofChild Care-AnExaminationofaBrokenSystem.pdf.

ChildCare.gov. "See Your State's Resources." https://childcare.gov/state-resources -home. Accessed February 1, 2022.

Chirinko, Robert S., and Daniel J. Wilson. "Can Lower Tax Rates Be Bought? Business Rent-Seeking and Tax Competition among U.S. States." *National Tax Journal* 63, no. 4.2 (2010): 967–993.

Chudacoff, Howard. "Success and Security: The Meaning of Social Mobility in America." *Reviews in American History* 10, no. 4 (1982): 101–112.

"Civil Liberties Act of 1988." *Densho Encyclopedia*, updated August 24, 2020. https:// encyclopedia.densho.org/Civil_Liberties_Act_of_1988.

Civil Liberties Public Education Fund Network. "Historical Overview of the Japanese-American Internment." http://www.momomedia.com/CLPEF/history.html. Accessed December 15, 2021.

Coleman-Jensen, Alisha, Matthew P. Rabbitt, Christian A. Gregory, and Anita Singh. "Household Food Security in the United States in 2019." US Department of Agriculture, 2019. https://www.ers.usda.gov/webdocs/publications/99282/err-275.pdf?v =1170.

Conexión. "About Conexión." http://conexion-all.org/about. Accessed November 14, 2022.

Congressional Budget Office. "The Budgetary Effects of the Raise the Wage Act of 2021," February 2021. https://www.cbo.gov/system/files/2021-02/56975-Minimum -Wage.pdf.

Congressional Budget Office. "The Effects on Employment and Family Income of Increasing the Federal Minimum Wage," July 2019. https://www.cbo.gov/system /files/2019-07/CBO-55410-MinimumWage2019.pdf.

Congressional Budget Office. "Estimated Impact of the American Recovery and Reinvestment Act on Employment and Economic Output in 2014." February 2015. https://www.cbo.gov/sites/default/files/114th-congress-2015-2016/reports/49958 -ARRA.pdf.

Congressional Research Service. "The Temporary Assistance for Needy Families (TANF) Block Grant: Responses to Frequently Asked Questions." Updated March 31, 2022. https://sgp.fas.org/crs/misc/RL32760.pdf.

Conwell, Russell. *Acres of Diamonds*. Digireads.com publishing, 2014 (original speech revised and delivered continually, ca. 1900–1925).

Coombs, Kyle, Arindrajit Dube, Calvin Jahnke, Raymond Kluender, Suresh Naidu, and Michael Stepner. "Early Withdrawal of Pandemic Unemployment Insurance: Effects on Employment and Earnings." *American Economic Association Papers and Proceedings*, 112 (2022):85-90.

Corak, Miles. "How to Slide Down the 'Great Gatsby Curve': Inequality, Life Chances, and Public Policy in the United States." Center for American Progress, December 2012. https://stonecenter.gc.cuny.edu/files/2012/12/corak-how-to-slide -down-the-great-gatsby-curve-2012.pdf.

Corley, Tracy, Elizabeth Haney, Ben Forman, and Catherine Tumber. "From Trans-actional to Transformative: The Case for Equity in Gateway City Transit-Oriented Development." MassInc, May 2020. https://2gaiae1lifzt2tsfgr2vil6c-wpengine.net dna-ssl.com/wp-content/uploads/2018/02/MassINC-ETOD-Paper-2020-FINAL.pdf.

Coughlin, Teresa A., Haley Samuel-Jakubos, and Rachel Garfield. "Sources of Pay-ment for Uncompensated Care for the Uninsured." Kaiser Family Foundation, April 6, 2021. https://www.kff.org/uninsured/issue-brief/sources-of-payment-for-uncom pensated-care-for-the-uninsured.

Council of Economic Advisors. "Economic Report of the President." Transmitted to the Congress January 1964.

Council of Economic Advisors. "Economic Report of the President." Transmitted to the Congress January 2016.

Cowen, Tyler. "Why CEOs Actually Deserve Their Gazillion Dollar Salaries." *Time*, April 11, 2019. https://time.com/5566816/ceo-pay-income-inequality.

Crump, Sarah, Jenny Schuetz, Trevor Mattos, and Luc Schuster. "Zoned Out: Why Massachusetts Needs to Legalize Apartments Near Transit." Boston Indicators,

October 21, 2020. https://www.bostonindicators.org/reports/report-website-pages/zoned-out.

Cunnyngham, Karen. "Reaching Those in Need: Estimates of State SNAP participation rates in 2018." US Department of Agriculture, May 2021. https://fns-prod.azureedge.us/sites/default/files/resource-files/Reaching2018.pdf.

Currie, Janet, and Maya Rossin-Slater. "Early-Life Origins of Life-Cycle Well-Being: Research and Policy Implications." *Journal of Policy Analysis and Management* 34, no. 1 (2015): 208–242.

Darity, William A. Jr., and Dania Frank. "The Economics of Reparations." *American Economic Association Papers and Proceedings* 93, no. 2 (2003): 326–329.

Darity, William A. Jr., Darrick Hamilton, Mark Paul, Alan Aja, Anne Price, Antonio Moore, and Caterina Chiopris. "What We Get Wrong about Closing the Racial Wealth Gap." Samuel DuBois Cook Center on Social Equity Insight Center for Community Economic Development, April 2018. https://socialequity.duke.edu/wp-content/uploads/2019/10/what-we-get-wrong.pdf.

Darity, William A. Jr., and A. Kirsten Mullen. *From Here to Equality: Reparations for Black Americans in the Twenty-First Century.* Chapel Hill: University of North Carolina Press, 2020.

Darity, William A. Jr., and A. Kirsten Mullen. "William Darity and A. Kirsten Mullen on Direct Payments to Close the Racial-Wealth Gap." *Economist*, May 18, 2021. https://www.economist.com/by-invitation/2021/05/18/william-darity-and-a-kirsten-mullen-on-direct-payments-to-close-the-racial-wealth-gap.

Davis, Elizabeth, and Aaron Sojourner. "Increasing Federal Investment in Children's Early Care and Education to Raise Quality, Access, and Affordability." The Hamilton Project, May 12, 2021. https://www.hamiltonproject.org/papers/increasing_federal_investment_in_childrens_early_care_and_education_to_raise_quality_access_and_affordability.

Davis, Karen. "Uninsured in America: Problems and Possible Solutions." *British Medical Journal* 334, no. 7589 (2007): 346–348.

Dawson, M., and R. Popoff. "Justice and Greed: Black and White Support for Reparation." *Du Bois Review: Social Science Research on Race* 1 no. 1 (2004): 47–91.

De La Cruz-Viesca, Melany, Zhenxiang Chen, Paul M. Ong, Darrick Hamilton, and William A. Darity Jr. "The Color of Wealth in Los Angeles." Federal Reserve Bank of San Francisco, 2016. https://www.frbsf.org/wp-content/uploads/sites/3/color-of-wealth-in-los-angeles.pdf.

Deloitte. "Missing Pieces Report: The Board Diversity Census of Women and Minorities on *Fortune* 500 Boards." 6th ed. 2021. https://www2.deloitte.com/content/dam

/Deloitte/us/Documents/center-for-board-effectiveness/missing-pieces-fortune-500
-board-diversity-study-6th-edition-report.pdf.

Derenoncourt, Ellora, and Claire Montialoux. "Minimum Wages and Racial Inequality." *Quarterly Journal of Economics* 136, no. 1 (2021): 169–228.

Desmond, Matthew. *Evicted: Poverty and Profit in the American City*. New York: Broad-
way Books, 2016.

Drucker, Jesse, and Danny Hakim. "How Accounting Giants Craft Favorable Tax Rules
from Inside Government." *New York Times*, September 19, 2021. https://www.nytimes
.com/2021/09/19/business/accounting-firms-tax-loopholes-government.html.

Drucker, Jesse, and Danny Hakim. "Private Inequity: How a Powerful Industry Con-
quered the Tax System." *New York Times*, September 8, 2021. https://www.nytimes
.com/2021/06/12/business/private-equity-taxes.html.

Dua, André, Kweilin Ellingrud, Michael Lazar, Ryan Luby, Matthew Petric, Alex
Ulyett, and Tucker Van Aken. "Unequal America: Ten Insights on the State of Economic Opportunity." McKinsey & Company, May 2021. https://www.mckinsey.com
/~/media/mckinsey/about%20us/covid%20response%20center/unequal%20america
%20ten%20insights%20on%20the%20state%20of%20economic%20opportunity
/unequal-america-ten-insights-on-the-state-of-economic-opportunity-vf.pdf.

Dube, Arindrajit, T. William Lester, and Michael Reich. "Minimum Wage Effects
Across State Borders: Estimates Using Contiguous Counties." IRLE Working paper
157-07, 2010. https://irle.berkeley.edu/files/2010/Minimum-Wage-Effects-Across-State
-Borders.pdf.

Earls, Eamon McCarthy. "MBTA Analysis: A look inside the MBTA." Pioneer Institute,
April 1, 2019. https://pioneerinstitute.org/blog/mbtaanalysis-a-look-inside-the-mbta.

Eavis, Peter. "Board Diversity Increase in 2021. Some Ask What Took So Long." *New
York Times*, January 3, 2021. https://www.nytimes.com/2022/01/03/business/corpo
rate-board-diversity.html.

Economic Policy Institute. "Family Budget Calculator." https://www.epi.org/resources
/budget/ November 21, 2021.

Economic Policy Institute. "Minimum Wage Tracker." https://www.epi.org/mini
mum-wage-tracker/#/min_wage. Accessed January 6, 2022.

"Economist Says Early Childhood Education Spending Has Big Payoff." Minnesota
Public Radio, May 10, 2017. https://www.mprnews.org/story/2017/05/10/arthur-rol
nick-early-childhood-ed-pays-off.

Edjemyr, Simon, and Kenneth A. Shores. "Pulling back the Curtain: Intra-District
School Spending Inequality and its Correlates." Unpublished manuscript, May 19,
2017. https://sejdemyr.github.io/docs/ejdemyr_shores_schoolineq.pdf.

Elango, Sneha, Jorge Luis García, James H. Heckman, and Andrés Hojman. "Early Childhood Education." NBER Working Paper 21766, November 2015. https://www.nber.org/system/files/working_papers/w21766/w21766.pdf.

Engelberg, Joseph, Pengjie Gao, and Christopher A. Parsons. "The Price of a CEO's Rolodex," *Review of Financial Studies* 26, no. 1 (2013): 79–114.

Eviction Lab. "Eviction Tracker." https://evictionlab.org/eviction-tracking. Accessed May 23, 2022.

Eviction Lab. "National Estimates: Eviction in America." May 11, 2018. https://evictionlab.org/national-estimates.

Eviction Lab. "Research." https://evictionlab.org/updates/research. Accessed November 14, 2022.

Faturechi, Robert, and Justin Elliott. "How the Trump Tax Law Created a Loophole That Lets Top Executives Net Millions by Slashing Their Own Salaries." *ProPublica*, August 19, 2021. https://www.propublica.org/article/how-the-trump-tax-law-created-a-loophole-that-lets-top-executives-net-millions-by-slashing-their-own-salaries.

Federal Bureau of Prisons. "Statistics on Race, Ethnicity, Gender, and Offense Type." https://www.bop.gov/about/statistics/statistics_inmate_race.jsp; https://www.bop.gov/about/statistics/statistics_inmate_ethnicity.jsp; https://www.bop.gov/about/statistics/statistics_inmate_offenses.jsp. Accessed May 31, 2022.

Federal Reserve Bank of Atlanta. "Wage Growth Tracker." https://www.atlantafed.org/chcs/wage-growth-tracker. Accessed March 2, 2022.

Federal Reserve Bank of Boston. "Working Cities Challenge." https://www.bostonfed.org/workingplaces/cities-challenge/massachusetts-one.aspx. Accessed May 9, 2022.

Federal Reserve Bank of Minneapolis. "Racism and the Economy." https://www.minneapolisfed.org/policy/racism-and-the-economy. Accessed April 5, 2022.

Federal Reserve Bank of Philadelphia. "Data Files—Real-Time Data Set (EMPLOY)." https://www.philadelphiafed.org/surveys-and-data/real-time-data-research/employ. Accessed February 15, 2022.

Federal Reserve Bank of Philadelphia. "Survey of Professional Forecasters." https://www.philadelphiafed.org/surveys-and-data/data-files. Accessed January 24, 2023.

Feenberg, Daniel, and James Poterba. "The Income and Tax Share of Very High-Income Households, 1960–1995." *American Economic Review* 90, no. 2 (2000): 264–270.

Fernández, Lilia. "Of Immigrants and Migrants: Mexican and Puerto Rican Labor Migration in Comparative Perspective." *Journal of American Ethnic History* 29, no. 3 (2010): 6–39.

First Nations Development Institute. "Stewarding Native Lands." https://www.first
nations.org/our-programs/stewarding-native-lands. Accessed November 12, 2022.

Foote, Christopher L., Jeffrey C. Fuhrer, Eileen Mauskopf, and Paul S. Willen. "A
Proposal to Help Distressed Homeowners: A Government Payment-Sharing Plan."
Federal Reserve Bank of Boston, 2009. https://www.bostonfed.org/publications
/public-policy-brief/2009/a-proposal-to-help-distressed-homeowners-a-government
-payment-sharing-plan.aspx.

Foote, Christopher L., Kristopher S. Gerardi, and Paul S. Willen. "Why Did So Many
People Make So Many Ex Post Bad Decisions? The Causes of the Foreclosure Crisis."
In *Rethinking the Financial Crisis*, edited by Alan Blinder, Andrew Lo, and Robert
Solow. New York: Russell Sage Foundation, 2012.

Fox, Liana, and Kalee Burns. "The Supplemental Poverty Measure: 2020." Census
Bureau, September 14, 2021. https://www.census.gov/library/publications/2021
/demo/p60-275.html.

Franklin, Benjamin. "On the Price of Corn, and Management of the Poor." *London
Chronicle*, November 29, 1766. Available via US National Archives at https://found
ers.archives.gov/documents/Franklin/01-13-02-0194.

FRED Economic Data. Federal Reserve Bank of St. Louis, Economic Research. https://
fred.stlouisfed.org/#. Accessed January 24, 2023.

Friedman, Benjamin. "Is Our Financial System Serving Us Well?" *Daedalus* 139, no.
4 (2010): 9–21.

Friedman, Benjamin. *Religion and the Rise of Capitalism*. New York: Knopf, 2021.

Friedman, Milton. *Capitalism and Freedom*. Chicago: University of Chicago Press, 1962.

Friedman, Milton. "The Social Responsibility of Business Is to Increase Its Profits."
New York Times Magazine, September 13, 1970. http://websites.umich.edu/~thecore
/doc/Friedman.pdf.

Fuhrer, Herbert. 1956. Invalid bed. US Patent 2,755,488, filed August 12, 1953, and
issued July 24, 1956.

Fuhrer, Mary B. *A Crisis of Community: The Trials and Transformation of a New England
Town, 1815–1848*. Chapel Hill: University of North Carolina Press, 2014.

Gabaix, Xavier, and Augustin Landier. "Why Has CEO Pay Increased So Much?"
Quarterly Journal of Economics 123, no. 1 (2008): 49–100.

Galbraith, John K. *The Good Society: The Humane Agenda*. New York: Houghton Mif-
flin, 1996.

Galbraith, John K. "Recession Economics." *New York Review of Books* 29, no. 1, February 4, 1982.

Gale, William. "Did the 2017 Tax Cut—the Tax Cuts and Jobs Act—Pay for Itself?" Brookings Institution, February 14, 2020. https://www.brookings.edu/policy2020 /votervital/did-the-2017-tax-cut-the-tax-cuts-and-jobs-act-pay-for-itself.

Gale, William, and Claire Haldeman. "The Tax Cuts and Jobs Act: Searching for Supply-Side Effects." *National Tax Journal* 74, no. 3 (2021): 895–914.

Galea, Sandro, Melissa Tracy, Katherine J. Hoggatt, Charles DiMaggio, and Adam Karpati. "Estimated Deaths Attributable to Social Factors in the United States." *American Journal of Public Health* 101, no. 8 (2011): 1456–1465. https://ajph.aphapublica tions.org/doi/pdfplus/10.2105/AJPH.2010.300086.

Gallup Polls. "Big Business." https://news.gallup.com/poll/5248/big-business.aspx. Accessed December 2, 2022.

Gallup Polls. "Confidence in Institutions." https://news.gallup.com/poll/1597/con fidence-institutions.aspx. Accessed December 2, 2022.

Gallup Polls. "Labor Unions." https://news.gallup.com/poll/12751/labor-unions .aspx. Accessed December 2, 2022.

Gallup Polls. "Most Important Problem." https://news.gallup.com/poll/1675/most -important-problem.aspx. Accessed January 18, 2022.

García, Jorge Luis, James J. Heckman, Duncan Ermini Leaf, and María José Prados. "Quantifying the Life-cycle Benefits of an Influential Early Childhood Program." *Journal of Political Economy* 128, no. 7 (2020): 2502–2541.

García, Jorge Luis, James J. Heckman, and Victor Ronda. "Boosting Intergenerational Mobility: The Lasting Effects of Early Childhood Education on Skills and Social Mobility." Center for the Economics of Human Development, 2021. https://heck manequation.org/www/assets/2021/11/F_Heckman_Perry-2021_OnePager_092321 .pdf.

Gates, Jimmie. "MDHS Confirms Most New Applicants Rejected for Welfare." *Clarion-Ledger*, April 20, 2017. https://www.clarionledger.com/story/news/2017/04/20/mdhs -confirms-most-new-applicants-rejected-welfare/100692926/. Accessed December 2, 2022.

Gelles, David. *The Man Who Broke Capitalism: How Jack Welch Gutted the Heartland and Crushed the Soul of Corporate America—and How to Undo His Legacy*. New York: Simon & Schuster, 2022.

Getsinger, Liza, Lily Posey, Graham MacDonald, and Josh Leopold. "The Housing Affordability Gap for Extremely Low-Income Renters in 2014." Urban Institute, April 2017. https://www.urban.org/sites/default/files/publication/89921/gap_map_report .pdf.

Ginther, Donna K., Janet M. Currie, Francine D. Blau, and Rachel T. A. Croson. "Can Mentoring Help Female Assistant Professors? An Evaluation by Randomized Trial." *American Economic Review Papers and Proceedings* 110 (2020): 205–209.

Glaeser, Edward, Jenny Schuetz, and Bryce Ward. "Regulation and the Rise of Housing Prices in Greater Boston." Pioneer Institute for Public Policy Research, January 5, 2006. https://www.hks.harvard.edu/sites/default/files/centers/rappaport/files/regulation_housingprices_1.pdf.

Glynn, Sarah Jane, Heather Boushey, Peter Berg, and Danielle Corley. "Fast Facts on Who Has Access to Paid Time Off and Flexibility." Center for American Progress, April 26, 2016. https://www.americanprogress.org/issues/economy/reports/2016/04/26/134814/fast-facts-on-who-has-access-to-paid-time-off-and-flexibility.

Goldhaber, Dan, Thomas J. Kane, Andrew McEachin, Emily Morton, Tyler Patterson, and Douglas O. Staiger. "The Consequences of Remote and Hybrid Instruction During the Pandemic." Harvard University Center for Education Policy Research, May 2022. https://cepr.harvard.edu/files/cepr/files/5-4.pdf.

Goldin, Claudia, and Lawrence F. Katz. "Why the United States Led in Education: Lessons from Secondary School Expansion, 1910 to 1940." In *Human Capital and Institutions: A Long-Run View*, edited by David Eltis, Frank D. Lewis, and Kenneth L. Sokoloff, 143–178. Cambridge: Cambridge University Press, 2009.

Goolsbee, Austan, Glenn Hubbard, and Amy Ganz. "A Policy Agenda to Develop Human Capital for the Modern Economy." Aspen Institute, February 4, 2019. https://www.aspeninstitute.org/longform/expanding-economic-opportunity-for-more-americans/a-policy-agenda-to-develop-human-capital-for-the-modern-economy.

Gordon, Robert J. "Perspectives on the Rise and Fall of American Growth." *American Economic Association Papers and Proceedings* 106, no. 5 (2016): 72–76.

Gray, Caroline, and Mark Hannah. "Modeling Democracy." Report from the Eurasia Group Foundation, May 18, 2021. https://egfound.org/2021/05/modeling-democracy-democracy-in-disarray.

Greenhouse, Steven. *Beaten Down, Worked Up: The Past, Present and Future of American Labor*. New York: Alfred A. Knopf, 2019.

Gribetz, Judah. "Holocaust Compensation." Annex to *In Re: Holocaust Victim Assets Litigation*. Case no. CV 96-4849 (E.D.N.Y. 2006). September 11, 2000. https://www.swissbankclaims.com/Documents_New/665994.pdf.

Griffin, Sarah, Serna Klempin, and Davis Jenkins. "Using Guided Pathways to Build Cross-Sector Pathways Partnerships." Columbia University Community College Research Center, October 2021. https://ccrc.tc.columbia.edu/media/k2/attachments/guided-pathways-cross-sector-partnerships.pdf.

Gruber, Joseph W., and Steven B. Kamin. "The Corporate Saving Glut and Falloff of Investment Spending in OECD Economies." *IMF Economic Review* 64, no. 4 (2016): 777–799.

Guyton, John, Patrick Langetieg, Daniel Reck, Max Risch, and Gabriel Zucman. "Tax Evasion at the Top of the Income Distribution: Theory and Evidence." NBER Working Paper 28542, March 2021.

Haerpfer, C., R. Inglehart, A. Moreno, C. Welzel, K. Kizilova, J. Diez-Medrano M. Lagos, P. Norris, E. Ponarin, B. Puranen. "World Values Survey Wave 7 (2017–2022)." JD Systems Institute & WVSA Secretariat, 2022. https://www.worldvaluessurvey.org /WVSDocumentationWV7.jsp.

Hahn, Heather, David Kassabian, and Sheila Zedlewski. "TANF Work Requirements and State Strategies to Fulfill Them." Urban Institute, March 2012. https://www.acf .hhs.gov/sites/default/files/documents/opre/work_requirements_0.pdf.

Hall, Peter A., and David Soskice. *Varieties of Capitalism: The Institutional Foundations of Comparative Advantage.* Oxford: Oxford University Press, 2001.

Hamdani, Kausar, Claire Kramer Mills, Edison Reyes, and Jessica Battisto. "Unequal Access to Credit: The Hidden Impact of Credit Constraints." Federal Reserve Bank of New York, 2019. https://www.newyorkfed.org/medialibrary/media/outreach-and -education/community-development/constraints-on-access-to-credit.pdf.

Hamilton, Darrick, and William Darity Jr. "Can 'Baby Bonds' Eliminate the Racial Wealth Gap in Putative Post-Racial America?" *Review of Black Political Economy* 37, nos. 3–4 (2010): 207–216.

Hamilton, Darrick, William A. Darity Jr., Anne E. Price, Vishnu Sridharan, and Rebecca Tippett. "Umbrellas Don't Make It Rain: Why Studying and Working Hard Isn't Enough for Black Americans." Samuel DuBois Cook Center on Social Equity, 2015. https://socialequity.duke.edu/wp-content/uploads/2019/10/Umbrellas_Dont _Make_It_Rain_Final.pdf.

Han, Jeehoon, Bruce D. Meyer, and James X. Sullivan. "The Consumption, Income and Well-Being of Single Mother Headed Families 25 Years After Welfare Reform." NBER Working Paper 29188, August 2021.

Hannah-Jones, Nikole, et al. "The 1619 Project." *New York Times Magazine*, August 14, 2019. https://www.nytimes.com/interactive/2019/08/14/magazine/1619-america -slavery.html 5/1/2022.

Hanushek, Eric, and Ludger Woessman. "The Economic Impacts of Learning Losses." OECD, September 2020. https://www.oecd.org/education/The-economic-impacts-of -coronavirus-covid-19-learning-losses.pdf.

Hanushek, Eric, and Ludger Woessman. *Universal Basic Skills: What Countries Stand to Gain.* Paris: OECD Publishing, 2015. https://www.oecd-ilibrary.org/docserver/978 9264234833-en.pdf.

Harknett, Kristen, and Daniel Schneider. "The Shift Project." https://shift.hks.har vard.edu. Accessed February 2, 2022.

Hartman, Steve. "Every Student at Five Chicago High Schools to Get Free College Tuition, Nonprofit Says." CBS News, February 25, 2022. https://www.cbsnews.com /news/nonprofit-pays-college-tuition-chicago-students-steve-hartman.

Hart, Oliver, and Luigi Zingales. "Companies Should Maximize Shareholder Welfare Not Market Value." *Journal of Law, Finance, and Accounting* 2, no. 2 (2017): 247–274. https://scholar.harvard.edu/files/hart/files/108.00000022-hart-vol2no2-jlfa-0022 _002.pdf.

Heckman, James J. "ABC/CARE: Elements of Quality Early Childhood Programs That Produce Quality Outcomes." The Heckman Equation, 2021. https://heckmanequa tion.org/www/assets/2018/06/F_Heckman_ABC_CARE_Quality_110117.pdf.

Heckman, James J. "Early Childhood Education: Quality and Access Pay Off." The Heckman Equation, 2017. https://heckmanequation.org/www/assets/2017/01/F _Heckman_Moffitt_093016.pdf.

Heidkamp, Maria, and Thomas Hilliard. "A Review of Community College-Employer Partnerships and Initiatives: Expanding Opportunities for Job Seekers with Disabil- ities." Employer Assistance and Resource Network on Disability Inclusion, 2014. https://production-askearn-org.s3.amazonaws.com/EARN_Review_Community _College_Employer_Partnerships_Initiatives_e1d4a2d8c3.pdf.

Heim, Joe. "Teaching America's Truth." *Washington Post*, August 28, 2019. https:// www.washingtonpost.com/education/2019/08/28/teaching-slavery-schools.

Henderson, Kaitlyn. "The Crisis of Low Wages in the US." Oxfam America, March 21, 2022. https://www.oxfamamerica.org/explore/research-publications/the-crisis-of -low-wages-in-the-us.

Herbold, Hilary. "Never a Level Playing Field: Blacks and the GI Bill." *Journal of Blacks in Higher Education* 6 (1994–1995): 104–108.

Heritage Foundation. "Index of Economic Freedom: United States." https://www .heritage.org/index/country/unitedstates. Accessed 5/2/2022.

Hicks, Natasha, Fenaba Addo, Anne Price, and William Darity Jr. "Still Running Up the Down Escalator: How Narratives Shape our Understanding of Racial Wealth Inequality." Samuel DuBois Cook Center on Social Equity, 2021. https://socialequity .duke.edu/wp-content/uploads/2021/09/INSIGHT_Still-Running-Up-Down-Escala tors_vF.pdf.

Hilger, Nate G. *The Parent Trap: How to Stop Overloading Parents and Fix Our Inequality Crisis*. Cambridge, MA: MIT Press, 2022.

Holzer, Harry J. "A 'Race to the Top' in Public Higher Education to Improve Education and Employment Among the Poor." *Russell Sage Foundation Journal of the Social Sciences* 4, no. 3 (2018): 84–99.

Holzer, Harry J., Diane Whitmore Schanzenbach, Greg J. Duncan, and Jens Ludwig. "The Economic Costs of Childhood Poverty in the United States." *Journal of Children and Poverty* 14, no. 1 (2008): 41–61.

Horatio Alger Society. "Bylaws." May 5, 2017. https://horatioalgersociety.net/216 _bylaws.html.

Horowitz, Juliana Menasce. "Support for Black Lives Matter Declined after George Floyd Protests, but Has Remained Unchanged Since." Pew Research Center, September 27, 2021. https://www.pewresearch.org/fact-tank/2021/09/27/support-for-black -lives-matter-declined-after-george-floyd-protests-but-has-remained-unchanged -since.

Horowitz, Juliana Menasce, Ruth Igielnik, and Rakesh Kochhar. "Most Americans Say There Is Too Much Economic Inequality in the U.S., but Fewer Than Half Call It a Top Priority." Pew Research Center, January 9, 2020. https://www.pewresearch .org/social-trends/2020/01/09/most-americans-say-there-is-too-much-economic -inequality-in-the-u-s-but-fewer-than-half-call-it-a-top-priority.

Howard-Hassman, Rhoda E., and Anthony P. Lombardo. "Framing Reparations Claims: Differences between the African and Jewish Social Movements for Reparations." *African Studies Review* 50, no. 1 (2007): 27–48.

"How Many Cities Are in the United States? 2022." World Population Review. https://worldpopulationreview.com/us-city-rankings/how-many-cities-are-in-the-us. Accessed November 12, 2022.

Hoyert, Donna L. "Maternal Mortality Rates in the United States, 2019." National Center for Health Statistics, 2021. https://www.cdc.gov/nchs/data/hestat/maternal -mortality-2021/E-Stat-Maternal-Mortality-Rates-H.pdf.

Huang, Nian-Sheng. "Financing Poor Relief in Colonial Boston." *Massachusetts Historical Review* 8 (2006): 72–103.

HUD Exchange. "CDBG State Program." https://www.hudexchange.info/programs /cdbg-state. Accessed November 14, 2022.

Hulse, Carl, and David M. Herszenhorn. "Defiant House Rejects Huge Bailout; Next Step Is Uncertain." *New York Times*, September 29, 2008. https://www.nytimes.com /2008/09/30/business/30cong.html.

Human Rights Watch. "Who Goes to Prison for Drug Offenses? A Rebuttal to the New York State District Attorneys Association." 1999. https://www.hrw.org/legacy /campaigns/drugs/ny-drugs.htm.

Humphrey, Hubert. Remarks to the National Alliance of Businessmen. Washington, DC, May 29, 1968. Available via Minnesota Historical Society. http://www2.mnhs .org/library/findaids/00442/pdfa/00442-02563.pdf.

Hunt, Vivian, Sundiatu Dixon-Fyles, Sara Prince, and Kevin Dolan. "Diversity Wins: How Inclusion Matters." McKinsey & Company, May 2020. https://www.mckinsey .com/~/media/mckinsey/featured%20insights/diversity%20and%20inclusion /diversity%20wins%20how%20inclusion%20matters/diversity-wins-how-inclusion -matters-vf.pdf.

Infield, Tom. "Deep Divisions in Views of America's Racial History." *Pew Magazine*, November 11, 2021. https://www.pewtrusts.org/en/trust/archive/fall-2021/deep-divi sions-in-views-of-americas-racial-history.

Inglehart, R., C. Haerpfer, A. Moreno, C. Welzel, K. Kizilova, J. Diez-Medrano, M. Lagos, P. Norris, E. Ponarin, B. Puranen. "World Values Survey Wave 3 (1995–1998)." JD Systems Institute & WVSA Secretariat, 2014. https://www.worldvaluessurvey.org/WVS DocumentationWV3.jsp.

Institute for Crime & Justice Policy Research. "World Prison Brief Data." https:// www.prisonstudies.org/world-prison-brief-data. Accessed December 2, 2022.

Institute of Medicine. "Spending on Health Care for Uninsured Americans: How Much, and Who Pays?" In *Hidden Costs, Values Lost: Uninsurance in America*," chapter 3. Washington, DC: National Academies Press, 2003. https://www.ncbi.nlm.nih.gov /books/NBK221653/.

Institute on Taxation and Economic Policy. "Who Pays Taxes in America in 2019?" April 2019. https://itep.sfo2.digitaloceanspaces.com/2019-Who-Pays-Taxes-in-Amer ica.pdf.

Internal Revenue Service. "Filing Season 2021 Child Tax Credit Frequently Asked Questions." 2022. https://www.irs.gov/credits-deductions/filing-season-2021-child -tax-credit-frequently-asked-questions-topic-a-2021-child-tax-credit-basics.

Internal Revenue Service. "Use the EITC Assistant." https://www.irs.gov/credits-deduc tions/individuals/earned-income-tax-credit/use-the-eitc-assistant. Accessed February 5, 2022.

International Monetary Fund. *World Economic Outlook: Managing Divergent Recoveries*. Washington, DC: International Monetary Fund, 2022. https://www.imf.org/en/Pub lications/WEO/Issues/2021/03/23/world-economic-outlook-april-2021.

International Trade Administration. "China—Country Commercial Guide: Market Challenges." Updated January 4, 2022. https://www.trade.gov/country-commercial -guides/china-market-challenges.

Irwin, Neil. "To Understand Rising Inequality, Consider the Janitors at Two Top Companies, Then and Now." *New York Times*, September 3, 2017. https://www.nytimes .com/2017/09/03/upshot/to-understand-rising-inequality-consider-the-janitors-at -two-top-companies-then-and-now.html.

Isaacs, Julia B. "International Comparisons of Economic Mobility." Brookings Institution, 2016. https://www.brookings.edu/wp-content/uploads/2016/07/02_economic _mobility_sawhill_ch3.pdf.

Isaacs, Julia B. "Starting School at a Disadvantage: The School Readiness of Poor Children." *Brookings Social Genome Project Research* 3, no. 5 (2012): 1–22.

Jacobs, Rose. "The Downfall (and Possible Salvation) of Expertise." *Chicago Booth Review*, November 30, 2020. https://www.chicagobooth.edu/review/downfall-and-possible -salvation-expertise.

Jardim, Ekaterina, Mark C. Long, Robert Plotnick, Emma van Inwegen, Jacob Vigdor, and Hilary Wething. "Minimum Wage Increases and Individual Employment Trajectories." NBER Working Paper 25182, October 2018. https://www.nber.org/system /files/working_papers/w25182/w25182.pdf.

Jepsen, Christopher, Kenneth Troske, and Paul Coomes. "The Labor-Market Returns to Community College Degrees, Diplomas, and Certificates." *Journal of Labor Economics* 32, no. 1 (2014): 95–121.

Jewish Vocational Services. "The History of JVS' Job Quality Index." https://www.jvs -boston.org/portfolio/job-quality. Accessed March 16, 2022.

Johnson, David S., and Jonathan D. Fisher. "Inequality and Mobility over the Past Half Century Using Income, Consumption and Wealth." In *Measuring Distribution and Mobility of Income and Wealth*, edited by Raj Chetty, John N. Friedman, Janet C. Gornick, Barry Johnson, and Arthur Kennickell, chapter 14. Chicago: University of Chicago Press, 2022.

Johnson, Rucker, and C. Kirabo Jackson. "Reducing Inequality through Dynamic Complementarity: Evidence from Head Start Public School Spending." *American Economic Journal: Policy* 11, no. 4 (2021): 310–349.

Johnson, Rucker, C. Kirabo Jackson, and Claudia Persico. "The Effects of School Spending on Educational & Economic Outcomes: Evidence from School Finance Reforms." *Quarterly Journal of Economics* 131, no. 1 (2016): 157–218.

Johnston, Katie. "Employers Can See Where Their Wages, Benefits Stand." *Boston Globe*, March 16, 2022.

Joint Economic Committee, Subcommittee on Fiscal Policy. *Income Security for Americans: Recommendations of the Public Welfare Study*. Washington, DC: US Government Printing Office, December 5, 1974.

Jost, John T., Mahzarin R. Banaji, and Brian A. Nosek. "A Decade of System Justification Theory: Accumulated Evidence of Conscious and Unconscious Bolstering of the Status Quo." *Political Psychology* 25, no. 6 (2004): 881–919.

Jost, John T., Sally Blount, Jeffrey Pfeffer, and György Hunyady. "Fair Market Ideology: Its Cognitive-Motivational Underpinnings." *Research in Organizational Behavior* 25 (2003): 53–91.

Jost, John T., Carlee Beth Hawkins, Brian A. Nosek, Erin P. Hennes, Chadly Stern, Samuel D. Gosling, and Jess Graham. "Belief in a Just God (and a Just Society): A System Justification Perspective on Religious Ideology." *Journal of Theoretical and Philosophical Psychology* 34, no. 1 (2013): 56–81.

Kahneman, Daniel, and Amos Tversky. "Prospect Theory: An Analysis of Decision under Risk." *Econometrica* 47, no. 2 (1979): 263–292.

Kaiser Family Foundation. "Status of Medicaid Expansion Decisions: Interactive Map." Updated November 9, 2022. https://www.kff.org/medicaid/issue-brief/status -of-state-medicaid-expansion-decisions-interactive-map.

Kaiser Family Foundation. "2020 Employer Health Benefits Survey," October 8, 2020. https://www.kff.org/health-costs/report/2020-employer-health-benefits-survey.

Kaiser-Schatzlein, Robin. "This Is How America's Richest Families Stay That Way." *New York Times*, September 24, 2021. https://www.nytimes.com/2021/09/24/opinion /biden-tax-loophole.html.

Karam, Rita T. "How Community Colleges Can Establish Better Partnerships with Employers." RAND, June 6, 2019. https://www.rand.org/blog/2019/06/how-commu nity-colleges-can-establish-better-partnerships.html.

Katz, Lawrence, and David Autor. "Changes in the Wage Structure and Earnings Inequality." In *Handbook of Labor Economics*, vol. 3A, edited by Orley Ashenfelter and David Card, chapter 26. Amsterdam: Elsevier, 1999.

Katznelson, Ira. *When Affirmative Action Was White: An Untold History of Racial Inequality in Twentieth-Century America*. New York: W. W. Norton, 2005.

Kearney, Melissa. "Welfare and the Federal Budget." EconoFact, July 25, 2017. https:// econofact.org/welfare-and-the-federal-budget.

Keisler-Starkey, Katherine, and Lisa Bunch. "Health Insurance Coverage in the United States: 2020." Census Bureau, September 14, 2021. https://www.census.gov /library/publications/2021/demo/p60-274.html.

Kijakazi, Kilolo, Rachel Marie Brooks-Atkins, Mark Paul, Anne E. Price, William A. Darity, and Darrick Hamilton. "The Color of Wealth in the Nation's Capital." The Urban Institute, 2016. https://www.urban.org/research/publication/color-wealth -nations-capital.

Kim, Dongwoo. "Worker Retirement Responses to Pension Incentives: Do They Respond to Pension Wealth?" *Journal of Economic Behavior and Organization* 173 (2020): 365–385.

King, Martin Luther Jr. April 1968 speech at unknown location. Video available at https://www.youtube.com/watch?v=pLV5y4utPKI.

King, Martin Luther Jr. *Where Do We Go from Here: Chaos or Community?* New York: Harper & Row, 1967.

Knack, Stephen, and Philip Keefer. "Institutions and Economic Performance: Cross-Country Tests Using Alternative Institutional Measures." *Economics and Politics* 7, no. 3 (1995): 207–227.

Kodrzycki, Yolanda, and Ana Patricia Muñoz, with Lynn Browne, DeAnna Green, Marques Benton, Prabal Chakrabarti, David Plasse, Richard Walker, and Bo Zhao. "Reinvigorating Springfield's Economy: Lessons from Resurgent Cities." Federal Reserve Bank of Boston, 2009. https://www.bostonfed.org/publications/public -policy-discussion-paper/2009/reinvigorating-springfields-economy-lessons-from -resurgent-cities.aspx.

Komlos, John. *Foundations of Real-World Economics: What Every Economics Student Needs to Know.* New York: Routledge, 2019.

Kopp, Emanuel, Daniel Leigh, Susanna Mursula, and Suchanan Tambunlertchai. "U.S. Investment Since the Tax Cuts and Jobs Act of 2017." IMF Working Paper 19/120, 2019.

Kraft, Patrick W., Milton Lodge, and Charles S. Taber. "Why People 'Don't Trust the Evidence': Motivated Reasoning and Scientific Beliefs." *Annals of the American Academy of Political and Social Science* 658, no. 1 (2015): 121–133.

Kraus, Michael W., Ivuoma N. Onyeador, Natalie M. Daumeyer, Julian M. Rucker, and Jennifer A. Richeson. "The Misperception of Racial Economic Inequality." *Perspectives on Psychological Science* 14, no. 6 (2019): 899–921. https://journals.sagepub .com/doi/pdf/10.1177/1745691619863049.

Kraus, Michael W., Julian M. Rucker, and Jennifer A. Richeson. "Americans Misperceive Racial Economic Inequality." *Proceedings of the National Academy of Sciences* 114, no. 39 (2017): 10324–10331. https://doi.org/10.1073/pnas.1707719114.

Krugman, Paul. "Doing Economics as if Evidence Matters." *New York Times*, October 11, 2021. https://www.nytimes.com/2021/10/11/opinion/nobel-prize-economics.html.

Krugman, Paul. "Profits without Production." *New York Times*, June 20, 2013. https://www.nytimes.com/2013/06/21/opinion/krugman-profits-without-production.html.

Krugman, Paul. "The Revolt of the American Worker." *New York Times*, October 14, 2021. https://www.nytimes.com/2021/10/14/opinion/workers-quitting-wages.html.

Krugman, Paul. "What Ever Happened to the Great Resignation?" *New York Times*, April 5, 2022. https://www.nytimes.com/2022/04/05/opinion/great-resignation-employment.html.

Kuznets, Simon. *Shares of Upper Income Groups in Income and Savings*. New York: National Bureau of Economic Research, 1953.

Larcker, David, and Brian Tayan. "Diversity in the C-Suite: The Dismal State of Diversity Among Fortune 100 Senior Executives." Stanford University Rock Center for Corporate Governance, April 28, 2020. https://papers.ssrn.com/sol3/papers.cfm?abstract_id=3587498.

Larson, William. "New Estimates of Value of Land of the United States." Bureau of Economic Analysis Working Paper, 2015. https://www.bea.gov/system/files/papers/WP2015-3.pdf.

Lazarus, Emma. "The New Colossus." Poets.org. https://poets.org/poem/new-colossus. Accessed December 2, 2022.

Lee, Charles R. "Public Poor Relief and the Massachusetts Community, 1620–1715." *New England Quarterly* 55, no. 4 (1982): 564–585.

Lempinen, Edward. "Ian Haney López: To Combat Racism, We Need to Talk about Economic Justice." *Berkeley News*, October 28, 2020. https://news.berkeley.edu/2020/10/28/ian-haney-lopez-to-combat-racism-we-need-to-talk-about-economic-justice.

Levesque, Elizabeth Mann. "Improving Community College Completion Rates by Addressing Structural and Motivational Barriers." Brookings Institution, October 8, 2018. https://www.brookings.edu/research/community-college-completion-rates-structural-and-motivational-barriers.

Levin, John, Elizabeth Cox, Christine Cerven, and Zachary Haberler. "The Recipe for Promising Practices in Community Colleges." *Community College Review* 38, no. 1 (2010): 31–58.

Levin, Josh. "The Welfare Queen." *Slate*, December 19, 2013. http://www.slate.com /articles/news_and_politics/history/2013/12/linda_taylor_welfare_queen_ronald _reagan_made_her_a_notorious_american_villain.html.

Levy, Alon. "Why It's So Expensive to Build Urban Rail in the U.S." *Bloomberg*, January 26, 2018. https://www.bloomberg.com/news/articles/2018-01-26/the-u-s-gets -less-subway-for-its-money-than-its-peers.

Liebman, Jeffrey, Kathryn Carlson, Eliza Novick, and Pamela Portocarrero. "Chelsea Eats Study: Card Spending Update." Rappaport Institute, May 2021. https://www .hks.harvard.edu/sites/default/files/Taubman/Research/ChelseaEatsCardSpending May2021.pdf.

Loh, Tracy, Christopher Coes, and Becca Buthe. "The Great Real Estate Reset: Separate and Unequal: Persistent Residential Segregation Is Sustaining Racial and Economic Injustices in the U.S." Brookings Institute, December 16, 2020. https://www .brookings.edu/essay/trend-1-separate-and-unequal-neighborhoods-are-sustaining -racial-and-economic-injustice-in-the-us.

López, Ian Haney. *Dog Whistle Politics: How Coded Racial Appeals Have Reinvented Racism and Wrecked the Middle Class*. New York: Oxford University Press, 2014.

Lopéz-Santana, Mariely, and Lucas Núñez. "Most Americans Support Biden's Expanded Child Tax Credit, Our Research Finds. But There Are Caveats." *Washington Post*, November 10, 2021. https://www.washingtonpost.com/politics/2021/11/10/ most-americans-support-bidens-expanded-child-tax-credit-our-research-finds-there -are-caveats.

Love, Bettina L., and Brandelyn Tosolt. "Reality or Rhetoric? Barack Obama and Post-Racial America." *Race, Gender and Class* 17, nos. 3–4 (2010): 19–37.

Lowe, Nichola. *Putting Skill to Work: How to Create Good Jobs in Uncertain Times*. Cambridge, MA: MIT Press, 2021.

Lyle, David S., and John Z. Smith. "The Effect of High-Performing Mentors on Junior Officer Promotion in the US Army." *Journal of Labor Economics* 32, no. 2 (2014): 229–258.

Malhotra, Neil. "Should Corporations Simply Maximize Shareholder Value?" *Forbes*, April 16, 2019. https://www.forbes.com/sites/neilmalhotra/2019/04/16/should-cor porations-simply-maximize-shareholder-value.

Malik, Rasheed. "Working Families Are Spending Big Money on Child Care." Center for American Progress, June 20, 2019. https://www.americanprogress.org/article /working-families-spending-big-money-child-care.

Maloney, Peter. "Electric Buses for Mass Transit Seen as Cost Effective." American Public Power Association, October 17, 2019. https://www.publicpower.org/periodi cal/article/electric-buses-mass-transit-seen-cost-effective.

Manyika, James, Jan Mischke, Jacques Bughin, Jonathan Woetzel, Mekala Krishnan, and Samuel Cudre. "A New Look at the Declining Labor Share of Income in the United States." McKinsey Global Institute, May 2019. https://www.mckinsey .com/~/media/mckinsey/featured%20insights/employment%20and%20growth/a %20new%20look%20at%20the%20declining%20labor%20share%20of%20income %20in%20the%20united%20states/mgi-a-new-look-at-the-declining-labor-share-of -income-in-the-united-states.pdf.

Marist Polls. "Exclusive *Point Taken*: Marist Poll." May 1, 2016. http://maristpoll .marist.edu/wp-content/misc/usapolls/us160502/Point%20Taken/Reparations /Exclusive%20Point%20Taken-Marist%20Poll_Reparations%20Banner%201_May %202016.pdf.

Markovits, Daniel. *The Meritocracy Trap*. New York: Penguin Books, 2019.

Marmot, Michael. "Social Determinants of Health Inequalities." *Lancet* 365, no. 9464 (2005): 1099–1104.

Massachusetts Business Alliance for Education. "The P-Tech Model of Early College High School: A Timely Opportunity for Massachusetts?" October 2021. https://www .mbae.org/wp-content/uploads/2021/10/The-P-TECH-Model-of-Early-College-High -School-MBAE-Report-update.pdf.

Mathur, Aparna. "Frayed Protection: The U.S. Social Safety Net Response to the Pandemic." Mossavar-Rahmani Center for Business and Government Working Paper, 2022.

Mazumder, Bhashkar. "Fortunate Sons: New Estimates of Intergenerational Mobility in the United States Using Social Security Earnings Data." *Review of Economics and Statistics* 87, no. 2 (2005): 235–255.

McGhee, Heather. *The Sum of Us*. New York: One World, 2021.

McKenzie, Brian. "Transit Access and Population Change: The Demographic Profiles of Rail-Accessible Neighborhoods in the Washington, DC Area." Census Bureau, SEHSD Working Paper No. 2015-023, 2015. https://www.census.gov/content/dam /Census/library/working-papers/2015/demo/SEHSD-WP2015-23.pdf.

McLaughlin, Michael, and Mark R. Rank. "Estimating the Economic Cost of Childhood Poverty in the United States." *Social Work Research* 42, no. 2 (2018): 73–83.

Meer, Jonathan. "A Minimum-Wage Study Faces Misplaced Skepticism." *National Review*, June 29, 2017. https://www.nationalreview.com/2017/06/seattle-minimum -wage-university-washington-study-critics-wrong.

Meer, Jonathan, and Michael Farren. "Subsidized—not Minimum—Wages Should Assist Workers during the Pandemic." *The Hill*, October 20, 2020. https://thehill.com/opinion/finance/512898-subsidized-not-minimum-wages-should-assist-workers-during-the-pandemic.

Merriam-Webster.com Dictionary. "Trickle-Down Theory." https://www.merriam-webster.com/dictionary/trickle-down%20theory. Accessed November 11, 2022.

Merrill, David. "No One Values Your Life More Than the Federal Government." Bloomberg, October 19, 2017. https://www.bloomberg.com/graphics/2017-value-of-life/.

Meyer, Bruce D., and James X. Sullivan. "Identifying the Disadvantaged: Official Poverty, Consumption Poverty, and the New Supplemental Poverty Measure." *Journal of Economic Perspectives* 26, no. 3 (2012): 111–136.

Mincer, Jacob. "Investment in Human Capital and the Personal Income Distribution." *Journal of Political Economy* 66 (1958): 281–302.

Mishel, Lawrence, and Jori Kandra. "CEO Pay Has Skyrocketed 1,322% since 1978." Economic Policy Institute, August 10, 2021. https://www.epi.org/publication/ceo-pay-in-2020.

Mississippi Department of Human Services. "Temporary Assistance for Needy Families Eligibility Guidelines." https://www.mdhs.ms.gov/economic-assistance/tanf/tanf-eligibility. Accessed December 2, 2022.

Mitchell, Olivia S. "Worker Knowledge of Pension Provisions." *Journal of Labor Economics* 6, no. 1 (1988): 21–39.

Moffitt, Robert A. "The Deserving Poor, the Family, and the U.S. Welfare System." *Demography* 52, no. 3 (2015): 729–749.

Moffitt, Robert A. "Explaining Welfare Reform: Public Choice and the Labor Market." *International Tax and Public Finance* 6 (1999): 289–315.

Mousa, Salma. "Building Social Cohesion between Christians and Muslims through Soccer in Post-ISIS Iraq." *Science* 369, no. 6505 (2020): 866–870.

Mullaney, Thomas. "Alliance of Businessmen: New Job Effort." *New York Times*, February 22, 1978.

Mullen, Kirsten, and William A. Darity Jr. "10 Things We Get Wrong about Reparations." *Rolling Stone*, June 19, 2021. https://www.rollingstone.com/culture/culture-commentary/juneteenth-reparations-misconceptions-1186060.

Munnell, Alicia, Geoffrey Tootell, Lynn E. Browne, and James McEneaney. "Mortgage Lending in Boston: Interpreting HMDA Data." *American Economic Review* 86, no. 1 (1996): 25–53.

Muñoz, Ana Patricia; Marlene Kim, Mariko Chang, Regine O. Jackson, Darrick Hamilton, and William A. Darity, Jr. "The Color of Wealth in Boston." Federal Reserve Bank of Boston, 2015. https://www.bostonfed.org/publications/one-time-pubs/color-of-wealth.aspx.

Nackenoff, Carol. "The Horatio Alger Myth." In *Myth America: A Historical Anthology*, vol. 2, edited by Patrick Gerster and Nicholas Cords. St. James, NY: Brandywine Press, 1997.

National Center for Education Statistics. "Total and Current Expenditures per Pupil in Fall Enrollment in Public Elementary and Secondary Schools, by Function and State or Jurisdiction: 2016–17," August, 2019. https://nces.ed.gov/programs/digest/d19/tables/dt19_236.75.asp.

National Renewable Energy Laboratory. "Fuel Cell Electric Bus Evaluations." https://www.nrel.gov/hydrogen/fuel-cell-bus-evaluation.html. Accessed November 12, 2022.

Naylor, Brian. "Stimulus Bill Gives 'Shovel-Ready' Projects Priority." National Public Radio *Morning Edition*, February 9, 2009. https://www.npr.org/templates/story/story.php?storyId=100295436.

Nellis, Eric, and Anne Decker Cecere. *The Eighteenth-Century Records of the Boston Overseers of the Poor*. Boston: The Colonial Society of Massachusetts, 2007.

Neumark, David. "The Higher Wages Tax Credit." In *Expanding Economic Opportunity for More Americans*, edited by Melissa S. Kearney and Amy Ganz, 196–212. Aspen, CO: The Aspen Institute, 2019.

Neumark, David, and William L. Wascher. "Minimum Wages and Employment." *Foundations and Trends in Microeconomics* 3, nos. 1–2 (2007): 1–182.

Newport, Frank. "Five Questions about Views of Business and Industry Sectors." Gallup Poll, September 24, 2021. https://news.gallup.com/opinion/polling-matters/354929/five-questions-views-business-industry-sectors.aspx.

Norton, Michael I., and Dan Ariely. "Building a Better America—One Wealth Quintile at a Time." *Perspectives on Psychological Science* 6, no. 1 (2011): 9–12.

Nowrasteh, Alex. "The 14 Most Common Arguments against Immigration and Why They're Wrong." Cato Institute, May 2, 2018. https://www.cato.org/blog/14-most-common-arguments-against-immigration-why-theyre-wrong.

Ocasio-Cortez, Alexandria. "Yep. Means testing = more bureaucracy . . ." Twitter, October 3, 2021, 10:27 a.m. https://twitter.com/AOC/status/1444685472349962245.

"Occupy Boston Timeline." *Boston Globe*, December 11, 2011. https://www.bostonglobe.com/metro/2011/12/11/occupy-boston-timleline/s9RZeAFlZI8yuhaambcDcM/story.html.

OECD. "Level of GDP Per Capita and Productivity." https://stats.oecd.org/index .aspx?DataSetCode=PDB_LV. Accessed December 2, 2022.

OECD. "Public Spending on Childcare and Early Education." https://www.oecd.org /els/soc/PF3_1_Public_spending_on_childcare_and_early_education.pdf. Accessed December 2, 2022.

OECD. "Tax Levels and Structures, 1965–2020." In *Revenue Statistics 2021: The Initial Impact of COVID-19 on OECD Tax Revenues*. Paris: OECD, 2021. https://www.oecd -ilibrary.org/sites/6e87f932-en/1/3/3/index.html?itemId=/content/publication/6e8 7f932-en&_csp_=989e3029323a6936ab9fa6df32f709e4&itemIGO=oecd&item ContentType=book. Accessed December 2, 2022.

OECD. "Trade Union Dataset." https://stats.oecd.org/Index.aspx?DataSetCode=TUD#.

OECD Data. "Education Spending." https://data.oecd.org/eduresource/education -spending.htm. Accessed December 2, 2022.

OECD Data. "Income Inequality." https://data.oecd.org/inequality/income-inequal ity.htm#indicator-chart. Accessed December 2, 2022.

OECD Data. "Tax on Corporate Profits." https://data.oecd.org/tax/tax-on-corporate -profits.htm. Accessed December 2, 2022.

Office of Management and Budget. "Historical Tables." Tables 8.5, 12.2, and 12.3. https://www.whitehouse.gov/omb/historical-tables. Accessed December 8, 2022.

Oliver, Melvin, and Thomas Shapiro. *Black Wealth/White Wealth*. New York: Rout-ledge, 1995, 2006.

O'Mara-Eves, Alison, Ginny Brunton, Sandy Oliver, Josephine Kavanagh, Farah Jamal, and James Thomas. "The Effectiveness of Community Engagement in Public Health Interventions for Disadvantaged Groups: A Meta-Analysis." *BMC Public Health* 15, art. no. 129 (2015). https://link.springer.com/article/10.1186/s12889-015-1352-y.

100 Black Men of America. "Mentoring." https://100blackmen.org/four-for-the-future /mentoring. Accessed November 14, 2022.

"Opportunity Atlas, The." https://www.opportunityatlas.org. Accessed May 23, 2022.

O'Reilly, Charles, and Brian Main. "Economic and Psychological Perspectives on CEO Compensation: A Review and Synthesis." *Industrial and Corporate Change* 19, no. 3 (2010): 675–712.

Osterman, Michelle J. K., Brady E. Hamilton, Joyce A. Martin, Anne K. Driscoll, and Claudia P. Valenzuela. "Births: Final Data for 2020." *National Vital Statistics Reports* 70, no. 17 (2022). https://www.cdc.gov/nchs/data/nvsr/nvsr70/nvsr70-17.pdf.

Owens, Lindsay. "I Listened in on Big Business. It's Profiting from Inflation, and You're Paying for It." *New York Times*, May 5, 2022. https://www.nytimes.com/2022 /05/05/opinion/us-companies-inflation.html.

Padeiro, Miguel, Ana Louro, and Nuno Marques da Costa. "Transit-Oriented Development and Gentrification: A Systematic Review." *Transport Reviews* 39, no. 6 (2019): 733–754.

Paluck, Elizabeth Levy, and Chelsey S. Clark. "Can Playing Together Help Us Live Together?" *Science* 369, no. 6506 (2020): 769–770.

Paluck, Elizabeth Levy, Roni Porat, Chelsey S. Clark, and Donald P. Green. "Prejudice Reduction: Progress and Challenges." *Annual Review of Psychology* 72 (2021): 533–560.

Paluck, Elizabeth Levy, and Jordan Starck. "Perspective Getting in a Democracy." *Psychological Inquiry* 32, no. 3 (2021): 178–179.

Parolin, Zachary, Megan Curran, Jordan Matsudaira, Jane Waldfogel, and Christopher Wimer. "Estimating Monthly Poverty Rates in the United States." *Journal of Policy Analysis and Management* 41, no. 4 (2022):1177–1203. https://static1.square space.com/static/610831a16c95260dbd68934a/t/61ef1fb9d816735dfc9b25c2/1643 061179107/Estimating-Monthly-Poverty-CPSP-2022.pdf.

Parrott, Jim, and Mark Zandi. "Overcoming the Nation's Daunting Housing Supply Shortage." Urban Institute, March 2021. https://www.urban.org/sites/default/files /publication/103940/overcoming-the-nations-daunting-housing-supply-shortage _0.pdf.

Perry, Andre. "Students Need More Than an SAT Adversity Score, They Need a Boost in Wealth." Brookings Institution, May 17, 2019. https://www.brookings.edu/blog /the-avenue/2019/05/17/students-need-more-than-an-sat-adversity-score-they-need -a-boost-in-wealth.

Perry, Andre, Jonathan Rothwell, and David Harshbarger. "Five-Star Reviews, One-Star Profits: The Devaluation of Businesses in Black Communities." Brookings Institution, February 2020. https://www.brookings.edu/wp-content/uploads/2020/02 /2020.02_DevOfBizInBlackCommunities_Perry-Rothwell-Harshbarger-final.pdf.

Personal Responsibility and Work Opportunity Reconciliation Act of 1996. Pub. L. No. 104-193, 110 Stat. 2105. https://www.congress.gov/104/plaws/publ193/PLAW -104publ193.pdf.

Pew Economic Mobility Project. "Does America Promote Mobility as Well as Other Nations?" Pew Charitable Trusts, November 2011. https://www.pewtrusts.org/-/media /legacy/uploadedfiles/pcs_assets/2011/critafinal1pdf.pdf.

Pew Economic Mobility Project. "Findings from a National Survey & Focus Groups on Economic Mobility." Pew Charitable Trusts, March 12, 2009. https://www.pewtrusts .org/-/media/legacy/uploadedfiles/pcs_assets/2009/survey_on_economic_mobility _findings(1).pdf.

Pew Research Center. "American's Trust in Scientists, Other Groups Declines." February 15, 2022. https://www.pewresearch.org/science/2022/02/15/americans-trust-in -scientists-other-groups-declines/.

Pew Research Center. "Americans' Views of Government: Low Trust, but Some Positive Performance Ratings." September 14, 2020. https://www.pewresearch.org/politics /2020/09/14/americans-views-of-government-low-trust-but-some-positive-perfor mance-ratings.

Pew Research Center. "Most Americans Point to Circumstances, Not Work Ethic, for Why People are Rich or Poor." March 2, 2020. https://www.pewresearch.org/politics /2020/03/02/most-americans-point-to-circumstances-not-work-ethic-as-reasons -people-are-rich-or-poor.

Pew Research Center. "On Views of Race and Inequality, Blacks and Whites Are Worlds Apart." June 27, 2016. https://www.pewresearch.org/social-trends/2016/06 /27/on-views-of-race-and-inequality-blacks-and-whites-are-worlds-apart.

Pew Research Center. "The Partisan Divide on Political Values Grows Even Wider." October 5, 2017. https://www.pewresearch.org/politics/wp-content/uploads/sites/4 /2017/10/10-05-2017-Political-landscape-release-updt..pdf.

Pew Research Center. "Partisans Are Divided Over the Fairness of the U.S. Economy— and Why People Are Rich or Poor." October 4, 2018. https://www.pewresearch.org /fact-tank/2018/10/04/partisans-are-divided-over-the-fairness-of-the-u-s-economy -and-why-people-are-rich-or-poor/.

Pew Research Center. "Religious Landscape Study: Political Affiliation." https://www .pewresearch.org/religion/religious-landscape-study/party-affiliation/ Accessed June 16, 2022.

Pew Research Center. "Religious Landscape Study: Views about Government Aid to the Poor." https://www.pewresearch.org/religion/religious-landscape-study/views-about -government-aid-to-the-poor. Accessed June 16, 2022.

Pew Research Center. "The State of American Jobs." October 6, 2016. https://www .pewresearch.org/social-trends/2016/10/06/the-state-of-american-jobs/.

Pew Research Center. "Views of the Economic System and Social Safety Net." December 17, 2019. https://www.pewresearch.org/politics/2019/12/17/views-of-the-econo mic-system-and-social-safety-net.

Pfeffer, Fabin T., and Alexandra Killewald. "Intergenerational Wealth Mobility and Racial Inequality." *SOCIUS Data Visualization* 5, nos. 1–2 (2019). https://journals .sagepub.com/doi/pdf/10.1177/2378023119831799.

Phalippou, Ludovic. "An Inconvenient Fact: Private Equity Returns and the Billionaire Factory." *Journal of Investing* 30, no.1 (2020): 11–39.

Piketty, Thomas, and Emmanuel Saez. "Income Inequality in the United States, 1913–1998." *Quarterly Journal of Economics* 118, no. 1 (2003): 1–41.

Piketty, Thomas, Emmanuel Saez, and Gabriel Zucman. "Distributional National Accounts: Methods and Estimates for the United States." *Quarterly Journal of Economics* 133, no. 2 (2018): 553–609.

Pope Francis. "Evangelii Gaudium: Apostolic Exhortation on the Proclamation of the Gospel in Today's World." November 24, 2013. https://www.vatican.va/content /francesco/en/apost_exhortations/documents/papa-francesco_esortazione-ap _20131124_evangelii-gaudium.html.

Popkin, Susan, Diane K. Levy, Mica O'Brien, and Abby Boshart. "An Equitable Strategy for Public Housing Redevelopment." Urban Institute, June 2021. https://www .urban.org/sites/default/files/publication/104467/an-equitable-strategy-for-public -housing-redevelopment_0.pdf.

Porter, Eduardo. "Patching Up the Social Safety Net." *New York Times*, March 17, 2015. https://www.nytimes.com/2015/03/18/business/patching-up-the-social-safety -net.html.

Porter, Michael, and Mark Kramer. "Shared Value." *Harvard Business Review* 89, nos. 1–2 (2011): 62–77.

Prentice, Deborah, and Levy Paluck. "Engineering Social Change Using Social Norms: Lessons from the Study of Collective Action." *Current Opinion in Psychology* 35 (2020): 138–142. https://doi.org/10.1016/j.copsyc.2020.06.012.

"President-Elect Obama: The Voters Rebuke Republicans for Economic Failure." *Wall Street Journal* editorial, November 5, 2008. https://www.wsj.com/articles/SB122 586244657800863.

Price, Anne. "Doing 'The Right Thing' Won't Close the Racial Wealth Gap." *Shelterforce*, February 8, 2022. https://shelterforce.org/2022/02/08/doing-the-right-thing -wont-close-the-racial-wealth-gap.

Prosperity Now. "Find a Children's Savings Program." https://prosperitynow.org/map /childrens-savings. Accessed November 12, 2022.

Putnam, Robert. *Bowling Alone: The Collapse and Revival of American Community*. New York: Simon & Schuster, 2001.

Quillian, Lincoln, Devah Pager, Ole Hexel, and Arnfinn Midtbøen. "Meta-Analysis of Field Experiments Shows No Change in Racial Discrimination in Hiring over Time." *Proceedings of the National Academy of Sciences of the United States of America* 114, no. 41 (2017): 10870–10875. https://www.pnas.org/content/114/41/10870.full.

Quincy, Josiah. Report to the Commonwealth of Massachusetts, 1821. https://www.primaryresearch.org/pr/dmdocuments/ootp_quincy_report.pdf.

Radcliffe, David. "The Art and Heart of Community Engagement." Federal Reserve Bank of Boston, May 2, 2019. https://www.bostonfed.org/workingplaces/news/2019/the-art-and-heart-of-community-engagement.aspx.

Rae, Matthew, Rebecca Copeland, and Cynthia Cox. "Tracking the Rise in Premium Contributions and Cost-Sharing for Families with Large Employer Coverage." Peterson-KFF Health System Tracker, August 14, 2019. https://www.healthsystemtracker.org/brief/tracking-the-rise-in-premium-contributions-and-cost-sharing-for-families-with-large-employer-coverage.

Rainie, Lee, Scott Keeter, and Andrew Perrin. "Trust and Distrust in America." Pew Research Center, July 22, 2019. https://www.pewresearch.org/politics/2019/07/22/trust-and-distrust-in-america.

Rappeport, Alan. "The Top 1 Percent Are Evading $163 Billion a Year in Taxes, the Treasury Finds." *New York Times*, September 8, 2021. https://www.nytimes.com/2021/09/08/business/irs-tax-avoidance.html.

Rappeport, Alan, and Emily Flitter. "Congress Approves First Bid Dodd-Frank Rollback." *New York Times*, May 22, 2018. https://www.nytimes.com/2018/05/22/business/congress-passes-dodd-frank-rollback-for-smaller-banks.html.

Reagan, Ronald. Remarks at the Annual Meeting of the National Alliance of Business. October 5, 1981. Ronald Reagan Presidential Library and Museum, Archives. https://www.reaganlibrary.gov/archives/speech/remarks-annual-meeting-national-alliance-business.

Reagan, Ronald. Remarks on the Air Traffic Controllers Strike. August 3, 1981. Available via UVA Miller Center: https://millercenter.org/the-presidency/presidential-speeches/august-3-1981-remarks-air-traffic-controllers-strike.

Reardon, Sean F., Kendra Bischoff, Ann Owens, and Joseph B. Townsend. "Has Income Segregation Really Increased? Bias and Bias Correction in Sample-Based Segregation Estimates." *Demography* 55, no. 6 (2018): 2129–2160.

Reeves, Richard. *Dream Hoarders: How the American Upper Middle Class Is Leaving Everyone Else in the Dust, Why That Is a Problem, and What to Do about It.* Washington, DC: Brookings Institution Press, 2017.

Reich, Robert. *The System: Who Rigged It, How We Fix It*. New York: Alfred Knopf, 2020.

Reinhart, Carmen M., and Kenneth S. Rogoff. *This Time is Different: Eight Centuries of Financial Folly*. Princeton, NJ: Princeton University Press, 2009.

Richter, Brian Kelleher, Krislert Samphantharak, and Jeffrey F. Timmons. "Lobbying and Taxes." *American Journal of Political Science* 53, no. 4 (2009): 893–909.

Rogers, Will. "And Here's How It All Happened." *St. Petersburg Times*, November 26, 1932.

Rosales, Steven. "Fighting the Peace at Home: Mexican American Veterans and the 1944 GI Bill of Rights." *Pacific Historical Review* 80, no. 4 (2011): 597–627.

Roth, Alvin E. "The Art of Designing Markets." *Harvard Business Review* 85, no. 10 (2007): 118–126.

Rothstein, Richard. *The Color of Law: A Forgotten History of How Our Government Segregated America*. New York: Liveright, 2017.

Rutz, David. "Twitter Erupts over Ocasio-Cortez's 'Tax the Rich' Dress." Fox News, September 14, 2021. https://www.foxnews.com/media/twitter-ocasio-cortez-met-gala-hypocrisy.

Saad, Lydia. "Socialism and Atheism Still U.S. Political Liabilities. Gallup Poll, February 11, 2020. https://news.gallup.com/poll/285563/socialism-atheism-political-liabilities.aspx.

Sabelhaus, John, and Jeff Thompson. "Racial Wealth Disparities: Re-considering the Roles of Human Capital and Inheritance." Working paper presented at the Federal Reserve Bank of Boston, "Racial Disparities in Today's Economy" conference October 4–6, 2021. https://www.bostonfed.org/-/media/Documents/events/2021/racial-disparities-in-todays-economy/Racial-Wealth-Disparities-Re-considering-the-Roles-of-Human-Capital-and-Inheritance.pdf.

Saez, Emmanuel. "Striking It Richer: The Evolution of Top Incomes in the United States." Unpublished manuscript, February 2020. https://eml.berkeley.edu/~saez/saez-UStopincomes-2018.pdf.

Sana, Mariano. "Public Opinion on Refugee Policy in the United States, 1938–2019: Increasing Support for Refugees and the Sympathy Effect." *International Migration Review* 55, no. 2 (2021): 574–604. https://doi.org/10.1177/0197918320954129.

Sarin, Natasha. "The Case for a Robust Attack on the Tax Gap." US Department of the Treasury, September 7, 2021. https://home.treasury.gov/news/featured-stories/the-case-for-a-robust-attack-on-the-tax-gap.

Saunt, Claudio. *Unworthy Republic: The Dispossession of Native Americans and the Road to Indian Territory.* New York: W. W. Norton, 2020.

Savage, Sarah, and Erin Graves. "Promoting Pathways to Financial Stability: A Resource Handbook on Building Financial Capabilities of Community College Students." Federal Reserve Bank of Boston, 2015. https://www.bostonfed.org/-/media/Documents/education/financial-capabilities/handbook/financial-capabilities-handbook.pdf.

Scharnhorst, Gary, and Jack Bales. *Horatio Alger Jr.: An Annotated Bibliography of Comment and Criticism.* Lanham, MD: Scarecrow Press, 1981.

Schedules That Work Act. H.R. 5004. 116th Cong. 2019. https://www.congress.gov/bill/116th-congress/house-bill/5004.

Scholz, John Karl, and Kara Levine. "U.S. Black-White Wealth Inequality." In *Social Inequality*, ch. 24, 895–929. New York: Russell Sage Foundation, 2004.

Schuetz, Jenny. "To Improve Housing Affordability, We Need Better Alignment of Zoning, Taxes, and Subsidies." Brookings Institution, January 2020. https://www.brookings.edu/wp-content/uploads/2019/12/Schuetz_Policy2020_BigIdea_Improving-Housing-Afforability.pdf.

Sebba, Leslie. "The Reparations Agreements: A New Perspective." *Annals of the American Academy of Political and Social Science* 450 (1980): 202–212.

Semuels, Alana. "Severe Inequality Is Incompatible with the American Dream." *Atlantic*, December 10, 2016. https://www.theatlantic.com/business/archive/2016/12/equality-of-opportunity/510227.

Shapiro, Thomas, Tatjana Meschede, and Sam Osoro. "The Roots of the Widening Racial Wealth Gap: Explaining the Black-White Economic Divide." Institute on Assets and Social Policy, February 2013. https://heller.brandeis.edu/iere/pdfs/racial-wealth-equity/racial-wealth-gap/roots-widening-racial-wealth-gap.pdf.

Shiller, Robert J. "Do Stock Prices Move Too Much to Be Justified by Subsequent Changes in Dividends?" *American Economic Review* 71, no. 3 (1981): 421–436.

Shiller, Robert J. *Irrational Exuberance.* Princeton NJ: Princeton University Press, 2000.

Shiller, Robert J. *Narrative Economics: How Stories Go Viral and Drive Major Economic Events.* Princeton NJ: Princeton University Press, 2019.

Shorrocks, Anthony, James Davies, and Rodrigo Lluberas. *Global Wealth Databook 2021.* Zurich: Credit Suisse Research Institute, 2021. https://www.credit-suisse.com/media/assets/corporate/docs/about-us/research/publications/global-wealth-databook-2021.pdf.

Shrider, Emily A., Melissa Kollar, Frances Chen, and Jessica Semega. "Income and Poverty in the United States: 2020." Census Bureau, September 14, 2021. https://www.census.gov/library/publications/2021/demo/p60-273.html.

Shrivastava, Aditi, and Gina Azito Thompson. "TANF Cash Assistance Should Reach Millions More Families to Lessen Hardship." Center on Budget and Policy Priorities, February 18, 2022. https://www.cbpp.org/research/family-income-support/tanf-cash-assistance-should-reach-millions-more-families-to-lessen.

Simonov, Andrey, Szymon K. Sacher, Jean-Pierre H. Dubé, and Shirsho Biswas. "The Persuasive Effect of Fox News: Non-Compliance with Social Distancing during the COVID-19 Pandemic." NBER Working Paper, July 2020. https://www.nber.org/papers/w27237.

Slemrod, Joel. "Is This Tax Reform, or Just Confusion?" *Journal of Economic Perspectives* 32, no. 4 (Fall 2018): 73–96.

Smith, Adam. *The Theory of Moral Sentiments*. London: Printed for A. Millar, in the Strand; Edinburgh: A. Kincaid and J. Bell, 1759. Available electronically at https://www.econlib.org/library/Smith/smMS.html.

Smith, Dave. "Most People Have No Idea Whether They're Paid Fairly." *Harvard Business Review*, December 2015. https://hbr.org/2015/10/most-people-have-no-idea-whether-theyre-paid-fairly.

Smith, Ember, and Richard Reeves. "SAT Math Scores Mirror and Maintain Racial Inequity." Brookings Institution, December 1, 2020. https://www.brookings.edu/blog/up-front/2020/12/01/sat-math-scores-mirror-and-maintain-racial-inequity.

Solomon, Danyelle, Connor Maxwell, and Abril Castro. "Systematic Inequality and Economic Opportunity." Center for American Progress, August 7, 2019. https://www.americanprogress.org/issues/race/reports/2019/08/07/472910/systematic-inequality-economic-opportunity.

Sovereign Wealth Fund Institute. "Top 100 Largest Financial Holding Company Rankings by Total Assets." https://www.swfinstitute.org/fund-rankings/financial-holding-company. Accessed December 2, 2022.

Sowell, Thomas. *Trickle Down Theory and Tax Cuts for the Rich*. Stanford, CA: Hoover Institution Press, 2012. https://www.hoover.org/sites/default/files/uploads/documents/Sowell_TrickleDown_FINAL.pdf.

Starr-McCluer, Martha, and Annika Sundén. "Workers' Knowledge of Their Pension Coverage: A Reevaluation." Federal Reserve working paper, January 1999. https://www.federalreserve.gov/pubs/feds/1999/199905/199905pap.pdf.

Stevens, Ann Huff, Michal Kurlaender, and Michel Grosz. "Career Technical Education and Labor Market Outcomes: Evidence from California Community Colleges." *Journal of Human Resources* 54, no. 4 (2019): 986–1036.

Stiglitz, Joseph E., with Nell Abernathy, Adam Hersh, Susan Holmberg, and Mike Konczal. *Rewriting the Rules of the American Economy: An Agenda for Growth and Shared Prosperity*. New York: W. W. Norton, 2015.

Stiglitz, Joseph E. *People, Power, and Profits: Progressive Capitalism for an Age of Discontent*. New York: W. W. Norton, 2019.

Stiglitz, Joseph E. *The Price of Inequality: How Today's Divided Society Endangers Our Future*. New York: W. W. Norton, 2012.

Sunstein, Cass R. *Sludge: What Stops Us from Getting Things Done and What to Do about It*. Cambridge, MA: MIT Press, 2021.

"Teaching the 1619 Project." Pulitzer Center on Crisis Reporting. https://1619educa tion.org/about-1619-project/teaching-1619-project. Accessed March 16, 2022.

Thompson, Jeffrey P., and Alice Henriques Volz. "A New Look at Racial Disparities Using a More Comprehensive Wealth Measure." Federal Reserve Bank of Boston, August 16, 2021. https://www.bostonfed.org/publications/current-policy-perspec tives/2021/a-new-look-at-racial-disparities-using-a-more-comprehensive-wealth -measure.aspx.

Thompson, Jeffrey P. and Gustavo Suarez. "Accounting for Racial Wealth Disparities in the United States." Federal Reserve Bank of Boston, December 2019. https://www .bostonfed.org/publications/research-department-working-paper/2019/accounting -for-racial-wealth-disparities-in-the-united-states.aspx.

Tikkanen, Roosa, and Melinda K. Abrams. "US Health Care from a Global Perspective, 2019: Higher Spending, Worse Outcomes?" The Commonwealth Fund, January 30, 2020. https://www.commonwealthfund.org/publications/issue-briefs/2020/jan /us-health-care-global-perspective-2019.

Tobenkin, David. "Employers Partner with Community Colleges to Fill the Talent Pipeline." Society for Human Resource Management. https://www.shrm.org/hr-today /news/all-things-work/pages/employers-partner-with-community-colleges-.aspx. Accessed November 6, 2021.

Tocqueville, Alexis de. *Democracy in America*, 2 vols., translated by Henry Reeve. Kindle Edition. Originally published 1835.

Tonidandel, Scott, Derek R. Avery, and McKensy G. Phillips. "Maximizing Returns on Mentoring: Factors Affecting Subsequent Protégé Performance." *Journal of Organizational Behavior* 28, no. 1 (2007): 89–110.

Ton, Zeynep. "The Case for Good Jobs." *Harvard Business Review*, November 30, 2017. https://hbr.org/2017/11/the-case-for-good-jobs.

Ton, Zeynep. "Why 'Good Jobs' Are Good for Retailers." *Harvard Business Review*, January–February 2012. https://hbr.org/2012/01/why-good-jobs-are-good-for-retailers.

Tversky, Amos, and Daniel Kahneman. "The Framing of Decisions and the Psychology of Choice." *Science* 211, no. 4481 (1981): 453–458.

Tversky, Amos, and Daniel Kahneman. "Judgment under Uncertainty: Heuristics and Biases." *Science* 185, no. 4157 (1974): 1124–1131.

University of Michigan Survey Research Center. "Survey of Consumers." Tables 32–33. https://data.sca.isr.umich.edu/data-archive/mine.php.

University of Minnesota Population Center. "Current Population Survey Data for Social, Economic, and Health Research." https://cps.ipums.org/cps.

US 100th Congress. H.R. 442. Civil Liberties Act of 1987. https://www.congress.gov/bill/100th-congress/house-bill/442?r=9.

US Department of Agriculture. "SNAP Participation Rates 2002–2014." https://www.ers.usda.gov/topics/food-nutrition-assistance/supplemental-nutrition-assistance-program-snap/charts/snap-participation-rates. Accessed February 17, 2022.

US Department of Agriculture. "SNAP Work Requirements." Updated May 29, 2019. https://www.fns.usda.gov/snap/work-requirements.

US Department of Agriculture. "What Can SNAP Buy?" Updated September 14, 2021. https://www.fns.usda.gov/snap/eligible-food-items.

US Department of Education. "Data Express. Data Dashboards." Accessed December 12, 2022. https://eddataexpress.ed.gov/dashboard/title-i-part-a/2020-2021?sy=2781&s=1035.

US Department of Education. "Graduation Rate Data" (Microsoft Excel spreadsheet). https://eddataexpress.ed.gov/sites/default/files/archive_files/Graduation%20Rate%20Data/EDE_GraduationRate.xlsx. Accessed May 23, 2022.

US Department of Health and Human Services. "TANF Caseload Data 1996–2015." Updated February 18, 2021. https://www.acf.hhs.gov/ofa/data/tanf-caseload-data-1996-2015.

US Department of Housing and Urban Development. "PIT and HIC Data Since 2007." 2007–2021 Point-in-Time Estimates by State, 2021. https://www.hudexchange.info/resource/3031/pit-and-hic-data-since-2007/.

US Department of Labor. "Handy Reference Guide to the Fair Labor Standards Act." September 2016. https://www.dol.gov/whd/regs/compliance/hrg.htm.

US Department of Transportation. "Departmental Guidance on Valuation of a Statistical Life in Economic Analysis." 2021. https://www.transportation.gov/office-policy/transportation-policy/revised-departmental-guidance-on-valuation-of-a-statistical-life-in-economic-analysis.

US Department of the Treasury. "Troubled Assets Relief Program (TARP)." https://home.treasury.gov/data/troubled-assets-relief-program.

US Equal Employment Opportunity Commission. "Annual Performance Report, Fiscal Year 2020." https://www.eeoc.gov/sites/default/files/2021-01/FY%202020%20APR.pdf.

US Equal Employment Opportunity Commission. "EEOC Budget and Staffing History 1980 to Present." https://www.eeoc.gov/eeoc-budget-and-staffing-history-1980-present.

US Government Printing Office. "Bond Yields and Interest Rates, 1933–2010." https://www.govinfo.gov/content/pkg/ERP-2011/pdf/ERP-2011-table73.pdf.

US Senate Historical Office. "The Enforcement Acts of 1870 and 1871." https://www.senate.gov/artandhistory/history/common/generic/EnforcementActs.htm.

Van Noy, Michelle, and James Jacobs. "Employer Perceptions of Associate Degrees in Local Labor Markets: A Case Study of the Employment of Information Technology Technicians in Detroit and Seattle." Community College Research Center Working Paper no. 39, February 2012. https://ccrc.tc.columbia.edu/media/k2/attachments/employer-perceptions-case-study.pdf.

Varian, Hal. *Microeconomic Analysis.* New York: W. W. Norton and Company, 1978.

Ventry, Dennis J. Jr. "The Collision of Tax and Welfare Politics: The Political History of the Earned Income Tax Credit, 1969–99." *National Tax Journal* 53, no. 4.2 (2000): 983–1026.

VentureRadar. "Top Electric Bus Companies." https://www.ventureradar.com/keyword/Electric%20buses. Accessed November 12, 2022.

Viscusi, W. Kip. *Pricing Lives: Guideposts for a Safer Society.* Princeton: Princeton University Press, 2018.

Vogels, Emily A. "56% of Americans Support More Regulation of Major Technology Companies." Pew Research center. July 20, 2021. https://www.pewresearch.org/fact-tank/2021/07/20/56-of-americans-support-more-regulation-of-major-technology-companies.

Vorenberg, Michael. "Abraham Lincoln and the Politics of Black Colonization." *Journal of the Abraham Lincoln Association* 14, no. 2 (1993): 23–45.

Wartzman, Rick. *The End of Loyalty: The Rise and Fall of Good Jobs in America*. New York: Public Affairs, 2017.

Washington Post-ABC News Poll. April 18–21, 2021. https://www.washingtonpost .com/context/april-18-21-2021-washington-post-abc-news-poll/72d8dab8-8a54 -4468-a964-b7326876814d.

Weaver, R. Kent. *Ending Welfare as We Know It*. Washington, DC: Brookings Institution Press, 2000.

"'Welfare Queen' Becomes Issue in Reagan Campaign." *New York Times*, February 15, 1976. https://www.nytimes.com/1976/02/15/archives/welfare-queen-becomes-issue -in-reagan-campaign-hitting-a-nerve-now.html. Accessed December 2, 2022.

Western, Bruce and Jake Rosenfeld. "Workers of the World Divide: The Decline of Labor and the Future of the Middle Class." *Foreign Affairs* 91, no. 3 (2012): 88–99.

"What Harm Do Minimum Wages Do?" *Economist*, August 15, 2020. https://www .economist.com/schools-brief/2020/08/15/what-harm-do-minimum-wages-do.

Wiatrowski, William J. "The Last Private Industry Pension Plans: A Visual Essay." *Monthly Labor Review*, December 2012. https://www.bls.gov/opub/mlr/2012/12/art1 full.pdf.

WID.World. "World Inequality Database." https://wid.world/data. Accessed 3/8/2022.

Wildasin, David E. "What's So Funny about Economics?" Personal webpage, 2006. http://davidwildasin.us/humor.html.

Williams, Joan, et al. "Stable Scheduling Increases Productivity and Sales: The Stable Scheduling Study." Worklife Law, University of California Hastings College of the Law, 2018. https://worklifelaw.org/publications/Stable-Scheduling-Study-Report.pdf.

Williamson, Jeffrey, and Peter Lindert. *American Inequality—A Macroeconomic History*. New York: Academic Press, 1980.

Wilson, James. *The Earth Shall Weep: A History of Native America*. New York: Grove Press, 2018.

Wilson, Megan. "Creative Placemaking—A Cautionary Tale." *Race, Poverty & the Environment* 20, no. 1 (2015): 101–105.

WIPO. *World Intellectual Property Indicators 2020*. Geneva: World Intellectual Property Organization, 2020. https://www.wipo.int/edocs/pubdocs/en/wipo_pub_941 _2020.pdf.

Wood, Laura. "10 Billionaires Like Oprah Winfrey Who Grew Up Poor." CNBC, September 11, 2017. https://www.cnbc.com/2017/09/11/10-billionaires-who-grew -up-dirt-poor.html.

World Bank, The. *World Bank Open Data*. https://data.worldbank.org/indicator/SI .POV.GINI. Accessed December 2, 2022.

Xu, Jiaquan, Sherry L. Murphy, Kenneth D. Kochanek, and Elizabeth Arias. "Deaths: Final Data for 2019." *National Vital Statistics Reports* 70, no. 8 (2021). https://www .cdc.gov/nchs/data/nvsr/nvsr70/nvsr70-08-508.pdf.

Zagorsky, Jay L. "Native Americans' Wealth." In *Wealth Accumulation & Communities of Color in the United States: Current Issues*, edited by Jessica Gordon Nembhard and Ngina Chiteji, 133–154. Ann Arbor: University of Michigan Press, 2006.

Zhou, Li. "The Case against Means Testing." *Vox*, October 15, 2021. https://www .vox.com/2021/10/15/22722418/means-testing-social-spending-reconciliation-bill.

Zillow. "Home Values" (CSV spreadsheet). https://files.zillowstatic.com/research /public_csvs/zhvi/Metro_zhvi_uc_sfrcondo_tier_0.33_0.67_sm_sa_month.csv?t =1641823391. Accessed January 10, 2022.

Zippel, Claire. "Tax Credits to Pay for Necessities, Education." Center on Budget and Policy Priorities, October 21, 2021. https://www.cbpp.org/blog/9-in-10-families-with -low-incomes-are-using-child-tax-credits-to-pay-for-necessities-education.

Zucman, Gabriel. "Global Wealth Inequality." *Annual Review of Economics* 11 (2019): 109–138. https://gabriel-zucman.eu/files/Zucman2019.pdf.

Zuk, Miriam, and Ian Carlton. "Equitable Transit Oriented Development: Examining the Progress and Continued Challenges of Developing Affordable Housing in Opportunity- and Transit-Rich Neighborhoods." Poverty and Race Research Action Council, March 2015. https://prrac.org/pdf/EquitableTOD.pdf.

Zundl, Elaine, Daniel Schneider, Kristen Harknett, and Evelyn Bellew. "Still Unstable: The Persistence of Schedule Uncertainty during the Pandemic." Shift Project, 2022. https://shift.hks.harvard.edu/wp-content/uploads/2022/01/COVIDUpdate_Brief _Final.pdf.

Index